VALUE, MONEY, PROFIT, AND CAPITAL TODAY

RESEARCH IN POLITICAL ECONOMY

Series Editor: Paul Zarembka

State University of New York at Buffalo, USA

Recent Volumes:

RESEARCH IN POLITICAL ECONOMY   VOLUME 39

VALUE, MONEY, PROFIT, AND CAPITAL TODAY

EDITED BY

RÉMY HERRERA

National Center of the Scientific Research (CNRS), France

United Kingdom – North America – Japan
India – Malaysia – China

Emerald Publishing Limited
Emerald Publishing, Floor 5, Northspring, 21-23 Wellington Street, Leeds LS1 4DL

First edition 2024

British Library Cataloguing in Publication Data
A catalogue record for this book is available from the British Library

ISBN: 978-1-80455-751-8 (Print)
ISBN: 978-1-80455-750-1 (Online)
ISBN: 978-1-80455-752-5 (Epub)

ISSN: 0161-7230 (Series)

PrintedandboundbyCPIGroup(UK)Ltd,Croydon,CR04YY

INVESTOR IN PEOPLE

CONTENTS

PART III
PROFIT TODAY

PART IV
CAPITAL TODAY

ABOUT THE EDITOR

Rémy Herrera (France) is an economist, researcher at the National Center of Scientific Research (CNRS). Graduated from a Business School (*École supérieure de Commerce*, 1988), the Institute of Political Studies (*Institut d'Études politiques*, 1990), and the University of Paris 1 *Panthéon-Sorbonne* (Master of Philosophy, 1994; PhD in Economics, 1996), he supervises students in PhD at the *Centre d'Économie de la Sorbonne*. He started working in the financial audit (1988), at the OECD (1992–1997) and for the World Bank (1999–2000). He was member of the CNRS National Committee (2000–2005) and of the Scientific Council of Paris 1 (2001–2006). He taught at various universities in France (especially at Paris 1 [1993–2013]) and abroad, including at the Universities of Aleppo (1998), Cairo (1999–2000), Vitoria in Brazil (2006), Complutense in Madrid (2009–2013), and Lingnan in Hong Kong (2018). He was adviser to research programs at the Chubu University (Nagoya). He is or has been associated with: the Third World Forum (Dakar), the Union of Radical Political Economics (New York), the International Initiative for Promoting Political Economics (London), the *Sociedad de Economía Política Latinoamericana* (São Paulo), and the *Asociación Nacional de Economistas de Cuba* (Havana). He was the World Forum of Alternatives (WFA)'s Executive Secretary. He is also member of the Global University for Sustainability and of the International Crisis Observatory. He organizes the "Marx in the Twenty-First Century" seminar at La Sorbonne. He regularly works with the Centre Europe-Tiers Monde (Geneva), supporting it in its advisory role to the Human Rights Council of the United Nations.

ABOUT THE CONTRIBUTORS

Joaquín Arriola (Spain) is a full Professor in the Department of Applied Economics at the University of the Basque Country (Spain). He has published various books, among them: *Los Nuevos Países Industrializados* (IEPALA, Madrid, 1988), *Internacionalismo y Movimiento Obrero – El eje Norte-Sur* (HOAC, Madrid, 1992; with P. Waterman), or *La Globalización o la razón del más fuerte (Asociación Paz y Solidaridad de Asturias, Oviedo*, 2011).

Juan Barredo-Zuriarrain (Spain) is an Assistant Professor in the Department of Applied Economics at the University of the Basque Country (Spain). He is also associate researcher at the Grenoble Research Center in Economics (University of Grenoble Alpes, France). He has published many articles in scientific reviews, including *Structural Change and Economic Dynamics* or *New Political Economy*.

William Paul Cockshott (United Kingdom) is a Scottish computer scientist and Marxist political economist. As a reader at the University of Glasgow, he has a BA in economics from Manchester University (1974), an MSc from Heriot Watt University (1976), and a PhD from University of Edinburgh (1982). He made significant contributions in computer science, as well as in economics, especially in the multidisciplinary area of economic computability. As the co-author of the book *Towards a New Socialism* (written with A. Cottrell), he advocates the use of cybernetics to build an efficient and democratic planning for a moneyless socialist economy.

Guido De Marco (Italy) is an independent researcher for the Association for the Redistribution of Labor in Rome. He holds a Master in Economics and was a Research Fellow of the Center for Economic Policy Analysis, New School for Social Research, as well as a PhD candidate at the New School for Social Research in 2001. He published "Fred Moseley, Money and Totality: A Macro-Monetary Interpretation of Marx's Logic in Capital and the End of the 'Transformation Problem'" (*Science & Society*), "A Critique of Moseley's *Money and Totality*" (*World Review of Political Economy*), and "Marx's General Rate of Profit: How Turnover time, Accumulation and Rate of Surplus Value Affect the Formation of Prices of Production" (*Capital & Class*, forthcoming). His book, *Marx and the Business*, is currently under review.

Weinan Ding (China). She is a PhD student in economics at the School of Marxism of the Tsinghua University in Beijing, People's Republic of China. Her PhD dissertation deals with the evolution of the rate of profit in France in the long period. Her main research direction is Marxist economics. The profit rate and long wave theory are subjects of her ongoing research.

Demba Moussa Dembele (Senegal), economist-researcher, is member of the Council for the Development of Social Science Research in Africa (CODESRIA) and the Third World Forum (FTM). He holds a PhD in Financial Economics from the Pierre et Marie Curie University, Paris; MBA in international trade and finance from the American University (Washington D.C.). He was a former research associate at the Institute of International Finance (Washington D.C.). Currently, he is the Chair of the African Association for Research and Cooperation in Support of Endogenous Development (ARCADE).

Zhixuan Feng (China) is a Professor at the School of Economics and Management of the Wuhan University. He received his PhD in Economics from the School of Economics at the Renmin University of China in 2016. His current research interests are underdevelopment theory, mathematical political economy, and macroeconomics. He is also a specialist in input–output analysis.

Bangxi Li (China) is an Associate Professor (tenure) of political economy at the Institute of Economics, School of Social Sciences, of the Tsinghua University, Beijing, P.R. of China. His research interests include mathematical political economy, post-Keynesian economics, input–output analysis, and the Chinese economy. His representative publication is entitled *Linear Theory of Fixed Capital and China's Economy: Marx, Sraffa and Okishio* (Springer, 2017).

Zhiming Long (China), economist, is an Associate Professor at the School of Marxism at the Tsinghua University in Beijing. He supervises PhD since 2017 in this same institution. He is chair professor of Tang Scholar since 2018. He has a PhD in Economics from the University of Paris 1, as well as two Master's degrees in economics from the University of Paris 1 and University of Paris 10. He is a specialist in growth theory, statistics, and (time-series analysis) econometrics.

Rosa Maria Marques (Brazil). Graduated from the University of Rio Grande do Sul (1974), the PUC-SP or *Pontifícia Universidade Católica de São Paulo* (1985), and the *Getúlio Vargas* Foundation (1996, PhD), with post-doctorates at the Universities of Grenoble (France) and of Buenos Aires (Argentine), she is a titular Professor in Economics at the PUC-SP. She is the former president of the Brazilian Society of Political Economy, member of the Brazilian Budget and Finance Commission of the National Council of Health, and President of the Brazilian Association of Health Economics.

Juan Pablo Mateo (Spain) is currently Associate Professor in the Department of Applied Economics, Structure & History, of the Complutense University of Madrid, and visiting scholar at the Institute for Research on World-Systems, in the University of California, Riverside (US). His research is focused on the theory of crisis, the tendency of the profit rate, and the core/periphery relation within the unequal development of world capitalism. His last book is *The theory of crisis and the Great Recession in Spain* (Palgrave, 2019), with articles in the Review of

Radical Political Economics, Capital & Class, Science & Society, and International Review of Applied Economics, among others.

Ernesto Molina Molina (Cuba), doctor in Economic Sciences, is a member of Merit of the Academy of Sciences of Cuba. He is titular Professor of political economy, history of economic thought and economic theory at the Higher Institute of International Relations (*Instituto Superior de Relaciones Internacionales Raúl Roa García*). He is also the President of the Scientific Society of Economic Thought at the National Association of Economists and Accountants of Cuba (*Asociación Nacional de Economistas y Contadores de Cuba*).

Gustavo Moura de Cavalcanti Mello (Brazil), doctor in Sociology from the *Universidade de São Paulo*, post-doctorate in Sociology from the UNICAMP and in Economics from the *Universidade de São Paulo,* is a Professor of the Department of Economics and the Postgraduate Programme of Social Policy at the *Universidade Federal do Espírito Santo* (UFES) and a researcher at the National Council for Scientific and Technological Development (CNPq).

Paulo Nakatani (Brazil). As a graduate in economics from the *Universities of Paraná* (1971), Paris 10 *Nanterre* (1981), *Picardie* (1982, doctorate), and Paris 13 (2002, post-doctorate), he is a titular Professor in the Economics department and the Graduate Studies in Social Policy from the *Universidade Federal do Espírito Santo,* and collaborates with MST's Florestan Fernandes national school. He is the member of the editorial board of the review of the Brazilian Society of Political Economy, of which he was President, and member of the International Observatory of Crises.

Christian Palloix (France) is a Professor emeritus at the University of Picardie Jules Verne, Amiens (France). As a teacher in Economics, he was successively appointed at the Universities of Grenoble (1963–1977), Alger (1977–1978), Oran (1978–1981), and Amiens (1981–2005). As a researcher, he participated in the research centers of IREP-Grenoble (1967–1981), CRMSI-Paris (1981–1986), CRIISEA-Amiens (1987–2021, including as Director), LEFMI-Amiens (since 2021). His research focuses on globalization and multinational corporations, industrial economics and productive systems, labor economics, and development (notably Algeria).

Alfredo Saad-Filho (Brazil) is a Professor of Political Economy and International Development at King's College, London. Previously, he was a Professor at SOAS University of London, and senior economic affairs officer at the United Nations Conference on Trade and Development (UNCTAD). He has published extensively on neoliberalism, the political economy of development, industrial policy, climate adaptation, democracy, alternative economic policies, Latin America, inflation and stabilization, and the labor theory of value and its applications.

Mauricio de Souza Sabadini (Brazil), doctor in economics from the University of Paris 1 *Panthéon-Sorbonne*, is a Professor at the Department of Economics and the Postgraduate Programme of Social Policy at the Federal University of

Espírito Santo (UFES). He is a researcher at the National Council for Scientific and Technological Development (CNPq) and Director (2016–2018), then president (2018–2020) of the *Sociedade Brasileira de Economia Política*.

Fabien Trémeau (France) is currently a PhD student at the University of Paris 1 *Panthéon-Sorbonne*. He Graduated in philosophy and sociology from the University of Paris 4 Sorbonne and from the Institute of European Studies in Paris. His research focuses on the value and the commodity fetishism in Marx's work. As a publisher, he is also the Founder and Director of the Éditions Critiques.

PRESENTATION

The new volume of *Research in Political Economy* that we deliver to the reader is devoted to the themes of value, money, profit, and capital within the theoretical and empirical framework of contemporary Marxism. To think about and discuss them, we brought together 18 economists – in addition to the author of these lines – from eight countries and four continents; economists who are, for some, experienced and internationally renowned personalities, and for others, young researchers starting their careers, but all working in their own way to broaden and deepen Marxism in order to apply its powerful methods to the interpretation and, above all, the transformation of the present world.

Even if we had to distinguish these four concepts of value, money, profit, and capital to better structure the exposition of the 13 contributions of the present volume, they are in fact narrowly related to each other in the analyzes provided by Marxism and its various currents. Let us briefly and basically recall here, in this presentation, how these distinct but linked notions are logically articulated by Marx and how they are dialectically chained in order to constitute the Marxian general theory of capitalist accumulation.

First, value: The law of value not only has the function of regulating exchanges but also commodity production and the reproduction of the capitalist system itself, based on private property. According to Marx, labor, as an expense of human power, is the source of value, determined by the labor time socially necessary for production. The commodity's dual character defines it, as we know, by both its use value, insofar as it has a social utility and satisfies human needs, and its exchange value, quantitative relation in which use values are exchanged for each other. Value in itself is the principle of this relation, lying on the labor crystallized in commodities, i.e., on what is common to all of them and allows them to be compared. Thus, the very substance of value resides in abstract labor, which is undifferentiated and noncomplex.

Secondly, money: The exchange relation involves money. If the commodity asserts itself as use value and in relation to another commodity as exchange value, the latter remains expressed with respect to the use value proper to this other good. Money brings commodities into relation under a common expression representing them as values, independently of the use values. The labor contained in them manifests itself as abstract labor. Extending the concept of value to the labor-power commodity leads to that of surplus value, key to the theory of exploitation. Observed in the fact of the capitalist's enrichment, surplus value is, as is known, an excess value produced by the wage earner, once reproduced the value of labor power, equivalent to salary. Unable to spring from an identity of value with itself, it arises from the process of production. Invisibilized under the appearance of free and equal exchanges of labor, it can only be identified at the level of global social labor because of the impossible distinction between the labor times devoted to the reproduction of value or to the production of value beyond the equivalent. The relation of exploitation, through the purchase of the use of labor power by the capitalist, is a monetary one. As value, the commodity is money, and its price is value in money form, fixed in its relation to a special "object," both commodity and non-commodity, which embodies labor in general and serves as general equivalent.

Thirdly, profit: One of the "phenomenal" forms of the surplus value is – with money's interest, in particular – profit. As capitalism developed, a mode of production completely enclosed in the logic of money for money was propelled. The desire grew among capitalists to substitute commodities with money which, from a medium in exchanges, became a purpose in itself. Money acquired the property of functioning as capital, whose movement is only intended for profit. For Marx, profit is not a simple difference between income and expenditure, but results from the social organization of capitalism which polarizes the distribution of property rights. It is the form taken by the value form of the surplus labor, that is, the surplus value produced by the workers and extorted from them, according to the degree of exploitation of the labor power. Profit is a transformed form of surplus value, from which come all the income of the owners of capital. As an excess in money of commodity value over the production costs, it has a monetary form, implying the realization of commodities. Always for Marx, the rate of profit, or quotient of the surplus value to total advanced capital, is subject to laws, for some, spatial (intersectorial equalization under the effect of competition), for others, temporal (downward trend, stemming from a rising value composition of capital). Profit is born in the process of production, where surplus value is created, but is realized only in the process of circulation, from which seem to be drawn its commercial and banking parts, even more mystified forms of the "new value" than industrial profit. Fetishism in capitalist relations is such that profit seems to be generated from trade or even money itself. In the movement of capital, the extortion of social labor is concealed – just like the increasingly parasitic distribution of the conflictual fractions of profit.

And fourth, capital: Marx's determination of the concept of surplus value, which passes through the technical distinction between constant capital and variable capital, as sums of money, opens the way to the analysis of capital. The latter is the specific social relation of capitalist economy according to which value as valorization process is enhanced through the exploitation of labor. The exchange $M - C$, where the goals of use value and exchange value intertwine, can become a capitalist relationship $M - C - M'$, where the accumulation of abstract wealth predominates. This social relation of capital is characterized by an inequality, because money is transformed into a commodity only with a view to the production of a higher quantity of value. As we have said, for Marx, a single commodity is indeed capable of producing a greater quantity of value; it is the labor power, which can produce more than its own value, since it daily works longer than the time required for its own production and thus contributes to capital's valorization. So we understand that capital does not exist without money. The term capital therefore also designates value itself in its process of self-valorization.

The four concepts of value, money, profit, and capital under consideration, being at the heart of all economic thought and its various problematics, constitute by this very fact major intellectual battlefields where the Marxist theoricians confront the many representatives of the mainstream in economics. As we unfortunately know too well, the striking dominance of the neoclassical mainstream is overwhelming today in academic institutions and their ideological apparatuses. Nevertheless, this hegemony, which is exercised to the detriment of all economic heterodoxies – and in the forefront of them Marxism – has in reality nothing of a scientific superiority, since the problems that neoclassicals encounter are numerous, serious, and so to speak insoluble when considering each of the four concepts we have chosen to examine. Let's take a closer look.

Contrary to the proponents of labor value who establish a distinction between value and price, these two notions are confused ("value-price") for the neoclassicals. The theory of labor value certainly poses serious difficulties, in particular those of the heterogeneity of forms of labor not always being determined solely by time, of the existence of capital which represents past labor, of the taking into account of productive labor alone in the value's measure, or of the regulation of profits according to principles different from those of wages. To try to solve this last problem, linked to the transformation of values into prices, the neoclassicals decide to let the market take its course and do its thing, which led them not only to reject the labor value, but also to ignore the issue of value. The latter, for the mainstream, depends on the utility of the good and on the satisfaction provided to the one who holds this good. It then results from the confrontation of supply and demand, but, no longer distinguishing itself from the price, the neoclassicals cannot say anything about it. In this respect, it is symptomatic that Gérard Debreu, who founded with Kenneth Arrow and others the modern version of the general equilibrium theory, so to speak no longer used the term "value" beyond the introduction of his *Theory of Value* (1959).

Simultaneously a unit of account, an intermediary in exchanges and a means of reserve, money is accepted by all. Its property is to serve as a link between individuals, which supposes trust between them and with regard to the institution issuing it. However, a phenomenon such as trust is a matter of inter-individual relations, not of the behavior of agents taken in isolation; and the legal guarantee required of the State for its issuance and circulation in society requires the action of a network of institutions that cannot be reduced to individual choices. Money is a social and political link that connects individuals to each other and to a community in which they can identify. It comes that taking trust into account is a huge problem for the neoclassicals' methodological individualism giving primacy to the individual over society. It should be noted, by the way, that there is no money in their theoretical reference, the Arrow-Debreu model. Money is not a "neuter" tool, as the mainstream claims or as the expression "to make money work" suggests, forgetting that only human beings work. Money is not natural. It is a complex, contradictory social reality – just as inflation in an economy reflects the intensity of the class struggle inside that country. Money is power, an attribute of national sovereignty. Its common appropriation by the peoples conditions the control of their collective future.

Whereas, for Marx, as we have seen, all the value created finds its origin in labor and nowhere else, the neoclassicals, on the contrary, support the ideas that it also comes from capital, defined with them as an aggregate representing the whole inputs (with the notable exception of the labor "factor") integrated in a "production function," and that this capital "factor" is remunerated up to its contribution to production through profit, the "normal" counterpart of this created value. The neoclassicals nevertheless come up against a logical problem related to the definition of profit. Since the latter is conceived, for them, as the difference between income and expenses, and that these same expenditures are supposed to include the remuneration of all the factors that contribute to production, then such a difference can no longer remunerate anything more, thus certainly not capital. Hence a mainstream theory that leads to consider that profit is zero and this permanently or, in the best case, momentarily. Yet, zero profit is obviously not going to be very pleasant to hear or easy to accept by the capitalist entrepreneur. Anyway, the fact is that the neoclassicals do not provide a theoretical analysis of the capitalist entrepreneur either.

If, following Marx, the term "capital" refers to the specific type of exploitation of the capitalist system and designates a social relationship between the owners of the means of production and the wage earners, it is conceived very differently among the neoclassicals, as we have just seen. However, a big problem is attached to this aggregation method, because capital as a factor of production is not a single good, but a heterogeneous set. Here, the solution they propose is not one, since it consists in evaluating, thanks to a system of prices, each of the goods that make up this capital, then in adding the different numbers obtained so as to obtain a sum representative of the "capital." And this is where the problem lies, because this unique number corresponds to a monetary "value," and not to a physical entity, whereas the production function is supposed to represent only technical relations between the arguments that it integrates. The neoclassicals are consequently faced with the impossibility of calculating the prices of the production factors, including that of capital, by deriving them from the factorial marginal productivities, while determining the latter presupposes that their prices are known, including for capital.

In view of such difficulties encountered by the neoclassical mainstream, insurmountable by the methodologies it deploys, we understand that their current has no lesson in scientificity to give to Marxism. It is even the latter which, in our opinion, constitutes the most powerful scientific instrument of analysis today at our disposal to account for the complex evolutions of the world and above all to envisage and organize the social transformations aimed at emancipating the workers. This is what we will collectively strive to show in the contributions that follow. These cover a vast spectrum of current topics relating to capitalist globalization, going from changes in the monetary policy's instruments and objectives, the rise of the credit system and the mutations of money, transnational corporations and their strategic behavior in the competition specific to oligopolies, relocations and the decomposition of value chains to produce ever more segments in low-wage countries, trends in profit rates or the recent forms taken by unequal exchange, up to the current crisis of capital, financialization, fictitious capital and the accelerating fictitious movements of capital (including the credit system and money capital), the role of crypto-currencies, the possibilities of monetary regionalization, and, beyond all that, the opportunities for post-capitalist alternatives that are opening up before us.

Rémy Herrera, January 23, 2023

PART I

VALUE TODAY

MONEY, CREDIT, AND FICTITIOUS CAPITAL IN MARX'S THEORY OF VALUE

Alfredo Saad-Filho

ABSTRACT

*This chapter offers a Marxist analysis of forms of value in capitalist econo-
mies, and their implications for accumulation, (in)stability, and economic
policy. The study focuses on seven key categories: money, capital, credit,
interest-bearing capital, fictitious capital, the domestic public debt, and macroeconomic management through monetary and fiscal policy. It argues, first,
that there is an intrinsic tendency toward the growing complexity of value
forms in capitalism. Its examination helps to locate the contradictions of
accumulation at increasingly complex levels, and the emergence of specifically
financial forms of instability. Second, state management of accumulation
through fiscal and monetary policy and the domestic public debt are essential
for the stabilization of the economy, but their effectiveness remains limited.
Third, monetary and financial structures, their relationship with production,
and capacity to stretch, transform, and (de)stabilize accumulation are historically and institutionally specific. Fourth, public policy can influence the
level and composition of output and employment, and the distributional and
other outcomes of accumulation. Examination of the capital relation from this
angle can shed light upon the drivers and modalities of accumulation of real
and financial assets, and the imperatives, forms, and limitations of state
regulation of accumulation.*

Keywords: Value; money; credit; fictitious capital; monetary policy;
domestic public debt

Value, Money, Profit, and Capital Today
Research in Political Economy, Volume 39, 3–18
Copyright © 2024 Alfredo Saad-Filho
Published under exclusive licence by Emerald Publishing Limited
ISSN: 0161-7230/doi:10.1108/S0161-723020230000039001

INTRODUCTION

This chapter offers a systematic analysis of the emergence of complex forms of value in capitalist economies from the point of view of Marx's theory of value. The work focuses on the following concepts: money, capital, credit, interest-bearing capital (IBC), fictitious capital, the domestic public debt (DPD), and macroeconomic management through monetary and fiscal policy. These concepts have been insufficiently examined in the Marxian literature.[1] Their analysis can offer insights supporting heterodox critiques of contemporary (financialized) capitalism, its fragilities and crises, and the role and limitations of economic policy.

The argument is developed in seven sections. This introduction is the first. The second offers a brief account of Marx's theory of money, and reviews the distinction between the circulation of money as money (Type 1) and the circulation of money as capital (Type 2).[2] The third explains IBC, the credit system, and the determination of the interest rate. This account of credit relations shows that dualist analyses separating "real production" from an ontologically distinct "financial sphere" are misguided. Production and finance are integrated across institutions, markets, assets, regulations, and policies; however, their interaction can lead to destabilizing outcomes. The fourth explains the emergence of fictitious capital, the capital markets, and the financial system. This section also suggests that there is an intrinsic (structural) tendency toward financialization in capitalism.[3] The fifth examines three modalities of state finance and their implications for accumulation, financial development, and the circulation and appropriation of value: taxation, monetization of deficits, and the DPD. The sixth reviews the necessity of state management of the accumulation of capital, the scope for fiscal and monetary policy, and their macroeconomic consequences, focusing on the DPD. This section argues that fiscal and monetary policy and the operation of the financial institutions can create liquid resources and shift them across distinct modalities of circulation, potentially changing the structure and outcomes of accumulation. The DPD is one of the most influential tools in this context. The final section summarizes the chapter and offers the relevant conclusions.

Identification of the key categories, tendencies, countertendencies, and policies concerning financial accumulation does not imply that the circuits of production, money, and finance can be examined purely logically. However, historical processes cannot be foregrounded at this stage both because of space limitations and because this chapter does not investigate specific monetary instruments, financial institutions, crises, or state policies. It merely seeks to outline a consistent framework for their examination drawing upon Marx's value categories. The framework developed below remains to be integrated into a broader understanding of the dynamics of accumulation in particular places and times. Despite these limitations, this chapter shows that Marx's value theory can be usefully deployed to locate the source of profit, interest, rent, and other sources of income. It can also suggest why and how capital accumulation takes increasingly financialized forms, how these must be accompanied by specific modalities of regulation, the limits of such regulation, and the changes in the forms of crisis under financialized capitalism.

THE CIRCULATION OF MONEY

In the Marxian literature, money is the measure of value and means of circulation (or means of exchange), and it performs the functions of means of payment, store of value, and international money. Several instruments can perform one or more of these functions, among them cash, debit and credit cards, certificates of deposit, treasury bills, and foreign currency. In practice, these instruments are arranged in a hierarchy with "money proper" at its pinnacle, as the only instrument that can serve across all functions, be exchanged for any asset, and settle all transactions.[4]

Drawing upon his reading of Tooke, Marx distinguishes between the circulation of *money as money* (Circulation Type 1) and *money as capital* (Circulation Type 2).[5] Money circulates as money when it is spent with no expectation of profit or even return. This includes unrequited transfers (e.g., gifts, tax payments, or the repayment of consumer loans) as well as the expenditure of revenue to buy goods and services for unproductive consumption, which will erase their use value and, with it, their value. This type of expenditure can be represented by simple commodity exchange, $C - M - C$, where C stands for commodities with equal value and different use values, and M is money.

Money circulates as capital when it is advanced with the expectation of profit, that is, it aims either to produce surplus value, or to capture it in exchange (Marx, 1981, p. 575). The creation of value can be represented by the circuit of industrial capital,

$$M - C <^{MP}_{LP} \ldots P \ldots C' - M'$$

where MP is means of production (land, buildings, machines, unprocessed goods, and so on), LP is labor power, $\ldots P \ldots$ is production, and $M' > M$. The capture of value in exchange can be represented by the circuit of IBC: $M - M'$ (see section "The Credit System").

When a capitalist purchases LP and MP, this is Circulation Type 2. However, while the purchase of MP preserves money-capital, as it realizes the advances of the (presumably capitalist) suppliers, the payment of wages destroys money-capital, as those resources become money as money in the hands of the workers (i.e., these funds shift into Circulation Type 1). When the workers spend their wages, they may realize advances of money-capital (e.g., if they buy products of capital at the supermarket, or repay their loans with commercial banks), or they might keep those resources in Circulation Type 1 (if they purchase commodities at the local farmers' market or pay their income taxes). Similarly, if it is assumed that the state neither extracts surplus value directly nor seeks to valorize its advances, public spending is unproductive and involves only money as money. This includes, in the first instance, purchases of consumables or consultancy services, infrastructure building and maintenance, welfare transfers, salaries, pensions, and the service of the DPD (see section "Public Finance and the DPD").

THE CREDIT SYSTEM

For Marx, IBC is credit extended to industrial, merchant, or money-dealing capitalist borrowers by specialized capitalist lenders, especially commercial, investment, and savings banks (the credit system). They provide money-capital for Circulation Type 2 (represented by the circuit $M - M'$), in order to create surplus value or to accelerate its realization (Marx, 1981, pp. 461, 477, 515–516). The loans must be repaid, plus interest, out of surplus value extracted in production or captured in exchange.[6] When the credit system supplies IBC, it deals in money as a "commodity *sui generis*,"[7] with the use value of self-expansion, i.e., its employment can facilitate the production of value. It follows that, in order to use IBC, one must be a capitalist rather than merely a borrower (Marx, 1981, p. 743). In contrast, households, rentiers, and the state can fund their unproductive expenditures (Circulation Type 1) with simple credit. Simple credit can be advanced by a wide variety of financial institutions, and the loans must be repaid out of revenue (wages, rent, or taxes; see Hudson, 2010).

The interest rate is the unit price of borrowed money-capital (Marx, 1981, pp. 687, 714). The market price of produced commodities is regulated by the law of value: it is rooted in the labor time socially necessary in production, and constrained by real wages, technologies, input costs, turnover times, supply and demand, and the pressure toward the intersectoral equalization of profit rates. In contrast, the price of IBC, a commodity that exists only in the sphere of exchange, is "irrational" or "accidental": interest is a share of the surplus value produced with the support of borrowed capital, and the interest rate is determined contingently by the regulatory, institutional and market relationships between lenders and borrowers. There is neither a "natural" rate of interest nor an economic law governing its movements.[8] Finally, the payment of interest leaves behind a residual that Marx calls profit of enterprise, which remunerates industrial and commercial capital.

IBC emerges from several sources. They include the pooling of hoards into the credit system, especially money as money held by workers and the state, and money-capital owned by industrial or commercial capitalists. These hoards accrue for several reasons, for example, lags between receipts and payments, for precaution, and to fund investment.[9] It follows that IBC is properly located at the level of the economy as a whole, rather than emerging from individual transactions between savers and investors or between lenders and borrowers, mediated by the banks. First, IBC draws upon the structural function of the loans in social reproduction, rather than the (infinitely diverse, possibly shifting, sometimes unrealized, and even fraudulent) motives of individual lenders and borrowers. Second, the outcome of each circuit (whether $M - C - M'$ or $M - M'$) depends upon the rhythm of accumulation at the social level (Marx, 1981, pp. 566–567).

Third, IBC can speed up commodity circulation and reduce turnover times; support more ambitious investments, technological advancements, and mergers and acquisitions than would be possible otherwise; and integrate all circuits of capital, as the credit system draws resources from everywhere and allocates IBC by socially determined criteria including profitability, risk, interest rates, policy guidance, and economic fashions or speculative frenzies.[10]

The expansion of IBC turns the credit system into the common source of money-capital for the bourgeoisie. The pool of IBC is managed by a cohort of professionals working on behalf of capital in general.[11] In IBC:

> ... [a]ll particular forms of capital, arising from its investment in particular spheres of production or circulation, are obliterated (...). [Capital] exists in the undifferentiated, self-identical form of independent value, of money (...). Here capital really does emerge, in the pressure of its demand and supply, as *the common capital of the class* (...). [It appears] as a concentrated and organized mass, placed under the control of the bankers as representatives of the social capital (...). The result is that, as far as the form of demand goes, capital for loan is faced with the entire weight of a class, as far as supply goes, it itself appears *en masse* as loan capital.[12]

Through its control of IBC, the credit system regulates the flows of resources in the economy, determines the level and composition of investment, output, employment, and trade, and helps to equalize as well as raise the general rate of profit. Even though the resources newly created by IBC are the property of specific capitalists, they come into being only because the social conditions of production have been transformed by IBC. Now, capital functions as social property and investment becomes independent of individual prior savings.[13] By the same token, interest is no longer an individual overhead: it becomes part of the general costs of production, an opportunity cost for every capital, and the regulator of prices of production (Saad-Filho, 2002, chapter 8). In doing this, the credit system "abolishes the private character of capital (...) within the confines of the capitalist mode of production itself" (Marx, 1981, pp. 567, 742).

FICTITIOUS CAPITAL AND THE FINANCIAL SYSTEM

Every investment brings an expected flow of returns that can take the form of profit, rent, dividends, interest, or other payments. In turn, any regular value flow can be capitalized, potentially giving rise to a (possibly immaterial) income-generating asset that can be represented by a tradable title of ownership. Marx calls these paper claims to (surplus) value yet to be produced *fictitious capital*.[14]

The capital that they represent is "fictitious" not because it is imagined, but because these claims replicate capital already deployed elsewhere, embody values already destroyed, or symbolize nontransferable or even nonexistent assets. These paper titles are only indirectly associated with real accumulation: they can be created regardless of the underlying assets or the constraints of value-production, and their returns depend on claims on (surplus) value to be produced elsewhere. Finally, they emerge through a reversal of the law of value, by which the returns "create" the income-generating assets, rather than vice-versa (De Brunhoff, 1998, p. 183).

Fictitious capital can take several forms, for example, shares, debt certificates, bonds, and public securities and, at a further remove (often as claims on claims), future contracts, collateralized debt obligations (CDOs), and a myriad of derivatives.[15] Two examples offer a template for the examination of most varieties of fictitious capital: shares and public securities.

Suppose, first, that a firm issues shares through an Initial Public Offering (IPO). The investors advance their money-capital to acquire tradable titles of ownership over the firm's capital (Circulation Type 2). At this point, the firm's capital seems to exist twice. It exists, first, as land, buildings, machines, technologies, inventories, brands, and so on, that, in combination with labor, can generate a flow of output and a stream of profits. Second, it *also* seems to exist as shares, with the peculiarity that, unless they have enough voting rights, the shareholders do not control the firm's real assets and cannot dispose of them: the shares are merely tradable claims on the firm's future profits, part of which will be distributed as dividends (Circulation Type 1). Correspondingly, the market value of the firm, represented by its share price, expresses the value of its real assets as well as its expected profits, which may fluctuate independently from each other and from the firm's output (Marx, 1981, pp. 597, 608–609; see also Hilferding, 1910, chapter 7).

The second case involves public securities (see section "Public Finance and the DPD"). In the simplest case, the state can fund its outlays, in part, by selling interest-bearing titles to banks and other capitalists.[16] The money-capital exchanged for public securities (Circulation Type 2) is destroyed, as it becomes money as money to be spent by the state (Circulation Type 1). Marx stresses that, in contrast with shares, that generally represent productive assets, government securities do not represent any assets in particular: they are merely the ghostly imprint of public expenditures past, of whatever nature, and they confirm the holder's claim on future social output through the taxes to be collected by the state. In the meantime, the buyers' money-capital is transformed into paper assets that can be traded in secondary markets. The market price of these securities is determined by the capitalized value of the expected payments to their holders:

> [Public securities] are capital only for the person who has bought them (…). They are not capital in themselves (…), [but] simply property titles which give the holder a claim to future surplus-value (…). The state has to pay its creditors a certain sum of interest each year for the capital it borrows. It this case the creditor cannot recall his capital (…), but can only sell the (…) title of ownership. The capital itself has been consumed, spent by the state. It no longer exists (…). [T]he capital from which the state's payment is taken as deriving, as interest, is illusory and fictitious. It is not only that the sum that was lent to the state no longer has any kind of existence. It was never designed to be spent as capital, to be invested, and yet only by being invested as capital could it have been made into a self-maintaining value. As far as the original creditor (…) is concerned, the share of the annual taxation he receives represents interest on his capital.[17]

Since future interest rates and the returns on fictitious capital cannot be guaranteed *ex ante*, the price of these titles is inherently speculative (Marx, 1981, p. 589). They are based on the underlying asset values (if any), expected macroeconomic variables, and the interactions and emerging beliefs of the traders ("the market"), which cannot be "correct" in any objective sense. They prevail only because the traders endorse them.[18]

Despite these intimations of artificiality, fictitious capital is not merely epiphenomenal. It can influence real accumulation by changing the distribution of assets and income flows, shifting resources across Circulations Types 1 and 2, facilitating new investments, and financing production, consumption and speculation, not least through the wealth effect. As it gives production greater flexibility, fictitious capital can even shift the threat of crisis (see section "The Scope and Limits of State Management of Accumulation"; Marx, 1981, p. 598; Fine, 2013–2014, pp. 50–51).

The financial system comprises the credit system and the capital markets (the institutions and exchanges dealing in fictitious capital, including shares, public securities, claims on foreign exchange and key commodities, especially oil, metals, bullion and foodstuffs, and the markets for options and derivatives). The component parts of the financial system interact closely. The credit system mobilizes resources, creates IBC *ex nihilo*, and supplies bundles of claims and cleverly designed derivatives for trading in the capital markets, which provide collateral for the entire economy, especially the financial institutions themselves. In turn, the capital markets amass investible funds and provide returns to all savers, while benefitting disproportionately the largest capitals.[19]

As the financial system expands, it can draw idle morsels of money as money and money-capital into (possibly very short term) "investment" in fictitious capital. In doing this, the financial system subsumes the hoarding function of money. More importantly, finance integrates every circuit of capital, commands all forms of fictitious capital and drives the capital markets, as it draws both resources and information from every firm and market (and, increasingly, every citizen), in order to trade claims based on different underlying assets with distinct returns, risks, and maturities. In doing this, finance seems to offer the possibility of automatic valorization of any advance, as if profit were an attribute of money, regardless of the mundane realities of lumpy technologies, uncertain changes in relative prices, and the challenges of managing unruly workers.[20]

This is illusory because financial claims do not directly produce (surplus) value. In contrast with commodities and tangible means of production, that (when purchased without the mediation of credit) appear only on the asset side of the balance sheet of social wealth, financial assets and bank loans have counterparts on the debit side: they appear simultaneously on the asset and liability sides. Consequently, their accumulation cannot, in and of itself, create wealth and, to the extent that running the financial system is costly, not least because of the remunerations involved, IBC and fictitious capital destroy value produced elsewhere (Marx, 1981, p. 945). This does not imply that there is a negative relationship between the size of the financial system and the rate of accumulation for, as was shown above, credit and fictitious capital can also raise profitability by permitting productive activities that would otherwise not take place. However, their net impact on accumulation depends on the institutional framework and on circumstances that can be examined only concretely.

PUBLIC FINANCE AND THE DPD

State expenditures are essential to secure the political, administrative, and infrastructural conditions for the accumulation of capital as a whole. These expenditures and their financing have unavoidable distributive implications, making them irreducibly political.

The financing of the state is based primarily on taxation, monetary expansion (seignorage), and the sale of securities. The most direct way for the state to cover its expenditures is to print inconvertible currency, but there is a risk of inflation in case of overissue (Saad-Filho, 2002, chapter 8).

If the state taxes income, expenditures, or wealth, the taxpayers must transfer resources to the Treasury. Given the definition of value of labor power as the costs of reproduction of the workforce, taxes must ultimately derive from surplus value.[21] It follows, then, that taxation shifts resources from Circulation Type 2 to Type 1; that is, it drains the economy's pool of capital and, in principle, reduces its growth potential. Conversely, the state spends money as money, and these resources may become capital and foster economic growth. The concrete impact of taxation and public spending on the rhythm and structure of accumulation depends on a myriad of variables. These outcomes cannot be fully controlled by government policy, and the intended outcomes may be partly neutralized by hoarding, financial innovations, or international capital flows.

Finally, if state spending is financed by the sale of securities, the buyers advance IBC in exchange for new fictitious capital. That IBC is converted into a public debt to be serviced, and its value is dispersed through (unproductive) public spending. From a social perspective, the DPD does not directly add value or increase the economy's capital stock: the bonds are liabilities for the state and assets for their holders, including banks, pension funds, firms, and individual investors.

The financial institutions purchase and distribute public securities in exchange for fees and interest payments. These are not their only sources of profit through the DPD. Public securities are both safe and highly liquid, since the Central Bank holds gold, foreign currency and other reserves, and the state can levy taxes and print domestic currency at will. For these reasons, public securities are "top quality" assets in bank balance sheets, and they can support the creation of new IBC, for example, by serving as collateral for the expansion of loans. In turn, these loans can fund both real and financial investment, bringing additional income to the banks.

The large size, liquidity, safety, and systemic significance of the DPD turns the interest rates on these securities into the benchmark for the prices and yield curves of many types of fictitious capital. In this way, public policy – operating through the financial system – can influence the returns on real and financial investments (including different forms of money, debt, and fictitious capital), the formation of prices of real and fictitious assets, the level and composition of output, employment and foreign trade, the (perception of) inflationary pressures, and the rate of profit of capital a whole (see section "The Scope and Limits of State Management of Accumulation").

The DPD offers financial institutions, firms, and wealthy individuals an instrument to help regulate their reserves, park funds temporarily available, obtain liquidity at short notice, and move seamlessly across different forms of fictitious capital. In doing this, the DPD also offers unparalleled scope for purely financial accumulation. Debt finance can also reduce taxation, protecting the mass of surplus value – although, in exchange, some of society's IBC must be transmogrified, on a strictly voluntary basis, into fictitious capital. This fictitious capital grants the state creditors claims upon a share of future tax revenues in the form of interest, drawing upon yet-to-be-produced surplus value. Those payments will convert money as money into money-capital, and replenish the stock of IBC:

> As with the stroke of an enchanter's wand, [the public debt] endows unproductive money with the power of creation and thus turns it into capital, without forcing it to expose itself to the troubles and risks inseparable from its employment in industry or even in usury. The state creditors actually give nothing away, for the sum lent is transformed into public bonds, easily negotiable, which go on functioning in their hands just as so much hard cash would. But furthermore, and quite apart from the class of idle *rentiers* thus created… the national debt has given rise to joint-stock companies, to dealings in negotiable effects of all kinds, and to speculation: in a word, to (…) gambling and the modern bankocracy.[22]

Marx's approach can capture the distributional implications of the DPD at two levels. At an abstract level, the DPD underpins the credit system and the functioning of the capitalist state. More concretely, the textbook arguments that state spending creates "demand" in general, and that the DPD is a liability of society to itself (the so-called "Ricardian equivalence") are misguided. Under the appearance of offering everyone opportunities to gain through financial investment, in return for the duty to share equally in the service of the DPD, the state chooses to impose taxes that are too low to fund its own expenditures; it then funds the remainder by borrowing primarily from the wealthiest citizens, to whom it pays interest. It follows that public sector borrowing rewards the wealthy for owning assets that should have been confiscated instead, and that the government pays interest disproportionately to the richest, instead of simply taxing them. In this way, the DPD supports the centralization of wealth in the hands of large capitalists and speculators, whose already vast fortunes expand further through transfers from the public purse. In turn, indebted states have less policy space, since their choices are constrained by the humor of the financial markets.[23]

This shows why the DPD is the most desirable modality of state finance from the point of view of capital. In contrast, taxation compulsorily drains the mass of surplus value, while the monetization of fiscal deficits bypasses the financial institutions entirely. This may help to explain the antipathy of finance toward monetization, the capitalist dislike of taxation (at least until state spending realizes some profits), and the universal applause which greets debt finance (at least while it can be serviced). Conversely, debt finance is disadvantageous for the state because this is the costliest modality of public finance, as it entails long-lasting repayment obligations.

In summary, the DPD is the foundation of capitalist finance and the keystone of the capital markets. It supports the institutions and processes that mobilize social resources, including the movements of money and capital across Circulation Type 1 and Circulation Type 2, as well as the creation, allocation and destruction of IBC and fictitious capital. In doing this, the DPD underpins both the *actual* emergence of capital in general through the financial system, and the management of accumulation by the state.

THE SCOPE AND LIMITS OF STATE MANAGEMENT OF ACCUMULATION

Any sophisticated capitalist economy has a monetary system based on inconvertible "money proper" backing up a financial system creating credit, supplying IBC and trading a plethora of monetary assets and fictitious capital. The financial system concentrates, allocates, manages, and represents capital as a whole; it also plays a key role funding the state. Most financial institutions are highly leveraged and closely linked together and to the state through complex chains of obligations. The largest institutions are also systemically important ("too big to fail"). The accumulation of capital in general is predicated on the stability of this arrangement, including the validation of the claims shuttling in and around the financial system.

The value relations in the economy and the chains of obligations attached to them, including the stocks and flows of IBC and fictitious capital, their composition, costs, rate of accumulation, and other macroeconomic variables can be (imperfectly) managed by specialist state institutions, especially the Treasury, the Central Bank, and the Ministry of Finance. They seek to regulate the credit system, the capital markets, the public finances (including the DPD), and manage the exchange rate and the conflicting claims of industrial capital, commercial capital, the rentiers, the workers, and other groups. These are complex tasks, since finance is prone to instability because price formation in the markets for IBC and fictitious capital is relatively autonomous from fundamental value relations. Consequently, shifts in interest rates or financial asset prices can feed upon themselves and propagate instability, instead of converging toward any type of "fundamental" values which, often, simply do not exist.

The DPD is one of the most important policy tools available to the state authorities. When the economy confronts financial instability or threats of uncontrolled devaluation and system-wide contraction, the state can change interest rates (that is, shift the price of IBC, the opportunity cost of capital and the pivot of the formation of prices of production), and deploy public securities to transform surplus (underperforming) capitals into fictitious capital created by the state itself ("sterilization"). That is, monetary and fiscal policy can guarantee private profit at collective expense.

The DPD is suited to the management of accumulation because changes in the discount rate and open market operations can reduce the risks of default, over-production, speculation, and inflation; resuscitate unviable fictitious capital and distressed financial institutions; modify real wages, the opportunity cost of investment, and the level and structure of demand; rebalance relative prices, the structure of financial claims, and the flows of money as money and money-capital; improve the allocation of real and financial capital, and stabilize the general rate of profit. In order to deliver these outcomes, the state offers to some capitalists a share in yet-to-be-produced surplus value, which will be channeled to them through the tax system. In exchange, those capitalists voluntarily surrender IBC or fictitious capital awaiting better opportunities for valorization, so their losses can be socialized by public policy. As Marx snappily put it:

> To uphold prices, and thus ward off the active cause of the distress, the State must pay the prices ruling before the outbreak of the commercial panic, and realize the value of bills of exchange which had ceased to represent anything but (...) failures. In other words, the fortune of the whole community, which the Government represents, ought to make good for the losses of private capitalists. This [is a] sort of communism, where the mutuality is all on one side.[24]

Monetary policy interventions can be supplemented by fiscal policy, that can irrigate directly Circulation Type 1 (for example, through welfare payments) and Circulation Type 2 (through subsidies or purchases from capitalist enterprises). In short, even though the state does not directly produce value, it can deploy policy tools to secure profitability elsewhere, and to reduce the risks of overproduction, underconsumption and disproportion; that is, to manage capital accumulation.[25]

Despite the stabilizing potential of monetary and fiscal policy, the authorities have only limited scope to neutralize the overaccumulation of capital through the regulation of short-term interest rates and the substitution of state-issued ficti-tious capital for surplus IBC. Even an inconvertible money system with floating exchange rates, that maximizes the scope for policy intervention, cannot ensure success. Stabilization policies are costly and, regardless of expense, the state remains unable to create surplus value directly, regulate real wages with preci-sion, resolve all social conflicts, honor all financial claims, guarantee financial stability, keep inflation always on target, or bypass the balance of payments constraint.

Monetary policy not only has limited effectiveness. To the extent that it does work, it supports an exclusionary mode of production and fosters a concentrating dynamic of accumulation predicated on despoliation, speculation and transfers of surplus value. This financialized form of accumulation centers on the protection of fictitious capital above all else, skewing the incentive structure and systemat-ically rewarding the most parasitic fractions of capital. In addition, the longer crises are avoided the more remote becomes the threat of failure. The incentives for technical innovation and the adoption of profit-maximizing managerial strategies decline, while the rewards for risky strategies of accumulation increase, which tends to reinforce the financialization of the economy as a whole.

In other words, while activist monetary and fiscal policies can deliver – within limits – macroeconomic stability, their successes eventually promote the over-accumulation of capital as a whole. As the economy grows, disproportions and bottlenecks emerge, financial structures become more fragile, and prices tend to increase. The contradictory demands of growth and stability, distributional and other conflicts, the balance of payments constraint and other limits to state policy can lock the economy into a stabilization-speculation trap that can be difficult to manage. Eventually, crises erupt spontaneously, or because contractionary policies have been imposed in order to limit the mushrooming economic imbalances.

In summary, Marx's analysis shows how the state can influence the structure and rhythm of accumulation; it also shows that it can lead to outcomes that are never entirely predictable, and that can be destabilizing. The ensuing tensions and displacements can help to explain disputes over the regulatory and institutional architecture, the choice of industrial, wage, exchange rate and other policies, and the development of the crisis tendencies inherent in capitalism. Marx's theory of value provides a unique window upon the processes of growth, instability, and crisis, and upon policy management in capitalism, through its distinctive focus on the tensions and displacements between the value system and the price system, by means of fictitious capital. This approach can help to inform the critique of political economy, as much as it can support the analysis of concrete economic policies.

CONCLUSION

This chapter reconstructs systematically the monetary, credit, and financial systems in Marx's value theory. These categories are essential for the analysis of interest, the formation of market prices, fictitious capital, financialization, and the management of accumulation by fiscal and monetary policy, where the domestic public debt plays a pivotal role. Investigation of these issues is centrally important for the study of contemporary capitalism; unfortunately, they have been relatively neglected in the Marxian literature.

The inquiry departs from the abstract concept of money as money, and it gradually incorporates money-capital and their distinctive forms of circulation, that Marx termed Type 1 and Type 2. This is followed by the systematic introduction of increasingly concrete concepts, especially credit, interest, interest-bearing capital, fictitious capital, and the financial system. The contradictions of real and financial accumulation posit the need for state management of capitalist reproduction that, in turn, allows the examination of monetary and fiscal policy and their limitations.

The analysis is grounded upon the recognition of the ontological unity between three sets of institutions that are commonly examined separately, or even in opposition: the (financial) markets and the state, production and finance, and the structures and institutions in the financial system. Value analysis illuminates their mutually constituting relationships, and lends support to the claim that political economy approaches can be more informative than mainstream theories of money, finance, and economic policy.

The development of capitalist production gives rise to IBC, the financial system, and fictitious capital. They tend to centralize the main sources of capital, and to manage the relationships between savers and investors, taxpayers and the state, and the economy and the rest of the world. In this way, finance supports the extraction of (surplus) value and helps to regulate output and employment. Finance also imposes the law of value through the general profit rate, supplies instruments allowing capital to hedge against risks and funds the public sector – but it also absorbs value produced elsewhere, concentrates income and wealth and creates specific forms of macroeconomic instability.

These tensions and displacements can trigger financial instability and devaluations of real and fictitious capital. They can be partly avoided, partly managed, and partly deferred by monetary and fiscal policy, which aims to regulate Circulations Type 1 and 2, the supply of IBC and fictitious capital, and the formation of prices. Ultimately, however, successful regulation breeds overproduction and overaccumulation. That is, value analysis shows that capitalist economies are fundamentally unstable, and it can inform studies of the scope for successful macroeconomic management and its limits.

Analysis of the contradictions of capitalism at different levels of complexity, and examination of monetary and fiscal policy, distinct forms of state finance and their implications for distribution and stability can illuminate the sectoral and political consequences of each modality of accumulation, as well as their contradictions. They can be outlined in principle and examined in practice. These are essential tasks for political economy.

NOTES

1. Hilferding's (1910) study was the most significant contribution to the field between the publication of *Capital 3*, in 1894, and the outstanding works by De Brunhoff (1976, 1978) and Rosdolsky (1977). These works inspired many ground-breaking contributions in the following period.

2. This approach draws upon a relatively literature, including Boger (1983), Ricciardi (1985), and Trindade (2006).

3. "Financialization" includes mutually reinforcing tendencies toward: (a) the expansion of the financial system, gauged by the volume and complexity of the assets that it produces, accumulates, and trades; (b) the transformation of the overaccumulation of financial assets into the typical form of overproduction; and (c) the imbrication of the state into the financial system. These tendencies are accompanied by countertendencies that can moderate, channel, or even reverse the destabilizing implications of financialization. They can include regulation, capital exports, and compensatory monetary policies.

4. Marx (1981, p. 492); see also De Brunhoff (1976, chapter 2), Fine and Saad-Filho (2016, chapters 2 and 3), Itoh and Lapavitsas (1999, chapters 3 and 4), Rosdolsky (1977, part II), and Saad-Filho (2002, chapter 8).

5. See Marx (1976, pp. 247–257, 1978, pp. 163–164, 1981, pp. 574–577, 592, 1986, pp. 304–309).

6. For simplicity, "interest payments" include the difference between borrowing and lending rates and the fees and charges on the loan.

7. See Marx (1981, pp. 459–460, 464, 471–478, 502–503, 517–518, 570–571, 626–627, 638, 658, 741).

8. Marx (1981, pp. 455–457, 475–478, 480–504, 638–639, 644–645). See also Fine (2013–2014, p. 52) and Itoh and Lapavitsas (1999, chapter 3).

9. These hoards are a "precipitate" of the circulation process, see Marx (1981, pp. 432–437, 528–529, 570–571, 626–627, 638–639, 658, 670, 701–702, 706–707, 741–742). See also Itoh and Lapavitsas (1999, chapters 3 and 4).

10. Marx (1981, pp. 566–567, 570–571, 626–627, 638, 658, 741). See also De Brunhoff (1978, p. 57).

11. In this article, capital in general and capital as a whole are synonymous.

12. Marx (1981, pp. 490–491; see also pp. 459–460), Marx (1981, p. 852), Chesnais (2004, p. 33), Harvey (1982, p. 286) and Henwood (1998, p. 238).

13. "[T]he industrial capitalist does not "save" his capital but rather disposes of the savings of others (...). [T]he credit that the reproductive capitalists give one another, and that the public give them, he makes into his own source of private enrichment. The final illusion of the capitalist system, that capital is the offspring of a person's own work and savings, is thereby demolished. Not only does profit consist in the appropriation of other people's labour, but the capital with which this labour of others is set in motion and exploited consists of other people's property, which the money-capitalist puts at the disposal of the industrial capitalist and for which he in turn exploits him" (Marx, 1981, p. 640). See also Marx (1981, pp. 368, 567, 569–570, 572, 678–679, 742–743).

14. Marx (1981, pp. 459–461, 595–599, 608). See also De Brunhoff (1976, pp. 95–96), Chesnais (2016, chapter 3), Durand (2017, chapter 3), Fine (2013–2014), Hudson (2010), and, especially, Perelman (2008).

15. Marx also calls fictitious capital the credit money created through the multiplier, or the issue of notes ("tokens of value") beyond the bank's metal reserve (Marx, 1981, p. 675). The most absurd form of fictitious capital is "human capital," since labor power is neither alienable from its owner nor collateralizable (De Brunhoff, 1998, p. 183; Ricciardi, 1985, pp. 8–9, 284).

16. For simplicity, it is assumed that the state has only domestic debt and no external liabilities.

17. Marx (1981, pp. 590, 595–596; see also pp. 598–599).

18. "What are commonly called competitive pressures in financial markets are in fact pressures to emulate market leaders (...). While this may speed the emergence of consensus (...), it may be as much through the exchange of disinformation and rumor as by the exchange of those prices and trading intentions that are the basis of neo-classical theories of financial markets (...). Because the business of financial firms is so dependent on reputation among other financial firms, pressures for conformity may seriously inhibit competitive behavior of the kind envisaged by neo-classical theorists" (Toporowski, 2000, p. 118).

19. Marx (1981, pp. 599–601). See also Chesnais (2004, p. 15), Hudson (2010) and Nesvetailova (2006, p. 45). For a Marxist account of derivatives, see Bryan and Rafferty (2006), Guttman (1996) and Norfield (2012, 2014). Options and futures are examined by Parsons (1988). Henwood (1998, p. 13) rightly argues that "fictitious capital (...) enables a whole class to own an economy's productive assets, rather than being bound to a specific property as they once were."

20. Marx (1981, pp. 338–341, 350–352, 355, 372–374, 378–381, 460, 498, 501, 516–518). See also Bellamy Foster (2010), Davis (2012, p. 50), Hudson (2010), Saad-Filho (2002, chapter 8) and Trindade (2006, pp. 85–86, 116–117).

21. See Fine, Lapavitsas, and Saad-Filho (2004). For a contrasting view, see Davanzati and Patalano (2017).

22. Marx (1976, p. 919).

23. There is a close relationship between domestic and international financial developments concerning the DPD. For example, "[a]long with the national debt there arose an international credit system" (Marx, 1976, p. 920), which imposes the supremacy of world money over national currencies.

24. Marx (1986, p. 405).
25. Keynes (1936, p. 238) famously claimed that: "It is not the ownership of the instruments of production which it is important for the State to assume. If the State is able to determine the aggregate amount of resources devoted to augmenting the instruments and the basic rate of reward to those who own them, it will have accomplished all that is necessary."

REFERENCES

Bellamy Foster, J. (2010). The financialization of accumulation. *Monthly Review, 62*(5), 1–17.

Boger, K. (1983). *Credit and inflation: Marx on fictitious capital and stagflation*. PhD thesis. New School for Social Research.

De Brunhoff, S. (1976). *Marx on money*. New York, NY: Urizen Books.

De Brunhoff, S. (1978). *The state, capital and economic policy*. London: Pluto Press.

De Brunhoff, S. (1998). Money, interest and finance in Marx's *Capital*. In R. Bellofiore (Ed.), *Marxian economics: A reappraisal* (Vol. 1). London: Macmillan.

Bryan, D., & Rafferty, M. (2006). *Capitalism with derivatives*. London: Palgrave.

Chesnais, F. (2004). Le Capital de placement: Accumulation, internationalisation, effets économiques et politiques. In *La Finance mondialisée*. Paris: La Découverte.

Chesnais, F. (2016). *Finance capital today*. Leiden: Brill.

Davanzati, G. F., & Patalano, R. (2017). Marx on public debt: Fiscal expropriation and capital reproduction. *International Journal of Political Economy, 46*, 50–64.

Davis, A. E. (2012). The new "voodoo economics": Fetishism and the public/private divide. *Review of Radical Political Economics, 45*(1), 42–58.

Durand, C. (2017). *Fictitious capital*. London: Verso.

Fine, B. (2013–2014). Financialization from a Marxist perspective. *International Journal of Political Economy, 42*(4), 47–66.

Fine, B., Lapavitsas, C., & Saad-Filho, A. (2004). Transforming the transformation problem: Why the 'New Interpretation' is a wrong turning. *Review of Radical Political Economics, 36*(1), 3–19.

Fine, B., & Saad-Filho, A. (2016). *Marx's Capital* (6th ed.). London: Pluto Press.

Guttman, R. (1996). Les mutations du capital financier. In F. Chesnais (Ed.), *La mondialisation financière*. Paris: Syros.

Harvey, D. (1982). *Limits to capital*. London: Verso.

Henwood, D. (1998). *Wall street*. London: Verso.

Hilferding, R. (1910, 1981). *Finance capital*. London: Routle dge and Kegan Paul.

Hudson, M. (2010). From Marx to Goldman Sachs: The fictions of fictitious capital, and the financialization of industry. *Critique, 38*(3), 419–444.

Itoh, M., & Lapavitsas, C. (1999). *Political economy of money and finance*. London: Macmillan.

Keynes, J. M. (1936). *The general theory of employment, interest, and money*. Retrieved from https://ebooks.adelaide.edu.au/k/keynes/john_maynard/k44g/index.html

Marx, K. (1976). *Capital* (Vol. 1). Harmondsworth: Penguin.

Marx, K. (1978). *Capital* (Vol. 2). Harmondsworth: Penguin.

Marx, K. (1981). *Capital* (Vol. 3). Harmondsworth: Penguin.

Marx, K. (1986). The financial crisis in Europe. *New York Daily Tribune*, 22 December 1857. In K. Marx & F. Engels (Eds.). *Collected works* (Vol. 15). London: Lawrence & Wishart.

Nesvetailova, A. (2006). Fictitious capital, real debts: Systemic illiquidity in the financial crises. *Review of Radical Political Economics, 38*(1), 45–70.

Norfield, T. (2012). Derivatives and capitalist markets. *Historical Materialism, 20*(1), 103–132.

Norfield, T. (2014). *British imperialism and finance*. PhD thesis. SOAS, University of London.

Parsons, J. E. (1988). Bubble, bubble, how much trouble? Financial markets, capitalist development and capitalist crises. *Science & Society, 52*(3), 260–289.

Perelman, M. (2008). *Fictitious capital and the crisis theory*. Retrieved from http://michaelperelman.files.wordpress.com/2008/09/fic1.doc

Ricciardi, J. M. (1985). *Essays on the role of money and finance in economic development*. PhD Thesis. University of Texas at Austin.

Rosdolsky, R. (1977). *The making of Marx's 'Capital'*. London: Pluto Press.

Saad-Filho, A. (2002). *The value of Marx*. London: Routledge.

Toporowski, J. (2000). *The end of finance capital market inflation, financial derivatives and pension fund capitalism*. London: Routledge.

Trindade, J. R. (2006). *Dívida pública e teoria do crédito em Marx: elementos para análise das finanças do estado capitalista*. PhD thesis. Universidade Federal do Paraná.

CRITIQUE OF VALUE CRITICISM

Fabien Trémeau

ABSTRACT

Since the 1990s, the German current of Value Criticism has been proposing to rework a critique of capitalism based on the mature works of Marx. Starting from the primary categories of capital – value, abstract labor, commodity fetishism – they intend to overcome the traditional contradictions of Marxism, capital/labor, proletariat/bourgeoisie, etc. The Canadian thinker Moishe Postone has, independently of value criticism, developed a thought that is close to the German current while distinguishing itself on certain important points. However, it is appropriate to question these new readings of Marx which, if they can be fruitful, pose many problems, both philosophical and political.

Keywords: Value; Value Criticism; abstract labor; commodity fetishism; philosophy; work

INTRODUCTION: VALUE CRITICISM, A NEW READING OF MARX

The *Wertkritik* or Value Criticism is a current of thought that originated in Germany at the end of the 1980s around Robert Kurz, Roswitha Scholz, Nobert Trenkle, and Ernst Lohoff. In 1986, this group participated in the creation of the review *Marxistische Kritik* (Marxist Criticism). The ideas developed in this review still remain largely within the framework of a traditional conception of Marxism. It is only in 1989, with the review *Krisis*, which takes the continuation of *Marxistische Kritik*, that appears a real questioning on the concepts of value and work which go against a certain Marxist tradition. The review *Krisis* intends to question the very foundations of capitalism by attacking its presuppositions (work, money, value) that "traditional Marxism"[1] would have, according to them, not known how to overcome. Starting from the critique of the foundations of the capitalist mode of production, which are value and work, and based on the concept of commodity fetishism, this group proposes a critique of the State, of the opposition proletarian/capitalist (and more

Value, Money, Profit, and Capital Today
Research in Political Economy, Volume 39, 19–29
Copyright © 2024 Fabien Trémeau
Published under exclusive licence by Emerald Publishing Limited
ISSN: 0161-7230/doi:10.1108/S0161-723020230000039002

generally of the class struggle), but also of the Enlightenment. In 1999, they published *Manifesto Against Work* in which they synthesized their theses, which were then quite popular in German-speaking countries. The review *Streifzüge* (forays) was founded in Vienna in the mid-1990s by Franz Schandl, and *Schwarzbuch Kapitalismus* (*The Black Book of capitalism*) by Robert Kurz, published in 1999, was quite successful and brought Value Criticism to a wider audience. In 1992, Roswitha Scholz developed a critique of the patriarchy in an article entitled "Value is the male,"[2] a criticism of the patriarchy while being based on the theses developed by *Krisis*, that she will name criticism of the dissociation-value (*Wert-Abspaltungskritik*):

> According to the theory of value-dissociation, it is therefore necessary to start from the fact that the modern relationship between the sexes must be analyzed in the context of commodity-producing patriarchy (just like value itself) and, consequently, not as a transhistorical fact, "parallel" to the different social formations. This does not mean that it is without prehistory. The fact remains that the relationship between the sexes reaches a completely new quality in commodity modernity, which must be taken into account at both the theoretical and analytical levels.[3]

In 2004, Robert Kurz, Claus Peter Ortlieb, Roswitha Scholz, and others were excluded from *Krisis* after heated debates,[4] notably on the relationship that theory should have with social movements. They found *Exit!*, a review in which they pursue and radicalize the critique of patriarchy from the point of view of value but also their critiques of the Enlightenment. The group Krisis notably around Lohoff and Trenkle and the Austrian magazine *Streifzüge* continue their work by trying to get closer to the social movements.

Value Criticism does not really recognize any predecessors. They recognize a certain filiation in the stakes with Isaak Roubine notably in his *Essays on Marx's theory of value* and the Frankfurt School notably with Adorno, but they claim an original reading of Marx's work. However, their reading of Marx's work is limited to *Capital*, more particularly Book I and the *Grundrisse*, leaving aside all of Marx's production prior to 1858, because, according to them, it is still impregnated by bourgeois economic thought and does not question the concept of work and value.

MOISHE POSTONE AND VALUE CRITICISM

Independently of Value Criticism, Moishe Postone, a Canadian philosopher and historian, developed ideas similar to the German current in the 1970s. In his book *Time, Work and Social Domination*, published in 1992, he criticizes traditional Marxism, which, according to him, is incapable of grasping the specificity of Marx's thought, and proposes a "reinterpretation of Marx's work" based on a rigorous reading of the *Grundrisse* and *Capital*. Like Value Criticism, it puts at the heart of its theory the specificity of labor under capitalism. There are many similarities between Value Criticism and Postone: an almost exclusive reading of Marx's mature work (mainly the *Grundrisse* and *Capital*); the centrality of the concept of commodity fetishism; the refusal of a naturalization of labor and value. However, if Kurz acknowledges that Postone was "the first to deconstruct and partly overcome the bourgeois ontology of labor,"[5] several disagreements can be pointed out on their theoretical positions. We will pass here on the style – undoubtedly more academic for Postone and more polemical for the *Krisis* group and Kurz – or on Postone's refusal to see a double Marx (exoteric and esoteric)[6] in order to come to two fundamental problems: the nature of abstract labor and the theory of crisis. Value Criticism is in general very polemical with the Marxist authors that it considers to have remained within the framework of the traditional Marxism; however, it has in spite of, its divergences, largely preserved the work of Postone. It is at the turn of the 2000s that Robert Kurz and Ernst Lohoff in particular began to point out, according to them, Postone's inconsistencies with regard to the theory of the crisis and the nature of abstract labor.

Value Criticism criticizes Postone for not having elaborated a theory of the crisis, a theory which, according to them, would follow naturally from his historically determined vision of value and labor, but above all from his understanding of the very dynamics of capital. Indeed, Postone – notably in his book *Time, Labor and Social Domination* – grasps the immanent dynamics of capital that constantly pushes it, under the effect of increasing productivity, to redefine the social hour of labor, which in turn serves as a referent for new productivity standards. Postone calls this the *treadmill effect*. In this race, the only way to counteract the decline in value per unit of commodity is to produce and sell more and more of it, but Postone reminds us that: "the new level of productivity, once generalized, yields the same amount of *value* per unit time as was the case prior to its increase."[7] Postone thus puts forward the contradictory character of capitalism which is based on value and work and which by its immanent dynamics denies them nevertheless more and more, it is not possible at an individual level to go against this process because according to him: "The reciprocal redetermination of increased productivity and the social labor hour has an objective, lawlike quality that is by no means a mere illusion or mystification."[8] However, Postone – and despite this treadmill effect – does not see an internal limit to capital but rather the opportunity for the proletariat to become aware of the contradiction between a society based on labor and its extinction by its own dynamics, which in fact renders it more and more useless in the production process. This point is widely criticized by the theorists of Value Criticism who accuse Postone of stopping halfway through his own critique and thus of proposing only rather standard and finally relatively traditional political solutions with regard to the history of Marxism. For the proponents of Value Criticism, the crisis is inscribed in the very process of capital, so there can be no other end than its final crisis, a theory that Postone rejects by opposing the vision of Robert Kurz:

> I don't quite agree with the way Kurz presents the idea of crisis, saying that either one argues that capitalism will collapse or one believes that it can continue indefinitely. I do not share this perspective, which seems to me to be strongly dichotomous. I also think that my work is more open and concerned with questions of ideology, subjectivity, and consciousness than Kurz's. I do not share this perspective, which seems to me to be strongly dichotomous.[9]

We are not dealing here with two visions that would start from the same presuppositions and simply diverge on the conclusions. This opposition reveals the only logical reading of *Capital* and consequently of the capitalist mode of production of Value Criticism. Ernst Lohoff summarizes perfectly the opposition to Postone on this point, but also shows the reading of Value Criticism:

> With increasing productivity, therefore, more and more commodities must be produced in one hour of work to represent the same measure of value. But this simply means that the worst-case scenario for the system of value valorization, namely the decrease in the absolute mass of value, can only be avoided if the mass of commodities produced increases at least as fast as the value represented by each commodity decreases. What could be more natural, then, than to ask whether the capitalist mode of production can guarantee this condition of existence under all circumstances? Although Postone explicitly refers to the passages in the *Grundrisse* where the question of an immanent limit to capital is addressed and where there is even talk of the collapse of the value-based mode of production, he erases the consequence, inscribed in the basic historical dynamics of capital, of a blind fundamental crisis process that takes place behind the backs of the protagonists. Postone knows how indispensable the extension of value production is to capitalism, but he undoubtedly assumes that the capitalist mode of production can guarantee what is indispensable to it until it is one day abolished by an emancipatory movement.[10]

This long quote shows us that the main reproach that Value Criticism makes to Postone concerning the crisis is that he makes a solely logical reading of the capitalist mode of production. For them, the logical contradiction of capitalism must necessarily lead to its final crisis and its end. The irruption of history by "a movement of emancipation" seems to them to be part of the old recipes of traditional Marxism. Beyond the easy attack against a set of past or recent experiences leading to the abolition of capitalism, Value Criticism concerned with carrying the fight against "traditional Marxism" does not even consider that history can arrive not by a proletarian revolutionary movement but by many other ways. Thus, in order to fight the "fall of the mass of value" other irruptions of history – other than a movement of emancipation – can appear: a localized or generalized war can be waged, which allows to destroy a great quantity of value; a policy very favorable to capital which could impose by force a drastic decrease of the remuneration of the labor force or even impose forced labor to external populations. What have we just described here, if not the concrete history of capitalism with the different world or colonial wars, the fascist states and imperialism. But Value Criticism does not seem to take into account real history and its multiple potential developments as a counterweight to the decline of the "mass of value." This absence of history suits Value Criticism well, since a purely logical reading – if it makes it possible to put the fundamental categories of capital back at the heart of the critique – becomes difficult to maintain in the face of the vagaries of history and its possibilities. The reproach made to Postone for hoping that a movement of emancipation will take charge of the abolition of capital is thus not only an argument to send him back to a certain form of traditional Marxism or to show that he does not go to the end of his theory of the crisis but gives the political vision of the crisis of Value Criticism. The collapse may be perfectly logical, but this does not mean that it will be concretely realized. This paradoxically a-historical reading in the sense that history is, so to speak, only the receptacle of a logic immanent to capital leads the proponents of Value Criticism to a certain quietism.

The other stumbling block between Postone and Value Criticism is his conception of abstract labor. This point is complex, let us simply say here that for Postone, and in a way consistent with his reading of Marx, value is born in the process of production, and consequently the commodity contains value objectively even before the exchange; however, abstract labor remains for him a social category that would therefore have no concrete reality. Thus abstract labor: "is a social determination, it cannot be a physiological category,"[11] while for Kurz abstract labor is a concrete reality, it is formed on the concrete basis of an undifferentiated expenditure of human energy. This point is essential for him because it allows him to combat the idea that value is formed in the process of circulation – an idea that he believes is shared by Roubine, Heinrich and Postone – and thus to assert a more consistent theory of the crisis, in the sense that it would start from a real basis.

REMARKS ON THE IDEALISM OF THE VALUE CRITICISM

Value Criticism is, in our opinion, a form of idealism in which the critique of alienation is cut off from realities and concrete data, hence the impasses as soon as it is a question of talking about practices that would allow for an emancipation or an exit from capitalism. Marx had already written about this flaw:

> Hitherto men have always formed wrong ideas about themselves, about what they are and what they ought to be. They have arranged their relations according to their ideas of God, of normal man, etc. The products of their brains have got out of their hands. They, the creators, have bowed down before their creations. Let us liberate them from the chimeras, the ideas, dogmas, imaginary beings under the yoke of which they are pining away. Let us revolt against this rule of concepts. Let us teach men, says one, how to exchange these imaginations for thoughts which correspond to the essence of man; says another, how to take up a critical attitude to them; says the third, how to get them out of their heads; and existing reality will collapse. (...) Once upon a time a valiant fellow had the idea that men were drowned in water only because they were possessed with the *idea of gravity*. If they were to get this notion out of their heads, say by avowing it to be a superstitious, a religious concept, they would be sublimely proof against any danger from water. His whole life long he fought against the illusion of gravity, of whose harmful consequences all statistics brought him new and manifold evidence. This valiant fellow was the type of the new revolutionary philosophers in Germany.[12]

This excerpt seems to us particularly relevant to Value Criticism. In our view, it is not possible to make a purely logical reading of capital without falling back into a form of idealism. Although for Robert Kurz abstract labor has a concrete reality – value does have a concrete substance – for all that it remains for him a way of better affirming the imminence of the end of capitalism. For Value Criticism the idea of crisis replaces the concrete analysis of the crisis. In none of Kurz's writings, and more broadly in the writings of Value Criticism, are there any concrete studies of this "inevitable" end of capitalism. It is quite necessary and legitimate to make a theoretical or philosophical reading of *Capital*, provided that we do not forget that the three volumes of *Capital* remain a meticulous study of the capitalism of its time. To criticize work and value is not enough to shake up history, unless, as the above quotation reminds us, we fall short of Marx.

Furthermore, we should ask ourselves if it is possible to free ourselves completely from fetishism. It is undoubtedly necessary to free ourselves from commodity fetishism, but can man become transparent to himself? This question is not really formulated by Value Criticism and therefore has no answer.[13] On the other hand, it seems paradoxical that the exacerbated objectivism of Value Criticism – in this case the commodity fetishism or the "automaton capital," has as a consequence a voluntarism of the individuals who become aware, via the critical theory, that they do not "want" anymore.

That said, the critique of the idealism of Value Criticism does not mean that we should deny the ideal character of the commodity, of value and of abstract labor. However, one must be careful not to rely on its critique alone, a way out of fetishism nor to think that a society totally transparent to itself would be possible. By breaking the dialectical link between the materiality of capitalism and its ideal functioning, Value Criticism locks itself into a dead end, falling short of the Hegelian dialectic of subject and object. Anselm Jappe writes on this subject that "Value is an a priori form, in the Kantian sense, because all objectivity manifests itself through it: it is a grid of reading of which the individual is not aware, but which is preliminary to all perception and constitutes its objects."[14] We can agree with Jappe and the value criticism that value forms consciousness, but only in part. There is a radicalization, even a totalitarian dimension of value in the proponents of Value Criticism as a constitution of the forms of consciousness that leads to a dead end. On the one hand, there are whole swathes of life not subject to value and market law, Paul Cockshott tells us that: "while we would conventionally say that Canada is a capitalist economy, the time-use statistics show that it is only at most 50 percent capitalist. Half the work done each day is still done in the home, and a significant part of the paid work, particularly that done by women, is done for the state not for private firms, and as such generates no profit."[15] Thus, in an advanced capitalist economy, only half of life is subject to commodification. Finally, the different sedimentations of the old modes of production and their regional particularities continue to exist within the commodity world. The very organization of work changes from country to country according to the weight of the past, which still governs by its force of inertia a part of habits and behaviors, even if they go against a purely capitalist logic. If we widen the point of view, it is easy to realize that capitalism in the United States, in Russia, in Sweden or in France does not produce the same "forms of consciousness," this is not due to the fact that there is no unity in the mode of production between these different countries, but that it expresses itself differently according to the historical soil in which it was born. These different national or regional sedimentations can be real brakes for capitalism. Gramsci already analyzed the resistance to Fordism in Europe by the fact that the classes of the old regime and their behaviors slowed down its introduction, a problem not encountered in the United States because of the absence of social strata inherited from the past:

Americanism, in its most developed form, requires a preliminary condition which has not attracted the attention of the American writers who have treated the problems arising from it, since in America it exists quite "naturally." This condition could be called "a rational demographic composition" and consists in the fact that there do not exist numerous classes with no essential function in the world of production, in other words classes which are purely parasitic. European "tradition," European "civilization," is, conversely, characterized precisely by the existence of such classes, created by the "richness" and "complexity" of past history. This past history has left behind a heap of passive sedimentations. (...) America does not have "great historical and cultural traditions;" but neither does it have this leaden burden to support. (...) The non-existence of viscous parasitic sedimentations left behind by past phases of history has allowed industry, and commerce in particular, to develop on a sound basis.[16]

To sum up, the totalitarian character of the commodity is thus, according to us, largely overestimated by Value Criticism: (1) a large part of everyday life, even within advanced capitalist economies, is not subject to commodification and to the laws of capital; (2) even within commodity relations, the many past sedimentations can slow down, or even oppose, its laws.

In spite of this, we could think that the commodification of forms of consciousness is a totalization in progress. In this case, even the past sedimentations and the non-marketing of large sectors of everyday life would be doomed either to disappear or to be themselves re-formed by the commodity. This vision could probably be shared by Value Criticism, since the latter is, according to us, a deterministic monism, although Anselm Jappe challenges it:

...one could object that the value criticism, even if it does not conceive of value in a purely economic sense, still sees in it a "monistic" principle: society would be completely determined by value, and thus by the exchange of equivalents (...). In truth, the Critique of value has quickly surpassed, in its development, such a conception (which would make any positive exit from capitalism unthinkable). The value exists, and can exist, only in a dialectical relation with the non-value, and this relation is necessarily antagonistic.[17]

This last sentence goes against other passages where, according to him, no subject or sector of society could claim to be totally antagonistic to value, i.e., not already formed by it: "These considerations lead to the conclusion that there is no subject ontologically opposed 'in itself' to capitalism, to which it would simply be subjected in an external way."[18] We can only note here the ambivalence or the contradiction of Anselm Jappe and more generally of Value Criticism on the possible exteriority or not to value and consequently of a possible place from which could emerge movements of emancipation not subjected to value. One gets the impression that on this question, Value Criticism is at least hesitant or adapts its discourse according to the context. What is disturbing in this monism of value is that it is necessary to succeed in explaining from where the critical discourse on it could emerge, in other words: what place to give to the critical theory if all discourse is already formed by the fetishism of the commodity? Unless we grant critical thought a power that would allow it to escape the determinism of value, it seems to us impossible in a materialist framework to think of the emergence of a critical reflexivity. This is, according to us, one of the unacknowledged reasons for this kind of critique and perhaps the cause of the pendulum swing between, on the one hand, the hyper-determinism of the "subject-automate" and, on the other hand, an idealist voluntarism.

STRUCTURE AND ACTION

From what we have just said, it emerges that Value Criticism is close to structuralism in the sense that the structuring of the social – by the law of value – predominates over all other determinations. The subject of history is "the automaton capital," so there is no human subject, the commodity fetishism makes humans "subjects" of the "automaton subject." For all that, Value Criticism refuses to be assimilated to structuralism and Robert Kurz has widely criticized the Althusserian reading of Marx. This criticism mainly concerns the place of the subject in history. As it is known, for Althusser the history is a "process without Subject"[19] or for Kurz, by not taking into account the commodity fetishism, Althusser falls back in: "the old Marxism of the labor movement in its completely unchanged essence, but by casting it in the new form of a 'law of the movement' structuralist and without subject."[20] Certainly the subjects are "functions" of this process without subject, but each one continues precisely to act according to its function within the structure, thus: "The bourgeoisie performs the functions without subject of the maintenance of the system, the proletariat performs (since it is a process of contradiction of the system) its antipodal function without subject of the critique of the system, and this is how the class struggle develops, also without subject, as systemic resultant."[21] Let us recall that Kurz and Value Criticism do not recognize antagonism between the social classes except within an already capitalist framework, for them the opposition capital/labor is already a struggle internal to the capital. The proletariat in this sense cannot be the subject of any change of structure since it is itself part of the structure, it is part of the very dynamics of the capitalist structure. For all that, Althusserian structuralism is not as different as the proponents of Value Criticism seem to believe. Certainly, as we have seen, their conception of the subject is different, but the difference is, according to us, on the historically determined character of the subject, Anselm Jappe recognizes in this respect that: "structuralist theory and system theory would be partially right, if they did not consider this absence of a human subject as a timeless constant."[22] However, there is indeed for Value Criticism an erasure of the human subject in favor of the "automaton capital," men are acted by it, although they are the creators of this subject. In this sense, Value Criticism remains in a very Feuerbachian conception of religious alienation. While for Feuerbach man has deposited in God the human power that alienates him in return, for Value Criticism men have created a mode of production based on value that alienates them in return with this difference that there is no human essence to be found behind the alienation of commodity fetishism since it is as soon as the subject is constituted that the alienation operates, that is why: "to overcome fetishism cannot therefore mean to restore its redicates to a subject that already exists in itself and whose essence has been alienated."[23] For all that, as well for the Althusserian structuralism as for

Value Criticism, the man is no more actor but is acted respectively by the structure and by commodity fetishism. However, Value Criticism radicalizes the structural to such an extent that it becomes almost impossible to think of action not determined by the structure-fetish. We have seen that the answers brought to this problem remain either without issue, or fall into a voluntarism that goes against the presuppositions of commodity-fetishism. The problem is complex, and in order to go deeper into it we need to return to the idealism of the value criticism. It is true that the foundation of the theory of Value Criticism rests on a social activity – abstract labor – which in turn subjects men to its law. From a materialist point of view, there is nothing wrong with this postulate, but we should not forget that even when men have become "subjects of the automaton subject," they still interact with matter, which Value Criticism does not seem to see. Thus, however alienated and subjected to commodity fetishism he may be, man continues to maintain a relationship with a world that remains external to him, and the fact that his consciousness is formed by value does not change the fact that he must confront this exterior. Unless we think that this exterior has no reality or consistency except in man's consciousness, or in other words that the form of consciousness creates the world in which man evolves – which would take us far below Marx's materialism – the real always offers a resistance and it is in this resistance that man's consciousness is formed.

CONCLUSION

To conclude, we would like to insist on the fact that we agree with Value Criticism that men have become the subjects of the capital Subject, but remaining locked in what we could call an idealist hyper-structuralism that tends to make the actor disappear, by identifying him with the efficiency of a hypostasized structure, in the case of capitalism, by constituting this one in subject, almost in world without thinking therefore the tension with this outside which opposes him, Value Criticism is condemned to propose only solutions tending strongly toward a subjective voluntarism. Marx in *The Eighteenth Brumaire of Louis Bonaparte* wrote this famous and often distorted sentence: "Men make their own history, but they do not make it just as they please; they do not make it under circumstances chosen by themselves, but under circumstances directly encountered, given and transmitted from the past."[24] We could start again from this sentence to say that history within commodity fetishism does not stop at making the history of the said fetishism, although it is the framework in which men act and evolve.

NOTES

1. "Traditional Marxism" is a term used by the Value Criticism German current as well as by M. Postone. For the latter, all the Marxist currents, whatever their theoretical contributions or radicality, remain prisoners of the capitalist categories or, to put it as Robert Kurz, are satisfied with the reading of the "exoteric Marx:" "Now, the truncated vision that the traditional Marxism of the workers' movement had of this systemic context consisted in the fact that it

criticized the "surplus value" in a purely superficial and sociological sense, namely in the sense of its "appropriation" by the "capitalist class." It was not the form of the value functioning in a loop and fetishistic way that was denounced as scandalous, but only its "unequal distribution." It is precisely for this reason that in the eyes of the representatives of the "fundamental critique of value" this "labor Marxism" remained trapped in the ideology of a simple "redistributive justice." See: Scholz (2019), p. 77.

2. This article is reproduced in the book *Le Sexe du capitalisme*, p. 15 *et seq.* and it was published in German in 1992 in the n° 12 of the review *Krisis*.

3. Scholz (2019), p. 87.

4. For Robert Kurz, the attempt to link up with social movements is premature, and encourages confusion about the goals of an "authentic" critique of value, which can be found in few if any current political or social movements. For this reason, attempts in this direction by *Streifzüge* or *Krisis*, according to him, only make the critique more bland and harmless.

5. Kurz (2019), p. 87.

6. For the *Krisis* group, this refusal of the double Marx prevents Postone from seeing the tensions in Marx's work between an ontologizing reading of labor and value and a historically determined reading. Moreover, this refusal would give Postone the role of righter of wrongs in the sense that he alone would present the "true Marx" against the other readings.

7. Postone (1993), p. 288.

8. See footnote 7, p. 290.

9. See: Postone (2012), p. 383.

10. Lohoff (2013), p. 28.

11. Postone (1993), p. 145.

12. Marx and Engels (2010), p. 24.

13. Some passages suggest that it would be possible in a post-capitalist society for the individual to free himself entirely from fetishism. "A society liberated from capitalism and from fetishism in general would be for the first time a society whose appearance, life and activity would effectively depend on its free will." See: Kurz (2002), p. 367.

14. Jappe (2003), p. 179.

15. Cockshott (2019), p. 161.

16. Gramsci (2000), p. 277–278.

17. Jappe (2011), p. 143.

18. Jappe (2003), p. 172–173.

19. Althusser (1982), "Idéologie et appareils idéologiques d'État," p. 76.

20. Read Kurz's article entitled *Subjektlose Herrschaft. Zur Aufhebung einer verkürzten Gesellschaftskritik*, and available on line: https://www.exit-online.org/textanz1.php?tabelle=autoren&index=22&posnr=135&backtext1= text1.php.

21. See footnote 20.

22. Jappe (2003), p. 215.

23. See footnote 22, p. 216.

24. Marx (2010), p. 103.

REFERENCES

Althusser, L. (1982). *Positions*. Essentiel, Paris: Éditions Sociales.
Cockshott, P. W. (2019). *How The World Works*. New York, NY: Monthly Review Press.
Gramsci, A. (2000). *The Antonio Gramsci reader, selected writings, 1916–1935*. New York, NY: New York University Press.
Jappe, A. (2003). *Les Aventures de la marchandise*. Paris: Denoël.
Jappe, A. (2011). *Crédit à mort. La décomposition du capitalisme et ses critiques*. Paris: Nouvelle Éditions Lignes.
Kurz, R. (2002). *Lire Marx*. Paris: Éditions Les Balustres.

Kurz, R. (2019). *La Substance du capital*. Paris: L'Échappée.

Lohoff, E. (2013). Krisis, Beitrag 2/2013. Retrieved from https://www.krisis.org/wp-content/data/ernst-lohoff-auf-selbstzerst%C3%B6rung-programmiert-2013-2.pdf

Marx, K. (2010). The eighteenth Brumaire of Louis Bonaparte. In *Karl Marx Frederik Engels Collected Works* (Vol. 11). London: Lawrence & Wishart.

Marx, K., & Engels, F. (2010). The German ideology in collected works. In *Karl Marx Frederik Engels collected works* (Vol. 5). London: Lawrence & Wishart.

Postone, M. (1993). *Time, labor and social domination*. Cambridge: Cambridge University Press.

Postone, M. (2012). Para una teoría crítica del presente: En conversación con moishe postone sobre las nuevas lecturas de Marx, la crisis y el antisemitismo. *Constelaciones, 4*. Retrieved from https://www.academia.edu/68119171/Para_una_Teor%C3%ADa_Cr%C3%ADtica_del_presente_En_conversaci%C3%B3n_con_Moishe_Postone_sobre_las_nuevas_lecturas_de_Marx_la_crisis_y_el_antisemitismo

Scholz, R. (2019). *Le Sexe du capitalisme*. Paris: Crises et Critique.

TURNING ONE'S LOSS INTO A WIN? THE US TRADE WAR WITH CHINA IN PERSPECTIVE

Zhiming Long, Zhixuan Feng, Bangxi Li and Rémy Herrera

ABSTRACT

This chapter aims to shed light on the hidden benefits and losses of US-China trade within the framework of unequal exchange theory. After presenting the evolutions of the trade balance between China and the United States, we propose two methods for measuring the unequal exchange between them: one considers the labor content directly incorporated into the exchange; the other focuses on the international values with input-output tables. This allows to present a synthesis of sectoral analyses. Our results show a significant unequal exchange in US-China trade over 1995–2014, the United States being actually the main beneficiary of this trade. Both methods exhibit the inequality in exchange tending to decrease over time; China's disadvantage has been gradually reducing from the 2000s. We finally suggest that the relative decline in the hegemonic status of the United States in this bilateral unequal relationship could help explain its decision to launch its trade war with China.

Keywords: International trade; trade war; unequal exchange; Marxism; labor value; input-output table

INTRODUCTION

After taking office in January 2017, the United States (hereafter, "US") President Donald Trump began setting trade barriers on the People's Republic of China (hereafter, "China"), effectively starting what it is commonly called a "trade war." Since the first half of 2018, this US-China confrontation has become a spiral of reciprocal increases in customs duties targeting certain products or sectors,

Value, Money, Profit, and Capital Today
Research in Political Economy, Volume 39, 31–50
Copyright © 2024 Zhiming Long, Zhixuan Feng, Bangxi Li and Rémy Herrera
Published under exclusive licence by Emerald Publishing Limited
ISSN: 0161-7230/doi:10.1108/S0161-723020230000039003

penalties against rival companies, tense bilateral negotiations with uncertain outcomes, then further reprisals, counter-offensives, and utterance of threats, which were not systematically followed by action. The extent of the conflict is such that hostilities have extended beyond the strict sphere of trade and into the monetary area through the devaluation of the yuan in the summer of 2019.

This dispute could affect the global system as a whole, and the reasons are multiple and complex: the supposed "unfair" competition of China due to low wages and an undervalued national currency boosting exports, on the one hand, and subsidies to domestic firms and heavy regulatory constraints hampering access to its domestic market and slowing down imports, in addition to "intellectual property theft," in the words of the US President, on the other.

Digging (almost) continuously for several decades, the trade balance between the two countries has been largely unfavorable for the US for several decades, and was the most likely pretext to start this trade war. Does the US trade deficit in goods and services not provide irrefutable evidence that the US President Trump was correct when he declared that China "gets away with theft" and that "hundreds of billions of dollars a year were lost dealing with China"? How could one deny the evidence that one country with a surplus induces a deficit in the other? Is it that simple? Is such logic well-founded? What is this "wealth," exactly? We are not questioning the idea that China benefits from its trade relations with the US, but rather questioning how fair these exchanges are.

The issue has arisen since heterodox theoreticians, such as Singer (1950), Prebisch (1959), and Emmanuel (1972), initiated the debate on unequal exchange, and has been echoed in the fields of international trade and development economics (Bacha, 1978; Evans, 1989; Peet & Hartwick, 2015). Unlike mainstream analyses, this theory focuses on possible unequal relationships in trade and income distribution by considering the terms of trade that determine the value added produced in a country by its labor during the working hours over a certain period of time, which configures the distribution of benefits among protagonists in trade. The difference in the added value of one unit of labor time between countries means that they obtain different amounts of currencies and wealth with the same amount of labor. Such a difference first refers to gaps in labor productivity, meaning that countries have different abilities in commodity production, but also, more importantly, different wage levels and capital intensities among countries, so that competitive equilibrium prices create differences in the value added per unit of labor time (Emmanuel, 1972). Moreover, if some countries have monopoly power in certain markets, the deviation from the competitive equilibrium prices due to changes in the terms of trade will create this difference in value added per unit of labor time (Clelland, 2014). This latter difference is not a gap in productive capacity, but a process of product distribution. As a matter of fact, industrialized countries will gain more value-added than developing countries will because they are involved in industries that have higher capital intensity and higher average wages, and are characterized by some monopoly capabilities. In other words, the mentioned phenomena will cause prices in international trade to deviate from their value, leading to an unequal exchange.

Unequal exchange, measurable by a wide variety of methods (Feng, 2018; Gibson, 1980; Nakajima & Izumi, 1995; Webber & Foot, 1984), reveals that, for a given traded volume, the total working time provided by the workers of an economy may be higher than that of the workers of its partner economy, thus causing a transfer of value from the one to the other, with the latter thereby appropriating the value produced by the other one. Only considering the transfer of international value – corresponding to the socially necessary working time required to produce a commodity – will reflect the effective redistribution of wealth effected between the two economies.

The chapter is structured as follows. First, the evolution of the US-China trade balance is presented. We propose two methods of measuring the unequal exchange between the countries. Second, we consider the content in labor directly incorporated into the exchange, and, inspired by Ricci (2019). Third, the research centers on the international value and mobilizing input-output tables. Last, it is the synthesis of the sectoral analysis.

BILATERAL TRADE BALANCE AND TRADE WAR

US-China trade in goods and services gained initial momentum after the US's diplomatic recognition of China in January 1979, following the latter's so-called "openness reforms" adopted in late 1978 under the influence of Deng Xiaoping. Following this, China became a member of the World Trade Organization in December 2001. However, the US began to show signs of a trade balance deficit with China from the very beginning of the 1970s, under the planned Maoist economy, and has continued to worsen, with rare exceptions.

Substantial accounting discrepancies are appearing over the exact amount of these trade deficits, particularly between the data disseminated by the US Department of Commerce and those provided by the China Customs Administration. The differences in the assessments are due to the way in which the authorities take into account re-exports, mostly from Hong Kong, transport costs (free on board or cost, insurance and freight), and travel expenses of the respective nationals of the two countries (Xu & Hang, 2018). Nevertheless, regardless of the accounting system, an increasingly deep deficit to the detriment of the US is observed.

If we select the statistical bases of the US Department of Commerce, we observe that the evolution of the trade balance between the US and China has been characterized by a very marked, almost continuous, deterioration since the 1980s.

This deterioration temporarily slowed down as a result of the crises that shook the US economy (from the bursting of the "new economy" or Dot-com bubble in 2001 to the 2008 Financial Crisis or Subprimes Crisis, which was systemic in reality and had effects on China in 2009 and even more so in 2012) (Herrera, Wim, Piqueras, Formento, & Nakatani, 2019), the appreciations of the yuan in

2005 and 2011, and the 2015–2016 Chinese stock market turbulence (Herrera & Long, 2021; Long & Herrera, 2017, and see Graph 1). The trade balance slowly degraded in the 1990s, then more bluntly in the years 2000–2010; it crossed the 100 billion USD mark in 2002, 200 billion USD in 2005, then 300 billion USD in 2011, before reaching the record deficit of 420 billion USD in 2018 for goods only (excluding services) (Graph 2). China then officially became the US's largest trading partner for goods, with a total of 660 billion USD exchanged: 120 billion USD in exports, and 540 billion USD in imports. Meanwhile, the trade in services exhibited a surplus in favor of the US at 41 billion USD.

It was in this same year, 2018, when the US launched the trade war against China. The initial measures, which consisted of abruptly increasing the customs tariffs borne from specific products imported from China (such as household equipment and photovoltaic solar panels), were enacted in January. From March, there were increases in the barriers to imports from China, affecting sectors such as metallurgy, the automobile industry, aeronautics, robotics, new information and communication technologies, and medical equipment. Then, in April, sanctions were imposed on Chinese firms, banning them from using inputs made in the US.

A year later, in June 2019, after tariff increases were extended to new sectors, China was no longer the US's largest trading partner (its NAFTA associates, Mexico and Canada, succeeded it). However, at the end of 2019, the significantly reduced trade deficit returned to −346 billion USD, which is below that observed in the last year of President Barack Obama's second term as President of the US in 2016. This inflection is clearly visible in monthly data in the first months of 2019 (Graph 3). Could it be then that D. Trump has won and, thus, was correct? The answer to this question requires knowing whether, as mainstream economists

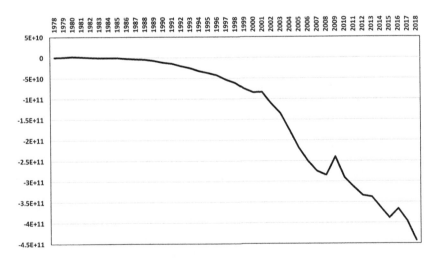

Graph 1.   US Trade Deficit in Goods With China: 1978–2018 (in Current Billion US Dollars). *Source:* U.S. Department of Commerce (various years).

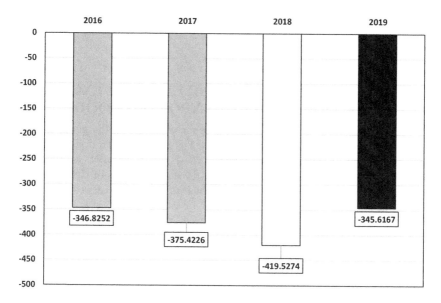

Graph 2.   US-China Bilateral Trade (Excluding Services): US Deficit Between 2016 and 2019 (in Current Billion US Dollars). *Source:* U.S. Department of Commerce (various years).

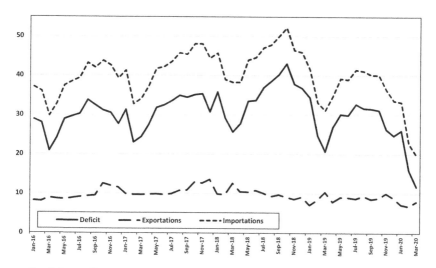

Graph 3.   Bilateral Monthly US-China Trade: Exports, Imports, and Deficit From January 2016 to March 2020 (in Current Billion US Dollars). *Source:* U.S. Department of Commerce (various years).

have claimed for a long time, the trade between the US and China is now "equal." We examine this further.

FIRST METHOD OF MEASURING UNEQUAL EXCHANGE: LABOR CONTENT OF EXPORTED GOODS

We first calculate the respective values in labor employed in the goods and services traded in the bilateral trade between the US and China. To do this, consider that, for the given year t, China exports $XL_{\text{CH } t}$ hours of work performed by Chinese workers and, in return, obtains $XL_{\text{US } t}$ working hours of US workers, to which are added $SL_{\text{US } t}$ working hours of these same US workers corresponding to the trade balance (seen from the point of view of China), that is, S_t dollars in monetary terms. The unequal exchange between the two countries can therefore be written as the ratio between the values in labor integrated in the respective exports of the two countries:

$$\rho_t = \frac{XL_{\text{CH } t}}{XL_{\text{US } t} + SL_{\text{US } t}} \tag{1}$$

where X represents the total exports of each country that we measure in hours of their domestic workers; the trade balance SL is measured in working hours of US workers. SL has a positive sign if it is a surplus registered by China, and negative if it is not.

Under these conditions, we must also estimate how many hours of work is equivalent to a US dollar alternatively in the US and in China:

$$XL = \frac{L}{Y}.X \tag{2}$$

where, for each of these two countries, L corresponds to the sum of the hours of work over the year, Y is its total product, X is the exports expressed in dollars, and XL represents these same exports measured in hours of work.

Similarly:

$$SL = \frac{L}{Y}.S \tag{3}$$

where SL is the trade balance, considered from the point of view of China, but also measured in hours of work.

Thus:

$$\rho_t = \frac{\frac{L_{\text{CH } t}}{Y_{\text{CH } t}}.X_{\text{CH } t}}{\frac{L_{\text{US } t}}{Y_{\text{US } t}}.X_{\text{US } t} + \frac{L_{\text{US } t}}{Y_{\text{US } t}}.S_t} \tag{4}$$

Firstly, for the US, L_{US} is obtained by multiplying the average number of hours worked per year and per worker, sourced from the OECD (various years,

2020), by that of the number of employed persons, whose data are sourced from the International Labor Organization (various years, 2020). In the case of China, the labor input L_c is the product of the number of workers employed, the database sourced from the National Bureau of Statistics (various years, 1993–2019), by that of the weekly hours of work of urban employees on average, sourced from the databases of the *China Labor Statistics Yearbooks* (NBS, 2007) and the *China Population and Employment Statistics Yearbooks* (NBS, 2008–2017) between 1998 and 2018 (a variable which is stable enough to allow recourse, retroactively from 1978 to 1997, to calculate the average for this period). The data are spread over the 52 weeks of the year.

Secondly, the product Y_{US} is obtained from the US Bureau of Economic Analysis. We use the total product instead of Gross Domestic Product (GDP) because we need to keep the production data consistent with those of exports and imports. As a matter of fact, the data of exports and imports are measured in total output; intermediate input and net value added are not differentiated. Just like for the US, to estimate Y_C for China, we use the total product, not GDP. However, data are available only for the years for which the input-output tables of the Chinese economy have published (NBS, various years), though the data are irregular. Among the possible different methods to complete this series, we use the value-added rate of the year with an input-output table in order to estimate the value-added rate of the year for which the data are missing, and then use the product of the value-added rate and GDP to find China's total output. The missing points are replaced by those of the nearest year or by the average of two equidistant points, if available. In order to homogenize the procedures for calculating unequal exchange ratios, we use the following two approaches: the first one, as described above, was built by ourselves; and the second one was derived from Ricci (2019) and verified by ours.

Thirdly, the labor contents directly included in the traded goods (XL_{CH} and XL_{US}) are estimated by using the data of the respective exports of the countries. The X_{US} and X_{CH} series are sourced from the database on trade provided by the United Nations (various years, 2020), with the same statistical scope. Under these circumstances, our series could be built from 1978 to 2018. The calculations were all carried out at current prices, and the conversion of the currencies between them was conducted using the official annual average exchange rate, given by the World Bank (various years, 2020).

Our results illustrate the existence of an unequal exchange between the US and China over the past four decades, operating in favor of the former and at the expense of the latter. The changes in the contents of labor integrated in the goods and services traded (Graph 4) were different in both countries: in China, they increased rapidly until the mid-2000s, then fell sharply before stabilizing at the start of the decade 2010; in the US, they increased much more moderately and continuously. The two curves converged at the end of the period. The extent of the unequal exchange is revealed when the ratio of the contents in labor of exports is calculated. Thus, we find that, between 1978 and 2018, one hour of work in the US was exchanged for nearly 40 hours of work in China, on average.

However, from the middle of the 1990s, that is, the years of deep reforms in China driven mainly by fiscal and budgetary matters, we observe a very marked

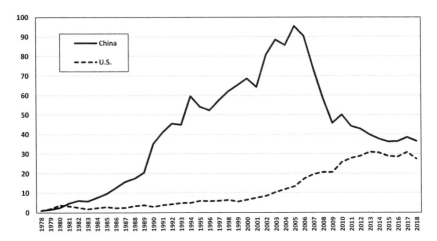

Graph 4.   Indices of Labor Contents Included in Bilateral Exports: China and the US, 1978–2018 (Index 1 in 1978). *Source:* Authors' calculations.

decrease in unequal exchange (Graph 5). As a matter of fact, in 2018, 6.4 hours of Chinese work were being exchanged for 1 hour of work from the US If we do not take into account the trade balance (trade surplus for China) over the 40 years examined, the Chinese worker had to work more than 121 hours to obtain 1 hour of US work, on average (Graph 6). Would the erosion of this advantage in the exchange of the US explain the trigger of its trade war?

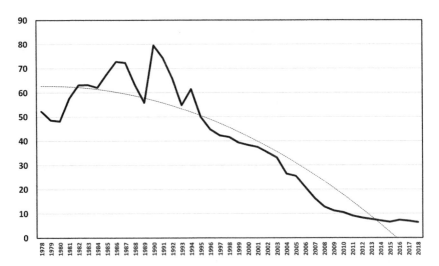

Graph 5.   Ratio of the Labor Exchange Included in US-China Trade, Bilateral Balance Included: 1978–2018. *Source:* Authors' calculations.

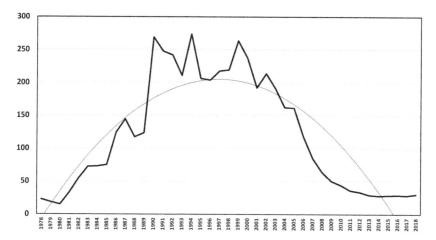

Graph 6. Ratio of Labor Exchange in US-China Trade, Excluding Bilateral Balance: 1978–2018. *Source:* Authors' calculations.

SECOND METHOD OF MEASURING UNEQUAL EXCHANGE: VALUE TRANSFER AND INPUT-OUTPUT TABLES

In the above, it was the comparison of the working hours required on average to manufacture the goods and services traded that allowed us to assess the unequal trade between the US and China markets. Nevertheless, the measurement of the appropriation of the produced wealth between the countries is only truly taken through the bilateral transfer of the necessary social work time, that is, the international value, which is empirically estimated here. Given the macroeconomic data available, it was only possible for us to calculate the living labor directly incorporated into exports with our first method, given gross product also includes materialized labor, crystallized in the various production methods.

To take these arguments into account, let us now adopt an alternative method, inspired by that of Ricci (2019), to examine more precisely the importance of this unequal exchange. Based on the New Interpretation of Labor Value Theory (hereafter, "New Interpretation") (Foley, 2000; Meng, 2015), we assume that, whatever the sector, the newly-created international value on the world market is equal to the total quantity of labor directly allocated as an input to this sector by the various countries of the world; that is, in each sector, assuming that its goods are homogeneous, the quantity of direct labor input allocated by each country is equivalent to the international value, which is obtained by multiplying the share of the country's production in that sector at the world scale by the total amount of international value created in that sector. If the prices of these homogeneous goods are similar, then the quantity of direct labor input corresponding to the international value in each country is itself equal to the product of the country's proportion in the total value added of the sector at the world level and the total amount of international value created in this sector.

In this framework, we derive the expression of the newly-created quantity of international value in country i and sector j, as follows:

$$l_{ij} = \left(\frac{e^p_{ij} Y_{ij}}{Y_{Wj}}\right) l_{Wj} \qquad (5)$$

where l_{ij} is the quantity of direct labor input considered as international value in country i and sector j; l_{Wj}, the total direct labor input into the global market for this sector j, in other words, the total international value newly created in the same sector j; Y_{ij}, the added value of sector j of country i, denominated in local currency; Y_{Wj}, the total added value of sector j on the world market, denominated in US dollars; and e^p_{ij} the exchange rate stated in purchasing power parity (PPP).

The reason why the expression of the exchange rate is essentially needed in PPP is because its use makes it possible to reflect the proportion of the product of a country in total production on the world market, and to reduce the eventual impact of fluctuations of the real exchange rate. The formula for calculating e^p_{ij} in PPP is as follows:

$$e^p_{ij} = e^p_i \frac{\sum_i e^m_i Y_{ij}}{\sum_i e^p_i Y_{ij}} \qquad (6)$$

where e^p_i is the exchange rate in PPP of the currency of a country i compared to the US dollar, and e^m_i the nominal exchange rate of this same national currency of country i against the dollar. Eq. (6) guarantees a normalization of the exchange rate in PPP of a country to ensure that the total added value at the world level calculated at the nominal exchange rates and in PPP are indeed equal. By applying such a process of monetary normalization, it is understood that the exchange rate in PPP will be different according to the sector in each country.

To calculate the difference existing between the world market price and the newly-created international value by each sector of the different countries, it is necessary to resolve two particularly important difficulties mentioned at the beginning of this current part: one is linked to the monetary translation of value; and the other is linked to the integration of materialized work in the means of production.

The first problem is that the unit of international value calculated by Eq. (5) is working time, while that of the world market price appears in monetary terms. Therefore, we need to convert the calculated international values into monetary units. This is in fact relatively easy to perform in the context of the New Interpretation of labor value because we can achieve this through the methods of Monetary Expression of Value or the Monetary Expression per Labor Time. Since, at the global level, the direct labor that is allocated in all sectors is equivalent to the quantity of the new added value created, the value of all sectors represented globally by value added in money can be expressed as the ratio of total value added to total direct labor, that is:

$$\mu = \frac{\sum\limits_{j} Y_{Wj}}{\sum\limits_{j} l_{Wj}} \tag{7}$$

μ being the monetary expression by working time or the unit of value.

A second problem to be solved is related to the fact that, in the previous calculation, we essentially consider the newly created part of the value of the merchandises, that is, living labor alone. However, in calculating the difference between the market price and the real value, we must take into consideration not only this living labor, but also the part that is associated with labor materialized in the means of production. In Ricci's method (2018), the total value of goods in country i and sector j is written:

$$V_{ij} = \mu l_{ij} + e_i^m C_{ij} \tag{8}$$

with C_{ij} the capital of sector j of country i corresponding to the purchase of the means of production in local currency; and $e_i^m C_{ij}$ is the total constant capital denominated this time in US dollars.

At the same time, the complete form of the market price for sector j in country i will be:

$$M_{ij} = e_i^m Y_{ij} + e_i^m C_{ij} \tag{9}$$

Using Eqs. (8) and (9), we can now obtain the difference between the world market price and the international value, according to the formula:

$$d_{ij} = M_{ij} - V_{ij} = e_i^m Y_{ij} - \mu l_{ij} = \left(\frac{e_i^m Y_{ij}}{l_{ij}} - \mu \right) l_{ij} \tag{10}$$

This difference is then multiplied by the proportion of exports from each sector and country in total production to calculate the estimated amount of value transferred through exports, as inputs, or as outputs. By considering both the gaps in other sectors and the quantities of products imported by them, we thus obtain the value transferred from or to other economic activities that is recorded by this sector. We can then arrive at an estimate of the net value transferred relating to this sector; that is, at the level of unequal exchange that corresponds to this sector.

In practice, when the world trade matrix constructed from the table of international inputs and outputs is calculated, the process that we have just analyzed can be carried out by the sequence of the following three stages: (1) once the amount of international value newly created in each sector and each country l_{ij} is obtained by Eq. (5), we use the total production of each sector M_{ij} in order to estimate the ratio between the value newly created and the total production

$\varphi_{ij} = l_{ij}/M_{ij}$ (*step 1*); (2) we multiply this ratio by the world trade matrix given in monetary terms to find the one in values, that is, in hours of work; and (3) the term $\frac{e_i^m Y_{ij}}{l_{ij}} - \mu$ in Eq. (10) is, at the very end, multiplied by this matrix of world trade in values so as to finally obtain that of transfers of international values.

Compared to other methods available in the literature, the one we use in this third part has serious advantages (Ricci, 2019). First, it provides a rigorous theoretical framework, based on a strict and logical interpretation of labor value, and is capable of being integrated into a unified model, the possible distinct forms taken by the unequal exchange between countries. Second, its empirical application does not require much data. Only the series concerning working time and value added are needed here to measure the difference between world market prices and international values since the axiomatic associated with the New Interpretation of the theory of labor value does not require additional assumptions on technology. Third, due to the very simplicity of measuring international values, the impact of missing data on the expected results is quite minor (more so for those of small Southern countries, whose weight in total value added is low), and does not significantly affect the accuracy of the calculations.

This procedure is carried out over the period 1995–2014 for 43 countries, representing more than 85% of world added value, and obviously including both the US and China. As our aim was to discuss the US-China trade war, we will thus focus on their bilateral relations. Our data on value added and inputs of direct working hours in the different sectors of each country are taken from the World Input-Output Database (WIOD) (Timmer et al., 2015). Its two versions, dating from 2013 to 2016, present different sectoral classifications for multi-country input-output tables: the first has 35 sectors and 40 countries and regions, and covers the period 1995–2009; and the second has 68 sectors and 43 economies, and covers the period 2000–2014. Thus, we use the first version between 1995 and 2009, and the second version from 2010 to 2014. For this last period, the input in working time by the hired employees is not provided. The missing points are estimated using International Labor Organization data (various years) and the same method as that used in the WIOD database. For those concerning the business sectors, we retain the data of higher levels in the sectoral classification. For those of temporal dimension, we replace the observations of the nearest year or use linear interpolation, if they are located between two equidistant years. PPP exchange rates are sourced from the World Bank (various years).

In the following, we only present the results for US.-China bilateral trade. They confirm those already collected using the first method (in *Part II*), and highlight the existence of inequality in trade between the two countries between 1995 and 2014. The recorded signs, positive for the US and negative for China, corroborate the idea that the transfer of international value occurs from the former country to the latter. This redistribution that operates for the benefit of the current world hegemony is particularly visible when this unequal exchange is expressed in proportion to the respective added values of the two countries (Graph 7). The amount of this unequal exchange, indicated in monetary terms in current dollars, even tends to increase from 1995 to 2014, reaching 100 billion USD at the end of the period (Graph 8), or just under 0.5% of total US value added.

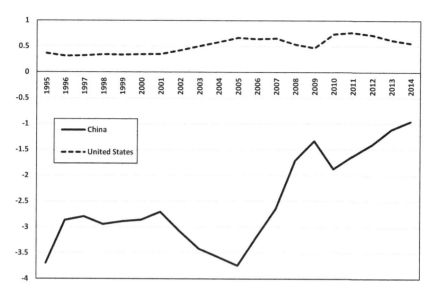

Graph 7. US-China Unequal Exchange in Proportion of the Respective Added Values of the Countries: 1995–2014 (in Percentages). *Source:* Authors' calculations.

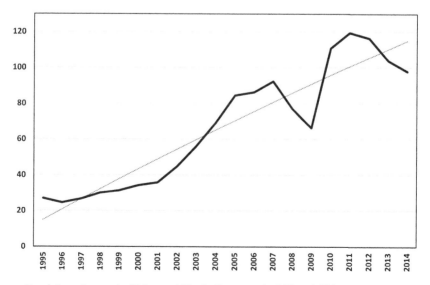

Graph 8. Amount of Unequal Trade Between the US and China: 1995–2014 (in Billions of Dollars). *Source:* Authors' calculations.

What we do observe, however, is that the US is finding it increasingly difficult to maintain its advantage and come out on top in this trade competition, and by extension bear all the implications of free trade, even when it once defined the rules as the hegemony of the capitalist world system (Herrera & Long, 2019), largely for their own benefit. As a matter of fact, China has managed to reduce the importance of this unequal exchange very significantly; the transfer of wealth to its disadvantage (and the US's advantage) gradually dissipated, from −3.7% to −0.9% of its total added value, between 1995 and 2014 (Graph 7). This result clearly supports the downward trends in the ratio of labor exchanges included in the bilateral trade previously observed (*Part II*). As can be seen in Graph 9, China needed to trade 50 hours of Chinese labor for one hour of US labor in 1995, but just over seven in 2014, if the bilateral trade balance is considered. Multiple overlapping factors explain these developments, some of the most influential of which are exchange rate fluctuations (marked by a yuan that is not systematically undervalued [Graph 10]) and productivity dynamics (reflecting technological catch-up [Graph 11]), but we reserve their study for future research.

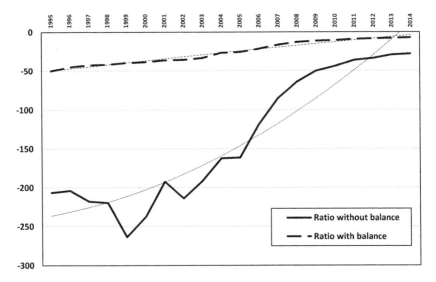

Graph 9.   Ratio of the Labor Exchange in US-China Trade, Balance Included or Not (According to the First Calculation Method): 1995–2014. *Source:* Authors' calculations.

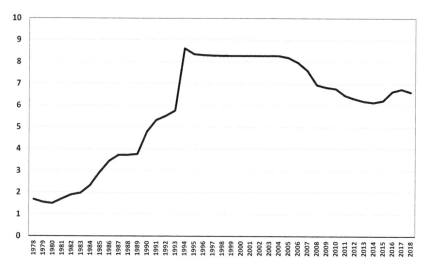

Graph 10.   Exchange Rate Dollar – Yuan: 1978–2018. *Source:* World Bank (various years).

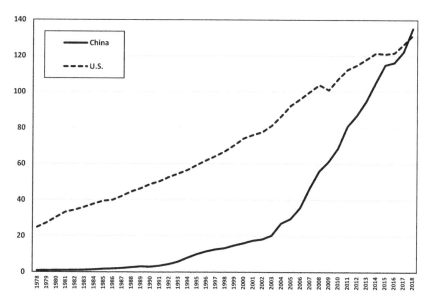

Graph 11.   Gross Product/Labor Ratio: China and the US, 1978–2018. *Source:* Authors' calculations (according to the first method, presented in Part II).

ELEMENTS OF SECTORAL ANALYSIS

It is nevertheless fundamental to note that these general results, jointly high-lighted by our two separate methods of calculating the unequal exchange between the US and China (*Parts II and III*) cover very pronounced disparities, depending on the sectors of activity that one chooses to examine.

Tables 1 and 2 thus present, for the last year of our second sample (2014), the amounts of cross sectoral transfers linked to unequal trade occurring in both directions during US.-China trade. Of the 55 sectors listed in the WIOD data-base, and whose input-output movements were not zero in 2014, more than three-quarters activities (78.2%, or 43 activities) recorded a transfer of value from China to the US The 20 largest transfers, measured in millions of USD, are listed in Table 1. The textile, clothing, and leather goods sectors largely lead with an amount of 71.2 billion USD transferred, followed by that of furniture and other supplies at 21.0 billion USD. These two activities account for almost 95% of total net transfers from unequal trade. The other sectors are far behind, but seven of

Table 1. Amounts of Bilateral Unequal Exchange Transfers From China to the US by Economic Sector in 2014 (in Million Dollars).

Rank	Title of the Economic Sector	Amount of the Transfer
1	Textile, clothing and leather goods manufacturing	71,165.3378
2	Manufacture of furniture and other supplies	20,977.5645
3	Manufacture of electrical equipment	3,256.4309
4	Air transport	2,838.4923
5	Manufacture of wood and wooden articles, cork, straw or spart (excluding furniture)	1,574.1495
6	Manufacturing of rubber and plastic articles	1,366.7739
7	Manufacturing of chemicals and derivatives	1,307.0527
8	Legal and accounting activities, head offices, and management consulting	1,295.6958
9	Manufacturing of general-purpose machinery and equipment (not elsewhere classified)	1,121.7315
10	Manufacturing of other non-metallic mineral products	996.4750
11	Manufacturing of food, beverage and tobacco products	732.9350
12	Manufacturing of fabricated metal products (except machinery and equipment)	695.6651
13	Other service activities	486.7961
14	Mines and quarries	456.9488
15	Land transportation and pipeline transportation	440.0414
16	Fishing and aquaculture	404.7337
17	Manufacturing of paper and paper products	315.2882
18	Wholesale trade (except motor vehicles and motorcycles)	159.5265
19	Telecommunications	147.8567
20	Public administration and social security	122.1474

Source: Authors' calculations.

Table 2. Amounts of Bilateral Unequal Exchange Transfers From the US to China by Economic Sector in 2014 (in Million Dollars).

Rank	Title of the Economic Sector	Amount of the Transfer
1	Manufacturing of computer, electronic, and optical products	6,907.3447
2	Agriculture and farming, hunting, and related services	3,127.2840
3	Manufacturing of motor vehicle, trailer, and semi-trailer	1,056.8188
4	Manufacturing of basic pharmaceutical products and pharmaceutical preparations	422.3682
5	Manufacturing of other transport equipment	383.7530
6	Forestry and logging	329.1851
7	Manufacturing of base metal	256.6966
8	Supply of electricity, gas, steam, and air conditioning	69.8080
9	Manufacturing of coke (coal) and refined petroleum products	19.1010
10	Water collection, treatment, and distribution	8.1942

Source: Authors' calculations.

them still reveal a transfer of an amount greater than a billion USD: electrical equipment (3.3 billion USD), air transport (2.8 billion USD), wood and wooden articles, cork, straw or spart excluding furniture (1.6 billion USD), rubber and/or plastic articles (1.4 billion USD), chemicals and their derivatives (1.3 billion USD), legal, accounting and management consultancy activities (1.3 billion USD), as well as miscellaneous general-purpose machinery and equipment not elsewhere classified (1.1 billion USD).

Conversely, 12 business sectors are at the origin of a value transfer that operated at the expense of the US in 2014 (Table 2), but only four are of an amount exceeding 400 million dollars: manufacturing of computer, electronic and optical products (6.9 billion USD), agriculture and livestock (3.1 billion USD), motor vehicles, trailers and semi-trailers (1.1 billion USD), and basic pharmaceuticals and pharmaceutical preparations (422 million USD).

As illustrated in Table 3, when compared as a share of the respective sectoral value added of the US or China, transfers reflecting these unequal exchanges appear to be the most costly for the Chinese economy in the manufacturing of furniture and other supplies (29.7%), and the manufacturing of textiles, clothing and leather goods (28.0%) sectors. Accompanying the industries already listed in Table 1, and added to that of air transport (12.1%), quite a number of services, ranging from the sector of legal, accounting and management activities (0.6%) to sanitation (0, 5%), via those of post and courier (0.2%) or printing and reproduction of recorded media (0.1%), are also characterized by such value transfers profiting in the US Those sectors that on the contrary, benefited China (Table 4) concern a much narrower range of business activities and reach smaller proportions in US value added. Although, it should be observed that there are significant transfers for the manufacturing of computer, electronic and optical products (2.6%), agriculture and livestock (1.8%) and forestry (1.4%).

Table 3. Proportion of Chinese Sectoral Value Added Transferred in Bilateral Trade From China to the US by Sector in 2014 (in Percentages of Chinese Sectoral Value Added).

Rank	Title of the Economic Sector	Share of Added Value
1	Manufacture of furniture and other supplies	29.6716
2	Textile, clothing and leather goods manufacturing	28.0065
3	Air transport	12.0741
4	Manufacture of electrical equipment	1.9620
5	Manufacture of wood and wooden articles, cork, straw, or spart (excluding furniture)	1.7162
6	Manufacturing of rubber and plastic articles	1.3709
7	Manufacturing of paper and paper products	0.6719
8	Legal and accounting activities, head offices, and management consulting	0.6278
9	Manufacturing of chemicals and derivatives	0.5943
10	Manufacturing of fabricated metal products (except machinery and equipment)	0.5658
11	Sanitation; collection, treatment and disposal of waste; materials recovery; other waste management services	0.4561
12	Manufacturing of other non-metallic mineral products	0.4429
13	Manufacturing of general-purpose machinery and equipment (not elsewhere classified)	0.4290
14	Fishing and aquaculture	0.4197
15	Other service activities	0.2034
16	Manufacturing of food, beverage, and tobacco products	0.1780
17	Postal and courier activities	0.1529
18	Land transportation and pipeline transportation	0.1434
19	Printing and reproduction of recorded media	0.1324
20	Scientific research and development	0.1323

Source: Authors' calculations.

CONCLUSION

By successively using two alternative methods of calculation, we have shown that the working hours integrated into the trade between the US and China were, by reference to the same volume traded, greater in the case of the latter than for that of the former. This reveals an unequal exchange in value. Such a phenomenon is highlighted over the last four decades with the first method (1978–2018) and over 20 years with the second method (1995–2014). To put it another way, the unmistakable finding that China has reaped monetary receipts from growing bilateral trade surpluses since the 1970s is nuanced by the fact that, in terms of working time incorporated into exports, it is mainly the US who benefited from these exchanges, as suggested by our calculations on sectors.

In such a paradoxical context, the outbreak of the trade war against China in 2018 could be interpreted as an attempt by the US President Trump to curb the continuous deterioration in the trade advantages the US has seen for decades

Table 4. Proportion of US Sectoral Value Added Transferred in Bilateral Trade From the US to China by Sector in 2014 (in Percentages of US Sectoral Value Added).

Rank	Title of the Economic Sector	Share of Added Value
1	Manufacturing of computer, electronic, and optical products	2.5777
2	Agriculture and farming, hunting, and related services	1.7649
3	Forestry and logging	1.3871
4	Manufacturing of motor vehicle, trailer, and semi-trailer	0.7536
5	Manufacturing of basic pharmaceutical products and pharmaceutical preparations	0.4452
6	Manufacturing of base metal	0.4300
7	Manufacturing of other transport equipment	0.3052
8	Water collection, treatment, and distribution	0.0883
9	Supply of electricity, gas, steam, and air conditioning	0.0257
10	Manufacturing of coke (coal) and refined petroleum products	0.0112

Source: Authors' calculations.

with China, its emerging rival. However, is the remedy likely to be worse than the disease?

A complexification arises in the analysis of the question that occupies us when we take into account recent changes in the configuration of value chains that have seen China play an integral and decisive part in the globalized supply networks of many economic sectors. Indeed, a substantial part of Chinese exports are made up of components that have been previously manufactured abroad before being delivered to China as inputs to assemble on its territory. However, as soon as these various imported components are subtracted from Chinese exports, the deficit in the US trade balance with China is halved.

REFERENCES

Bacha, E. (1978). An interpretation of unequal exchange from Prebisch-Singer to Emmanuel. *Journal of Development Economics, 5*(4), 319–330.

Clelland, D. (2014). The core of the apple: Degrees of monopoly and dark value in global commodity chains. *Journal of World-Systems Research, 20*(1), 82–111.

Emmanuel, A. (1972). *Unequal exchange: A study of the imperialism of trade.* New York, NY: Monthly Review Press.

Evans, D. (1989). Alternative perspectives on trade and development. In H. Chenery & T. N. Srinivasan (Eds.), *Handbook of development economics* (Vol. 2, pp. 1241–1304). North Holland: Elsevier.

Feng, Z. (2018). International value, international production price and unequal exchange. In K. Tomoko, Y. Linhui, C. Qiang, & Z. Feng (Eds.), *Economic growth and transition of industrial structure in East Asia.* Singapore: Springer.

Foley, D. (2000). Recent developments in the labor theory of value. *Review of Radical Political Economics, 32*(1), 1–39.

Gibson, B. (1980). Unequal exchange: Theoretical issues and empirical findings. *Review of Radical Political Economics, 12*(3), 15–35.

Herrera, R., & Long, Z. (2019). *La Chine est-elle capitaliste?* Paris: Éditions Critiques.

Herrera, R., & Long, Z. (2021). *Dynamique de l'économie chinoise: croissance, cycles et crises.* Paris: Éditions Critiques.

Herrera, R., Wim, D., Piqueras, A., Formento, W., & Nakatani, P. (2019). *200 Years of Marx – Capitalism in Decline (International Observatory of the Crisis).* Hong Kong: Our Global U.

International Labour Organization. (2020). *ILOSTAT database.* Retrieved from https://ilostat.ilo.org/data/

Long, Z., & Herrera, R. (2017). Capital accumulation, profit rates and cycles in China from 1952 to 2014. *Journal of Innovation Economics & Management, 2*(23), 59–82.

Meng, J. (2015). Two kinds of melt and their determinations: Critical notes on Moseley and the new interpretation. *Review of Radical Political Economics, 47*(2), 309–316.

Nakajima, A., & Izumi, H. (1995). Economic development and unequal exchange among nations: Analysis of the U.S., Japan and South Korea. *Review of Radical Political Economics, 27*(3), 86–94.

National Bureau of Statistics (NBS) of China. (1993–2019). *China Statistics Yearbooks.* Beijing: China Statistics Press.

National Bureau of Statistics (NBS) of China. (2007). *China Labor Statistics Yearbooks.* Beijing: China Statistics Press.

National Bureau of Statistics (NBS) of China. (2008–2017). *China Population and Employment Statistics Yearbooks.* Beijing: China Statistics Press.

National Bureau of Statistics (NBS) of China. (various years: 1981, 1987, 1990, 1992, 1995, 1997, 2000, 2002, 2005, 2007, 2010, 2012, 2015, 2017). *Input-Output Tables of China.* Beijing: China Statistics Press.

Organisation of Economic Cooperation and Development (OECD). (2020). *OECD database.* Retrieved from https://data.oecd.org/emp

Peet, R., & Hartwick, E. (2015). *Theories of development: Contentions, arguments, alternatives.* New York, NY: Guilford Publications.

Prebisch, R. (1959). Commercial policy in the underdeveloped countries. *American Economic Review, 49*(2), 251–273.

Ricci, A. (2019). Unequal exchange in the age of globalization. *Review of Radical Political Economics, 51*(2), 225–245.

Singer, H. W. (1950). The distribution of gains between investing and borrowing countries. *American Economic Review, 40*(2), 473–485.

Timmer, M., Dietzenbacher, E., Los, B., Stehrer, R., & De Vries, G. (2015). An illustrated user guide to the World Input-Output database: The case of global automotive production. *Review of International Economics, 23*(3), 575–605.

United Nations. (2020). *U.N. Comtrade database.* Retrieved from https://comtrade.un.org/data/

U.S. Department of Commerce. (various years). *Trade in goods with China.* Washington, DC: U.S. Census Bureau, Economic Indicator Division.

Webber, M. J., & Foot, S. P. H. (1984). The measurement of unequal exchange. *Environment and Planning A: Economy and Space, 16*(7), 927–947.

World Bank. (2020). *World Bank Open Data.* Retrieved from https://data.worldbank.org/

Xu, X., & Hang, Y. (2018). Understanding Sino-U.S. trade imbalance: A statistical perspective. *Economic Perspectives, 7*, 27–36.

PART II

MONEY TODAY

COLONIAL LEGACY, MONETARY POLICY, AND RESOURCE MOBILIZATION FOR DEVELOPMENT IN AFRICA

Demba Moussa Dembele

ABSTRACT

This chapter aims to demonstrate how the colonial legacy in general, and in its monetary area in particular, has been one of the major obstacles to African countries' ability to mobilize financial resources for their development. In fact, the monetary systems inherited from colonialism serve as an instrument to plunder African resources and extract surplus for capital accumulation in former colonial powers. One of the best examples is found in the relationships between France and its former colonies in West and Central Africa. The monetary system imposed on those countries is essentially perpetuating the Colonial Pact, under which the role of the colonies is to serve the political, economic, and strategic interests of the colonial power. For African countries, the monetary arrangement, illustrated by the use of CFA franc as their currency, has been a major obstacle to capital accumulation, productive capacity building and effective structural transformation of their economies. Unless African countries break free from the CFA monetary system and reclaim their sovereignty, there will be no development. The struggle for monetary sovereignty in former French colonies is now part of a broader continental struggle to reclaim Africa's sovereignty over its resources and the formulation of its development policies.

Keywords: Colonialism; CFA; center/periphery; exploitation; unequal exchange; capital accumulation; sovereignty; development; resource mobilization

Value, Money, Profit, and Capital Today
Research in Political Economy, Volume 39, 53–71
Copyright © 2024 Demba Moussa Dembele
Published under exclusive licence by Emerald Publishing Limited
ISSN: 0161-7230/doi:10.1108/S0161-723020230000039004

INTRODUCTION

One of the most intractable challenges faced by African countries has been the difficulty to mobilize the financial resources needed for their development. Indeed, despite its immense natural resources, Africa has not been able to put together efficient policies aimed at mobilizing enough domestic and external financial resources. This failure has to do, in large part, with the economic models and structures inherited from colonialism.

In reality, the formal independence achieved by most African countries did not fundamentally change the relationships with former colonial powers, especially in the economic and financial areas. These former colonial powers continue to dominate and control key sectors of their former colonies' economies. One of them is the area of monetary policy. If in Western countries and in most countries in the Global South, monetary policy plays a central role in mobilizing domestic and external financial resources, this is not the case in many African countries, especially in former French colonies.

THE COLONIAL LEGACY

The reason is the legacy of colonialism. Indeed, with the exception of Ethiopia, African countries were all under colonial rule from the late nineteenth century to the mid-twentieth century, when most of them became formally independent, either through negotiations or wars of Liberation, like Algeria and former Portuguese colonies. During the period of colonial rule, the economies of African countries were completely integrated into the economic systems of the colonial powers. Indeed, during that period, African natural resources were used for capital accumulation in Europe, which contributed to its industrialization. In other words, colonization was a period of intense plunder of Africa's resources, hence laying the roots of its "backwardness" and underdevelopment (Rodney, 2001).

In the colonial French system, there was a Colonial Pact, under which, African colonies were to serve the economic, political and geopolitical interests of the colonial power, namely France. This means that the role of the colonies was to enrich the colonial power and serve to give it prestige and influence within the most powerful group of nations (N'Guessan, 2001).

Under colonization, the colonies had no economic policies of their own. This was especially the case in terms of monetary policy. The colonial powers controlled the Central Banks and the monetary policy, like money supply, as well as interest and exchange rate policies. It was only after independence that many former African colonies set up their Central Banks, created their own currencies and gained control over their monetary policies. Even then, their currencies were pegged to those of former colonial powers and their monetary policies almost aligned with theirs.

However, in the former French colonies in West and Central Africa, independence did not put an end to the Colonial Pact, which took other name and form. To this very day, more than 60 years after the end of colonialization, the unequal relations forged during that period still exist. In several former French colonies, France still retains a strong sway on economic, political, and security issues. This is particularly the case for the former colonies using the CFA franc (Nubukpo et al., 2016).

THE CFA FRANC SYSTEM

The CFA[1] franc was created in December 1945, by the first post-war French government under General de Gaulle. The goal was to reassert France's control over its African colonies, weakened during the Occupation by Nazi Germany.

Of course, African colonies had no say in this decision. After the wave of independence, beginning in the late 1950s, several countries left the system and created their own currencies. This was notably the case in North Africa, with Morocco and Tunisia, followed later by Algeria. In Sub-Saharan Africa, Guinea and Mali were the first to leave the CFA system in the early 1960s. They were followed in the mid-1970s by Madagascar and Mauritania. However, Mali rejoined the Franc Zone in 1984. Currently, there are 15 African countries in the Franc Zone, eight in West Africa, six in Central Africa, plus the Comoros.[2]

The CFA countries are in a vast geographical zone, stretching from West to Central Africa. Most of them are resource-rich, as oil producers (Congo, Gabon, Equatorial Guinea, Chad), located in the Gulf of Guinea, where are found the continent's largest crude oil reserves, according to several expert sources. Other countries are rich in strategic raw materials, such as uranium in Niger, which is under the exclusive control of the French company AREVA. Not to forget that other countries, like Cote d'Ivoire, have large quantities of agricultural products, such as cocoa and coffee, also under the control of French agro-industrial companies.

The location of these countries and their resources show their economic, political and strategic importance for France. This explains why successive French governments are doing whatever they can to continue their country's control over the fate of its former colonies through the CFA system and other kinds of agreements, including trade and military agreements.

THE ROLE OF THE CFA SYSTEM

If one is to believe the official discourse from French authorities, the CFA franc was supposed to help bring "stability" to African economies, which would help attract foreign investments and foster economic growth and development. It was also supposed to contribute to the integration of these countries through closer trade ties. However, they are all "pure myths" (Pigeaud & Sylla, 2018). The reality tells a different story. It shows that the survival of the CFA franc system, more than 60 years after formal independence of African countries, has served two main objectives. The first objective is to maintain French political domination over its former colonies. The second objective is to reinforce the exploitation of African economies, by allowing French companies to continue the extraction of surplus through huge profits made in plundering the resources of the former colonies.

This unequal relationship can be understood in the context of the center/ periphery system of global capitalism so powerfully analyzed by the late great Marxist economist, Professor Samir Amin.[3] In his work, he explained that there is one global capitalist system, composed of a center and of a periphery. The center is composed of the major industrialized countries, while the periphery involves roughly all countries of the Global South (Amin, 1986). In that system, those countries serve as a source of capital accumulation for the center. This is particularly true in this era of globalized capitalism, which has not only accentuated the unequal exchange and the transfer of value between the center and the periphery but also intensified the plunder of the resources of the planet by the center (Amin, 2018).

Africa, with its immense natural resources, remains one of the primary sources of that plunder and capital accumulation for Western countries. This explains why the former French colonies in West and Central Africa are still under French control via several economic, financial and monetary agreements. The CFA franc system, with its four pillars (see Box 1), illustrates best this control, to the great benefit of the French economy.

BOX 1 The Four Pillars of the Franc Zone.[4]

i. Fixed exchange rate between the CFA franc and the French franc (now with the euro).
ii. Free transfer of capital between African countries and France, but not between African countries.
iii. Centralization of reserves, half in the French Treasury and half in the BCEAO (*Banque Centrale des États de l'Afrique de l'Ouest*, or Central Bank of West African States).
iv. The unlimited "guarantee" of convertibility of the CFA franc by the French Treasury.

THE ADVANTAGES TO FRANCE'S ECONOMY

With this system, France pays with its own currency for its imports from CFA countries. This results in saving foreign exchange that could be used for other international obligations. This privilege became especially advantageous when the

French franc was weak and unstable relative to the US dollar and other major currencies. Now, with the weakening of the euro relative to the dollar, France and other countries of the Eurozone get access to goods and services from CFA countries without the costs associated with inflation imported from the dollar zone.

The fixed exchange rate and the free movement of capital between France and African countries give French companies a double advantage. They are not exposed to foreign exchange risks, and they freely transfer their profits made in Africa, without incurring any capital control.

The obligation of African countries to deposit half of their exchange reserves in the French Treasury is a feature of the CFA system that gives France another key advantage over African economies. In return, the Treasury provides "a guarantee" of convertibility to the CFA franc. But this "guarantee" works only if there is a global deficit of exchange reserves for all the eight countries. In reality, it is the exchange reserves accumulated by African countries that serve as a guarantee for the CFA franc (Koulibaly, 2011).

Nevertheless, beyond the economic and financial benefits, the CFA franc system provides France with a geopolitical advantage against its potential competitors in Europe. It is obvious that without its lingering influence with its former African colonies, France would have a status lower than that of the United Kingdom and Germany.

If France reaps many benefits from the CFA franc system, by contrast, it has been costly to African countries.

THE COSTS OF THE CFA SYSTEM TO AFRICAN COUNTRIES

Each of the pillars of the CFA franc has carried a number of costs to African economies.

The Costs of Fixed Exchange Rate

The fixed exchange rate between the CFA franc and the French franc (now with the euro) is supposed to be a factor of "stability" for CFA countries, because it is associated with the absence of foreign exchange risks and low inflation, both of which could be positive factors in attracting foreign investors, compared to other African countries with their own currencies. But the reality shows a different picture, as illustrated in Table 1.

As this table shows, non-CFA countries, including Ghana and Mauritania in West Africa, have received more foreign direct investments (FDIs) than CFA countries, like Cameroon and Cote d'Ivoire, which are the largest economies in Central Africa and West Africa, respectively. Therefore, the fixed exchange rate with the euro and the absence of exchange risks associated with it has not been an

Table 1. FDI (Dollars per Capita) in CFA and Non-CFA Countries.

Country	2015	2016	2017	2018	Average
Cameroon	6.9	27.8	33.1	27.8	23.4
Cote d'Ivoire	21.3	24.2	39.8	36.4	30.4
Ethiopia	26.1	38.5	37.8	30.3	33.2
Ghana	114.6	122.4	111.8	100.4	112.3
Mauritania	124.1	65.1	137.1	16.1	85.6

Source: African Development Bank Statistical Yearbook (2020).

advantage for CFA countries in attracting more FDIs compared to countries with their own currencies exposed to exchange risks.

On the contrary, the fixed exchange rate with the euro has been a big handicap for the African exporting economies. The war in Ukraine and its consequences have made this handicap more glaring. With the high inflation ripping through the Eurozone and the weakening of the euro against the US dollar, African countries using the CFA franc are under the threat of high prices of imported goods and services, especially energy and food prices. The latest statistics show that inflation is approaching double digits in the West African Economy and Monetary Union (WAEMU), with a level of 8.1% in July 2022 compared to July 2021. This is bad news for exporting companies which have lost their competitive edge, even within the Economic Community of West African States (ECOWAS). In addition, with the devaluation of the euro relative to the US dollar, the CFA franc is also dragged down, with dire consequences for the countries, in terms of their external debt and some of their US dollar-denominated imports, like crude oil.

The Costs of Inflation Targeting

For CFA countries, the fixed exchange rate system is associated with tight monetary policies as the African central banks, like BCEAO (*Banque Centrale des États de l'Afrique de l'Ouest*, or Central Bank of West African States), and BEAC (*Banque des États de l'Afrique centrale*, or Bank of Central African States), tend to adopt monetary policies similar to those of the European Central Bank (ECB). This explains why African central banks have made price stability their main objective, with an inflation target of 2% to 3%.

According to Article 8 of its Statutes, revised in 2010, the BCEAO claims:

> The main objective of monetary policy of the Central Bank is price stability. The inflation target is set by the Monetary Policy Committee. Without prejudice to this objective, the Central Bank supports the economic policies of the West African Economic and Monetary Union (WAEMU) with an eye to healthy and sustainable growth.[5]

For countries, which need to build productive capacities, to transform their raw materials, create jobs and wealth for their citizens, it is absurd to set price stability as priority, even if nobody would support runaway inflation. This decision is one more indication of the loss of sovereignty over African countries' monetary and economic policies. It has nothing to do with the economic and social priorities of the WAEMU. In addition, in the BCEAO, monetary policy is no longer set by the Council of Ministers, composed of ministers running key economic and financial departments in the governments of the member States. Monetary policy is now set by a group of "experts" assembled in a new institution called Monetary Policy Committee (MPC). These "experts," imbued with neoliberal ideology, tend to care more about the concerns of foreign investors than about the consequences of their policies for the population of the member countries.

Yet, several critics have disputed inflation targeting as a sound policy, especially for developing countries. Indeed, for these countries, targeting inflation may lead to stifling growth. As a matter of fact, the record of more than 60 years of independence shows that low inflation is not necessarily synonymous with high growth, much less with development.

Heinz and Ndikumana (2010) give several examples showing that double-digit inflation can be beneficial to economic growth, while an inflation below 5% can be harmful to growth. Indeed, in Africa, countries like Ghana, Ethiopia, and Nigeria, among others, which have higher rates of inflation, compared to CFA countries, attract more foreign direct investments and have generally enjoyed higher growth rates. Kako Nubukpo expresses a view similar as Heinz and Ndikumana. He claims that several studies have indicated that an inflation of up to 8% in the CFA countries could generate economic growth that is higher than the one obtained with the targeted inflation of 2% (Nubukpo, 2016).

Rémy Herrera, for his part, condemns inflation targeting as an "absurd" policy imposed by the ECB on African countries – via their central banks –, thus punishing their economies and peoples (Herrera, 2022). He goes on to sharply criticize the fixed exchange rate policy between the euro, which is a strong currency serving the interests of highly developed countries, and the CFA franc, which is used by African countries, most of which are least developed countries. Such asymmetrical relationships are likely to be detrimental to African countries' economies.

Other critics remind proponents of inflation targeting that what is called the "Glorious Thirty Years," of high growth and "full employment," between 1945 and 1975, took place in a period when inflation was in double digits in many Western countries and in the rest of the world (Agbohou, 1999).

Inflation targeting has been dealt a major blow over the last two years with the outbreak of Covid-19 and the consequences of the war in Ukraine. When major central banks launched the "Quantitative Easing" (QE) policies, during the pic of the pandemic, they did not care much about inflation. On the contrary, they were concerned about growth and employment. Interest rates were down to zero or close to zero in the United States and Europe.

However, the great lesson from the war in Ukraine is that inflation is fundamentally linked to what happens to the real economy. It is mainly the disruptions in supply chains, more than excess money supply, that are behind the current surge of inflation in most parts of the world. Despite the tightening of monetary policy in the United States and Europe, through the increase in interest rates, inflation levels are approaching double digits. They are likely to remain high as long as the disruptions in supply chains persist. There are even fears of stagflation, a combination of recession and high levels of inflation.

Capital Flight

Another feature of the CFA system that has been very costly to CFA countries is capital flight. For one thing, the free movement of capital between African countries and France opens the door to huge capital flight, especially in times of political instability. Whenever there are rumors of devaluation, there are massive capital flights. There was a massive capital flight between 1993 and 1994, before and after the devaluation of 50% of the CFA franc relative to the French franc (Agbohou, 1999).

Recent assessment shows that Cote d'Ivoire, Cameroon and Congo are the CFA countries experiencing the highest levels of capital flight. Between 1970 and 2008, Cote d'Ivoire has lost 66.2 billion in 2008-US dollars. It is the third largest country suffering from capital flight after Nigeria and Angola. In the Franc Zone, it is followed by Cameroon, with 33.2 billion US dollars, and Congo, with 27 billion US dollars (Pigeaud & Sylla, 2018).

Nevertheless, capital flight from CFA countries is part of a wider phenomenon bleeding Africa (AfDB & GFI, 2013). And West Africa is the region leading in illicit financial flows (see UNCTAD, 2020b; UNECA, 2015). It is the extractive sector the main source of illicit capital flight. Most CFA countries have a large extractive sector under the control of multinational corporations. The free transfer of capital is also used by the African wealthy people to move their savings to Paris and other Western capitals, thus depriving their countries of much-needed resources (Nubukpo, 2016; Pigeaud & Sylla, 2018).

The Overall Costs of the CFA System

Overall, except for the inflation rate, which is lower than the average in Africa, the CFA franc system has given no significant advantage to former French colonies. On the contrary, this system is associated with several costs as analyzed above. Therefore, there is little wonder the majority of CFA countries are ranked among the "poorest" countries in the world, according to the rankings made by the United Nations. In West Africa, seven of the eight countries using the CFA are called "least developed countries" (LDCs). In Central Africa, two out of the six CFA countries are also among the least developed countries. Therefore, among the 14 African countries using the CFA franc, 9 are LDCs, almost two-thirds of them.

It is in light of all the above that the tide has turned against the CFA franc as one of the lingering symbols of French domination.

THE CASE FOR MONETARY SOVEREIGNTY

The CFA system deprives African countries of their sovereignty over their monetary policies. The monetary policies adopted by CFA central banks are totally disconnected from their countries' economic fundamentals. In reality, the CFA franc is not an African currency. It is a French currency circulating in African countries, as the renowned Cameroonian economist Joseph Tchundjang Pouemi so rightly said 40 years ago:

> France is the only country in the world to have succeeded in circulating its currency – only its currency – in politically free countries (...). The CFA franc is not created by any African State, it is created by the French State. Therefore, it is the French franc itself.[6]

One of the best illustrations of this assertion is the devaluation of the CFA franc in January 1994. The decision was unilaterally made by the French government, with the help of the International Monetary Fund (IMF), whose Managing Director at the time was a French national, Mister Michel Camdessus, who was a former Director of the French Treasury. African Presidents were summoned to Dakar (Senegal) and informed of the decision (Agbohou, 1999; Dembele, 2015a).[7]

This is why one of the most powerful arguments against the CFA system is that it is a denial of African countries' sovereignty; because, essentially, money is an attribute of sovereignty for a country. In addition, money has economic, political and social dimensions. It symbolizes power, both economic and political. Indeed, from a political economy perspective, one cannot spate economics from politics. As a matter of fact, fundamentally, a monetary policy aims to achieve economic and social objectives set by the political entity. Therefore, when a country has no control over its currency, it has lost both its sovereignty and the power to decide for its economic and social policies; in other words, the power to decide on its development (Nubukpo, Ze Belinga, Tinel, & Dembele, 2016).

This is the predicament former French colonies using the CFA franc system have been going through since their formal "independence." Their economic policies are decided by external forces, whether by France or by international financial institutions, like the IMF and the World Bank. And as to be expected, this dependency put these countries in the category of the poor countries. This is illustrated by their human development indicators, which are at the lowest scale, according to the Human Development Index (HDI) published by the United Nations Development Program (UNDP). One illustration of this is that of the 33 African countries classified as the "least developed countries" (LDCs) by the

United Nations, nine are countries having the CFA franc as their currency (UNCTAD, 2020a).

The opponents of the CFA system have therefore developed solid arguments against that system. One of the most powerful arguments that resonates profoundly in the African public opinion is that the CFA franc is a symbol of domination and denial of sovereignty. The second strong argument is that the CFA is an instrument of underdevelopment. This is why there has been a rising tide against this system, considered as a symbol of servitude (Nubukpo et al., 2016).

THE STRUGGLE FOR MONETARY SOVEREIGNTY IN WEST AFRICA

In West Africa, there are currently two groups of countries using eight different currencies. As already indicated, the CFA franc is used by the West African Economic and Monetary Union (WAEMU). The second group is composed of seven States using their own national currencies. They have formed the West African Monetary Zone (WAMZ). These countries and the CFA countries, all together, are members of the Economic Community of West African States (ECOWAS). Since the mid-1980s, this grouping has launched a process aimed at adopting a single currency in order to strengthen its economic integration.

The ECOWAS Project: Regional Monetary Union

The goal is to eliminate the eight currencies in circulation, that is, the CFA franc and the seven national currencies.[8] This would lead to the creation of a single currency issued by a regional central bank to recover sovereignty monetary policy and to serve the structural transformation of the region's economies, which have vast natural resources that would create wealth for its citizens and be one of the strong engines of growth for the continent.

But the road to a single currency has been a bumpy and long one, due to several obstacles. The political obstacles are illustrated by the reluctance of CFA countries to give up that currency for a regional currency. Another political obstacle is the fear for those countries to be under the leadership of Nigeria, given its weight. Indeed, Nigeria accounts for 70% of the ECOWAS gross domestic production (GDP), and its population is more than half of the population of the Community (Demba, 2015). This fear is shared by France and even the European Union, because they know that under Nigeria leadership, they would inevitably lose control over their former colonies. This is why France is openly working to stall the ECOWAS monetary project, as we will see later.

The second set of obstacles is economic in the form of convergence criteria that are deemed necessary in order to adopt the single currency (Box 2).

BOX 2 Convergence Criteria in ECOWAS.

Criteria of First Rank

- Keep inflation rate at less than 10%.
- Ratio of State budget deficit (excluding grants) to GDP at 3%.
- Respect the maximum limit for central bank financing at 10% of past year fiscal deficit.
- Maintain a level of exchange reserves covering at least 3 months of importations.

Criteria of Second Rank

- Maintain a positive real interest rate.
- Not accumulate new domestic payments arrears and liquidate the old ones.
- Reach a level of taxation revenue of at least 20% of GDP.
- Maintain the ratio salary mass to tax revenues at less or 35%.
- Public investments financed by domestic resources with at least 20% of fiscal revenues.

Those criteria are too stringent. Some critics call them copies of the Maastricht criteria used by the European Union for its single currency, the euro. Now, critics say the Eurozone is in crisis due to the stringent Maastricht criteria. The Greece debt crisis being one of the most glaring symbols of that crisis (Maucourant, 2016).

The mistake made by the ECOWAS countries is to copy a model which has nothing to do with their economic realities. This explains why, despite several deadlines, its members have not yet been able to fulfill the neoliberal-inspired criteria. However, the ECOWAS Heads of State seem to be determined to overcome the obstacle posed by the criteria.

The Abuja Decision of June 2019

This explains why on June 29, 2019, during their Summit in Abuja (Nigeria), the ECOWAS countries adopted what could be called a "bold" decision to adopt a single currency called "eco," which should have been operational by 2020. The other elements of the decision were the following:

- the future central bank will be a federal central bank;
- the exchange regime will be flexible, with the targeting of global inflation;
- the exchange rate will be determined by a basket of currencies: US dollar, the euro, the British pound, the Chinese yuan, and the Japanese yen.

However, this decision was criticized as unrealistic because it was impossible for any country to fulfill even some of the criteria before 2020. The decision also

ran soon into trouble with the French government's attempt to undermine the
project, with the complicity of its allies in the region, Cote d'Ivoire and Senegal.
In December 2019, the French President Emmanuel Macron and the President of
Cote d'Ivoire, Alassane Ouattara, announced an agreement to change the name
of the CFA franc into "eco," just like the name adopted by the ECOWAS. This
agreement drew a strong rebuke from Nigeria and the other non-CFA countries.

France's Cosmetic Changes

Despite the critiques against the Ouattara-Macron agreement, France went
ahead, anyway and in May 2020, it introduced some changes in its relations with
the CFA countries:

(1) The deposit of 50% of their reserves in the French Treasury is no longer
    required;
(2) French representatives in the BCEAO institutions will be removed.

But in analyzing these changes, one can see that they are more cosmetic than
substantial. For example, French representatives in the BCEAO institutions will
be replaced by international "experts" who will be selected with the participation
of the *Banque de France*, the French central bank. Which means, people who will
continue to defend and protect French interests.

In addition, there are three key elements that remain in place in the "new"
arrangement between France and the CFA countries:

(1) the fixed exchange rate with euro is maintained;
(2) the free transfer of capital between African countries and France remains;
(3) France will be a "guarantor" of the new arrangement.

Which means that it will still have some control over CFA-eco economic
policies.

Clouds Over the ECOWAS Project

Nevertheless, even without the French attempt to undermine the single currency
of the ECOWAS, the project of the latter is in big doubt. For one thing, the
political will seems to be lacking in the regional leadership. Even more worrisome
are the dramatic changes in the international context with the consequences of the
Covid-19 pandemic and the war in Ukraine. This explains why since mid-2020,
all ECOWAS countries have suspended the compliance with the convergence
criteria. The decision to adopt the single currency was pushed back to 2027. But
even this new date is in doubt. It is very difficult to see how the current context
will change in five years to allow the ECOWAS countries to fulfill their

commitment. The world is in big turmoil. There is a big geopolitical upheaval whose consequences are yet to be known.

The world economy is confronted with the biggest threat of inflation in decades. Several ECOWAS countries are experiencing double-digit inflation. This is the case for Nigeria and Ghana, among others. The CFA countries are also experiencing high levels of inflation, never seen before. Therefore, the economic clouds are too heavy for the ECOWAS monetary project in the foreseeable future.

However, beyond economic constraints, one of the biggest problems is the political will, which seems to be lacking at the moment in the ECOWAS. Since money is fundamentally a political issue, without a committed Pan-African leadership, it is difficult to see how to move this project forward.

But the ECOWAS is not the only economic community working toward a single currency. It is also the case for the East African Community (Box 3).

BOX 3 The East African Community (EAC) Common Currency.

According to the Ugandan First Deputy Prime Minister and Minister for East African Community (EAC) Affairs, Rebecca Kadaga, if everything goes according to technical experts, the EAC will have a single currency by 2031. She said the member States are now working on the finer details to choose a country to host the East African Monetary Institute that will later become the East African Central Bank.

Already, Ms. Kadaga noted Uganda, Tanzania, Burundi, and Kenya have submitted requests to host this institute, and the four countries are being reviewed for a decision.

The EAC now has seven member states, including Uganda, Tanzania, Kenya, Rwanda, Burundi, South Sudan, and the Democratic Republic of Congo, which formally joined the bloc in April. However, only four, apart from the Democratic Republic of Congo, have so far ratified the Single Currency Protocol.

The Monetary Union is the third step in the EAC regional integration that is expected to be capped by a political federation.

However, a 2020 report by the United Nations Economic Commission for Africa (UNECA) has cast doubt on the EAC capacity to attain a single currency by 2024. The reason: the sharp divergences in monetary policies among member countries.

Any progress made in the monetary projects in West and East Africa or in any other regional community is likely to give a big boost to the continental monetary projects.

The African Union's Monetary Projects

In connection with its Agenda 2063, the African Union has launched a process leading to the creation of an African Central Bank and an African Monetary Fund. The ultimate goal of these projects is to create a common African currency in order to help the continental integration.

A common African currency over which African countries have full sovereignty is one of the keys to achieving Agenda 2063 of the African Union. For one thing, there is no possibility for Africa to move forward with the multiplicity of currencies, many of which are too weak. But the most important argument for a common currency is the issue of industrialization. If regional economic communities strive to transform domestically their natural resources, they need to have monetary policies in step with this objective. A monetary policy that could serve that objective is a policy that is fully under the control of member countries. African economists have said time and again that the African economic projects could not move forward without a common currency over which African countries exert full sovereignty and control.

The project has attracted more than 40 African central banks. There is a secretariat located at the BCEAO in Dakar, Senegal (Dembele, 2015a).

For participating banks, despite the probable loss of monetary flexibility for member countries, the single currency for the continent is supposed to provide several benefits. These include, among others, the elimination of the costs associated with currency exchange, the elimination of exchange rate risks in economic and financial transactions between countries in the Union, as well as the promotion of price and employment stabilization and growth of real output.

Members States adopted an African Monetary Cooperation Program (AMCP) in September 2002. The program is based on a framework for macroeconomic convergence, highlighting the convergence criteria. However, the convergence criteria, inspired by orthodox monetary theories, are more stringent than the ones adopted by the ECOWAS. These criteria have a remote relationship with the economic realities of African countries. If such criteria are maintained, it is fair to say that the adoption of an African single currency is not likely to happen in the foreseeable future.

However, a Pan-African payment and settlement system has been adopted (Box 4) to facilitate intra-African trade and financial transactions.

BOX 4 The Pan-African Payment and Settlement System (PAPSS).

The PAPSS was launched on July 7, 2019, in Niamey (Niger). Its aim is to overcome the fragmented payment, clearing and settlement systems in Africa in order to facilitate intra-African trade and financial transactions.

Currently, more than 80% of intra-African payments go through Europe or the United States, resulting in high transfer and compliance costs to the continent. The establishment of the African Continental Free Trade Area (AfCFTA) has added to the need and urgency of providing an enabling continental payment and settlement infrastructure that will support the objectives of the AfCFTA. At a time when cross-border trading is high on the agenda with AfCFTA and now a reality, the single continental market makes it necessary for home grown payment gateway to facilitate trade and investment among African countries.

Therefore, PAPSS was adopted in July 2019 in Niamey by the African Union Heads of State as the payment and settlement system to support the implementation of AfCFTA. It is a financial market infrastructure that has been developed and initiated through a collaborative effort of the AfCFTA Secretariat, Afreximbank (African Exportimport Bank) and the African Union Commission.

According to its Executive Director, the system started with a pilot phase in the West African Monetary Zone (WAMZ), where Central Banks of Nigeria, Ghana, Liberia, Guinea, the Gambia, and Sierra Leone successfully performed live transactions between each other. With this successful pilot-run, the next phase is to bring any central banks and commercial banks on board. The system is expected to be in the five regions of Africa before the end of 2023, all central banks signed up by end of 2024, and all commercial banks by end of 2025.

Currently, the system is composed of eight central banks, seven switches, and more than 30 commercial banks. More commercial banks will join soon as they are almost finalized the on-boarding and integration process. Altogether, it is designed to ensure instant payments for goods and services between African jurisdictions. Payments are initiated and settled in the local currencies of initiators and beneficiaries effectively eliminating the need for third (hard) currencies to consummate trades within Africa.

Once it begins to operate at scale, PAPSS should save Africa countries an estimated 5 billion US dollars annually in payment transaction costs, while it plays an increasingly significant role in accelerating the continent's transactions underpinning the operationalization of AfCFTA.

ABOUT THE MODERN MONETARY THEORY

Still within the framework of a major break with conventional neoliberal approach to Africa's development, the modern monetary theory (MMT) may open new and innovative way of mobilizing resources for development.

The popularity of MMT is based on the growing discredit of orthodox monetary theories. This is especially the case for monetarism, whose most prominent intellectual leader was Milton Friedman of the University of Chicago. But the 2008 international financial crisis has laid bare its shallowness (Krugman, 2009).

The MMT was exposed in a book by US economist Stephanie Kelton. Titled *The Deficit Myth (2020)*, it has become a bestseller in the United States and in many parts of Europe. The MMT is founded on some basic principles. One of them is that a fiscal deficit for a sovereign State is a myth. In fact, from the MMT perspective, a government, which issues a sovereign currency, such government: (1) does not face a "budget constraint"; (2) cannot "run out of money"; (3) can always meet its obligations by paying in its own currency; and (4) can set the interest rate on any obligations it issues. This means that a sovereign government cannot have any constraint on financing its policies.

Clearly, the MMT supports strong government intervention. However, the only constraint on public spending is concern about inflation, which may occur if both the public and private sectors spend too much at the same time. But that risk could be avoided by raising taxes on the private sector, hence limiting its spending capacity.

The growing popularity of the MMT, which is associated with the Keynesian economics, coincides with the demise of the neoliberal paradigm, in particular the collapse of market fundamentalism, a crisis accentuated by the coronavirus pandemic (The Economist, 2020).

There are two interesting aspects of MMT from the perspective of our struggle in Africa. The first aspect is that its application is possible only in a context of monetary sovereignty. Which is consistent with our struggle to end French neocolonial monetary control. The second aspect is that MMT puts the State at the center of monetary policy, as key agent in the decision-making. This is also consistent with the struggle to rehabilitate the State in African countries, to rebuild developmental States as called for by several institutions (UNCTAD, 2007; UNECA, 2011, 2014).

CONCLUSION

This paper has exposed how the CFA franc continues to symbolize the colonial French legacy of domination and exploitation of 14 of its former colonies in West and Central Africa. The experience has shown the CFA franc system has almost exclusively benefited France and its economy.

Indeed, the CFA franc system is an instrument of political domination and a tool of economic exploitation. It facilitates capital accumulation for French companies while impoverishing African countries. With that system, these companies get a privileged access to African resources and make huge profits that are freely repatriated without being subjected to capital controls. This shows that the CFA franc system is an instrument of surplus extraction from African countries through the plunder of their natural resources. This illustrates well the center/periphery unequal relationships cogently analyzed by the late Samir Amin.

However, in addition to being an economic and financial instrument, the CFA franc system has a geopolitical dimension. It is part of the Colonial Pact, which still exists today in a new form, familiarly called "*Françafrique.*" In this system, the role of the colonies is to serve the economic, political and geostrategic interests of the colonial power. For African countries, the CFA franc system also symbolizes not only the loss of monetary sovereignty, but the loss of political sovereignty as well, because money is fundamentally a political issue.

In light of this, the opposition to the CFA franc and French neocolonialism has been growing over the last several years. That opposition has gained momentum lately with the contribution of prominent intellectuals and high profile activists as well as the involvement of some current and former leaders and policymakers.

The struggle for monetary sovereignty has compelled France and its puppets in West Africa to propose a fake "reform," whose ultimate aim is to undermine the process toward a single currency in the Economic Community of West African States (ECOWAS). But the struggle for a sovereign currency in West Africa is irreversible because there can be no possibility of development without an independent and sovereign currency. In addition, the struggle in West Africa is part of a wider struggle at the continental level, with the monetary projects and payment systems that the African Union is promoting in order to serve the objectives of its Agenda 2063.

NOTES

1. CFA meant "*Colonies françaises d'Afrique*" (French colonies in Africa) at the time of its creation. However, today, even though the acronym remains the same, it has two different meanings: *Communauté financière africaine* (African financial community) in West Africa; and *Coopération financière d'Afrique* (African Financial Cooperation) in Central Africa.

2. In West Africa, the countries are Benin, Burkina Faso, Cote d'Ivoire, Guinea-Bissau, Mali, Niger, Senegal and Togo, with the BCEAO (*Banque Centrale des États de l'Afrique de l'Ouest*, or Central Bank of West African States). In Central Africa, there are Cameroon, Central African Republic, Chad, Congo, Equatorial Guinea and Gabon, with BEAC (*Banque des États de l'Afrique centrale*, or Bank of Central African States).

3. Dembele (2011).

4. However, this system has undergone some changes in 2020, which will be explained later.

5. Dembele (2015a).

6. Pouemi (1980).

7. Also: Dembele (2015b, 2022).

8. These currencies are: cedi (Ghana); dalasi (Gambia); dollar (Liberia), escudo (Cape Verde); Guinean franc; leone (Sierra Leone) and naira (Nigeria).

REFERENCES

African Development Bank (various years). Abidjan: Statistical Yearbook.

African Development Bank & Global Financial Integrity. (2013). *Illicit financial flows and the problem of net resource transfers from Africa*. Joint Report by the African Development Bank (AfDB) and Global Financial Integrity (GFI). Abidjan and Washington D.C.

Agbohou, N. (1999). *Le Franc CFA et l'euro contre l'Afrique*. Paris: Éditions Solidarité Mondiale.

Amin, S. (1986). *La Déconnexion: Pour sortir du système mondial*. Paris: La Découverte.

Amin, S. (2018). *Modern imperialism, monopoly finance capital, and Marx's law of value*. New York, NY: Monthly Review Press.

Demba (2015). Draft report. In Association of African Central Banks (AACB) (Ed.), *Draft report of the experts group on the refinement of the convergence criteria of the African monetary cooperation programme*. Malabo (Equatorial Guinea): African Monetary Cooperation Program (AMCP).

Dembele, D. M. (2011). *Samir Amin, intellectuel organique au service de l'émancipation du Sud*. Dakar: Council for the Development of Social Science Research in Africa (CODESRIA).

Dembele, D. M. (2015a). *Franc Zone and underdevelopment in Africa*. Dakar: ARCADE Publications.

Dembele, D. M. (2015b). *Contribution à la déconstruction des théories conventionnelles sur le développement de l'Afrique*. Paris: L'Harmattan.

Dembele, D. M. (2022). The Neoliberal narrative of growth in Africa: The Afro-optimistic discourse. In F. Lopez-Castellano, C. Lizarraga, & R. Manzanera-Ruiz (Eds.), *Neoliberalism and unequal development*. London: Routledge.

Heinz, J., & Ndikumana, L. (2010). *Is there a case for formal inflation targeting in Sub-Saharan Africa?* PERI Working Paper Series, n° 2018.

Herrera, R. (2022). *Money: From the power of finance to the sovereignty of the peoples*. New York, NY: Palgrave Macmillan.

Kelton, S. (2020). *The Deficit myth: Modern monetary theory and the birth of people's economy*. London: John Murray.

Koulibaly, M. (2011). *La Souveraineté monétaire des pays africains*. Paris: L'Harmattan.

Krugman, P. (2009, September 2). How did economists get it so wrong? *New York Times Magazine*.

Maucourant, J. (2016). Des Rapports entre monnaie et souveraineté : une analyse socio-historique. In K. Nubukpo, M. Ze Belinga, B. Tinel, & D. M. Dembele (Eds.), *Sortir l'Afrique de la servitude monétaire: à qui profite le franc CFA?* (pp. 59–78). Paris: La Dispute.

N'Guessan, T. (2001). « La zone franc: essai de bilan économique et institutionnel ». In *L'avenir de la zone franc. Perspectives africaines* (dir. M. Kassé et H. Ben Hammouda), CODESRIA et Karthala.

Nubukpo, K. (2016). Le Franc CFA et le financement de l'émergence en zone franc. In K. Nubukpo, M. Ze Belinga, B. Tinel, & D. M. Dembele (Eds.), *Sortir l'Afrique de la servitude monétaire: à qui profite le franc CFA?* (pp. 123–133). Paris: La Dispute.

Nubukpo, K., Ze Belinga, M., Tinel, B., & Dembele, D. M. (Eds.). (2016). *Sortir l'Afrique de la servitude monétaire. A qui profite le franc CFA?* Paris: La Dispute.

Pigeaud, F., & Sylla, N. S. (2018). *L'Arme invisible de la Françafrique : Une histoire du franc CFA*. Paris: La Découverte.

Pouemi, T. J. (1980). *Monnaie et servitude : la répression monétaire de l'Afrique*. Paris: Éditions Jeune Afrique.

Rodney, W. (2001/1972). *How Europe underdeveloped Africa*. Nairobi/Kampala/Dar-es-Salaam: East African Educational Publishers.

The Economist. (2020, July 24). *The Covid-19 pandemic is forcing a rethink in macroeconomics*.

United Nations Conference on Trade and Development (UNCTAD). (2007). *Economic development in Africa: Recovering policy space, domestic resource mobilization and developmental state*. Geneva/New York, NY: United Nations.

United Nations Conference on Trade and Development (UNCTAD). (2020a). *The Least developed countries report 2020*. Geneva/New York, NY: United Nations.

United Nations Conference on Trade and Development (UNCTAD). (2020b). *Economic development in Africa report 2020: Tackling illicit financial flows for sustainable development in Africa*. Geneva/New York, NY: United Nations.

United Nations Economic Commission for Africa (UNECA). (2011). *Managing development: The role of the state in economic transformation*. Economic report on Africa. Addis-Ababa.

United Nations Economic Commission for Africa (UNECA). (2014). *Dynamic industrial policy in Africa: Innovative institutions, efficient processes and flexible mechanisms*. Economic report on Africa. Addis-Ababa.

United Nations Economic Commission for Africa (UNECA). (2015). *Illicit financial flows: Report of the high level panel on illicit financial flows from Africa*. Addis-Ababa: Mbeki Panel.

SURPLUS PRODUCTION AND UNEQUAL DEVELOPMENT IN LATIN AMERICA: A COMPARATIVE STUDY WITH THE US FROM A POLITICAL ECONOMY PERSPECTIVE

Juan Pablo Mateo

ABSTRACT

This chapter analyzes the process of surplus generation in Latin America based on the Penn World Tables, also with a comparison with the United States. The reference period is 1950–2019, revealing long-run evolution as well as certain differences between a State-driven industrialization strategy, the turn toward neoliberalism beginning in the 1980s, and a neo-developmentalist period in the twenty-first century. The research shows a steep decline in the rate of profit in Latin America until the early 1990s, with stabilization thereafter but without reversal of the downward trend. However, the turning point in terms of capital accumulation, surplus generation, and productivity indicators occurred in the early 1980s. In addition, divergence vis-à-vis the United States has been growing in the capacity to generate surplus, labor productivity, and GDP per capita.

Keywords: Profit rate; neoliberalism; Latin America; productivity; surplus; developmentalism

Value, Money, Profit, and Capital Today
Research in Political Economy, Volume 39, 73–93
Copyright © 2024 Juan Pablo Mateo
Published under exclusive licence by Emerald Publishing Limited
ISSN: 0161-7230/doi:10.1108/S0161-723020230000039005

INTRODUCTION

This chapter addresses the process of surplus generation in a number of Latin American (Latam) countries using the Penn World Tables (PWT 10.0) and following a Marxist approach. The economies considered are Argentina (ARG), Bolivia (BOL), Brazil (BRA), Chile (CHL), Colombia (COL), Ecuador (ECU), Mexico (MEX), Peru (PER), Paraguay (PRY), and Uruguay (URY); Venezuela has been excluded due to statistical distortions in recent years.

Analysis of capital valorization is carried out through various indicators for the region, highlighting the particularities of the different countries and comparing them with the US economy, taken as reference as the main developed area. The time-span for study is the period 1950–2019, according to the availability of information in the PWT. This allows the identification of several stages: a phase of State-driven industrialization; neoliberal restructuring following the external debt crisis, and a *neo-developmentalist* phase in the twenty-first century.

This research aims to analyze Latin America's process of capital valorization from a long-term perspective, including the evolution over time and the relative levels of diverse variables, for which US acts as a mirror. Questions to be pursued include these: Can any trend be discerned in the profitability of capital? Has the trend in terms of the capacity to generate surplus (the basis of measures such as GDP) been one of convergence or divergence? Is it possible to identify any particular feature of Latin America as a region situated on the periphery of the world economy?

Complementarily, a second purpose of this chapter is to present data series in order to evaluate the relevance of the PWT for long-run analyses of peripheral economies. In this regard, several problems arise, including the impossibility of disaggregating variables by sectors, meaning that unproductive activities cannot be considered and that residential assets cannot be deducted for the stock of fixed capital. This represents perhaps the main limitation of the present study.

Analysis is based on the centrality of surplus generation for both productive development and the business cycle, which takes conceptual priority over other spheres of the economy such as finance, income distribution, or the economic policy framework. This perspective is consistent with the "historical materialism" foundation of the Marxist approach, since the process under study is an objective one that conditions (and indeed governs) decisions made by individuals, groups, or companies (see Mateo, 2019). This process of valorization shows a tendency toward disequilibrium and is characterized by turbulence and instability (Shaikh, 2016), all of which is manifested in geographically unequal development where the national dimension – the space of capital valorization – plays a crucial role, thus justifying the comparison of various countries. Capitalism certainly operates at an eminently global dimension in terms of the laws of its functioning and how these unfold; but it can also assume particular forms within both central and peripheral areas.

On the other hand, the level and evolution over time of the valorization of capital within a country or region must be properly contextualized, as it is not independent of the dynamics of capital accumulation in the region into which it is inserted. In the case of the peripheral economies of Latin America – given their broad dependence on imports of high technology assets, as well as on export markets and foreign capital inflows –, the study of price deflators and exchange rates acquires a qualitatively distinct relevance as compared to developed regions (Astarita, 2010; Mateo, 2020).

The chapter is organized as follows. The second section addresses theoretical and methodological issues on the estimated variables, as well as a review of the literature on the profit rate in Latin America. In the third section, the evolution over time of the process of surplus generation is analyzed, first with respect to price deflators and the exchange rate; second, the profit rate is examined, together with the numerator (profit) and denominator (capital) of this ratio. Finally, in the fourth section, a comparison is undertaken of the capacity to generate surplus in Latin America and in the United States.

THEORETICAL AND METHODOLOGICAL ASPECTS

Surplus Production

The analysis of surplus and its quantification constitutes a central element in the Marxist economic approach. A surplus, which assumes the form of "surplus value" in the regime of capitalist production, refers to the theory of value – the foundation of the various currents of economic thought. Within this theory, the idea of a "process of generation (or production) of surplus" by the labor force should be emphasized, the efficiency of which can be approximated from what I term the "labor productivity of surplus" (LPS). This category is associated with the framework of social relations of production (and the capital stock) wherein labor acquires its productive capacity, and also with a ratio – the profit rate – which shows the degree of capital valorization. Therefore, the systematic study of the generation of surplus value must synchronously address the center/periphery structure as well as diachronically analyze the process of economic reproduction over time, characterized by phases of growth and crisis.

In this framework, the development of productive forces is linked to the capacity of a country to produce a large amount of surplus – i.e., to valorize the accumulated capital stock – on a long-term basis, and to materialize this surplus in a certain way, both sectorially and in terms of goods and services (Mateo, 2020). Thus, the general rate of profit (r) is an indicator of the valorization capacity of the total social capital, as this relates profit (P) to the capital stock (K).

$$r = \frac{P}{K} \qquad (1)$$

Here P is calculated as a residual between the net domestic product (NDP) and wages (w); K includes all assets in net terms (including housing, as disaggregated data on assets are not available). However, considering the inflationary phases of several Latam countries, K will not be taken here at $t - 1$, as is customary in the literature.[1]

Hypothetically, this ratio can be expected to be higher in peripheral areas (p) than in central or developed ones (c), than is, $r_p > r_c$, unlike what may occur with more concrete expressions of profitability that consider net profit after taxes or interest payments, and with a closer relationship to investment.[2] The volume of profit (P^*) is accounted for by its purchasing power of capital assets (Shaikh, 2016); thus, I will take this deflator (P_k), with $P^* = P/P_k$. The ability to generate surplus per hour of labor (or employment, L), which I denote as the above-mentioned labor productivity of surplus (LPS), is expressed as follows:

$$\text{LPS} = \frac{P^*}{L} = \frac{P}{P_k L} \qquad (2)$$

This indicator is also the so-called "margin over wages," or difference between labor productivity (q_L) and the real wage (wr), where $\text{LPS} = q_L - \text{wr}$, which constitutes the purpose of the progressive mechanization of the productive process, or the capital-labor ratio ($\vartheta = K^*/L$).

$$r = \left(\frac{q_L - \text{wr}}{\vartheta} \leftrightarrow P_y = P_k = P_c \right) \qquad (3)$$

In the economic analysis, it is important to consider the essential causality, which runs from the mechanization of the productive process to the margin on wages, that is: $\vartheta \rightarrow q_L - \text{wr} = \text{LPS}$. The ability to generate surplus is the basis of labor productivity in general terms, as the ratio of output ($Y = \text{GDP}$, at constant prices) and employment (L), in turn associated to the GDP per capita.

International Comparison

The process of value generation has in the first place a social and eminently national dimension. The value of labor power, which is taken as given, is theoretically fixed at the national level, since both its movement and the institutional framework in which its formation and conditions of utilization by capital are regulated are mainly established at the level of each country (see Mateo, 2020).

This has two implications. First, the generation of value is not an individual phenomenon, whether at the level of a person, a company, or even a sector of activity. Second, the generation of world surplus requires a second step: the transformation of (national) value into world value, therefore expressed in "world money" (dollars). Consequently, the comparative study requires consideration of the contingent aspects of the capacity to produce surplus, such as the monetary sphere, as money must validate individual labor; in other words, incorporating both prices and exchange rates, in which the concrete labor of workers will be transformed into domestic and international value.

In this regard, and briefly, it can be assumed that the economies of Latam experience higher as well as more volatile average inflation. In turn, productive underdevelopment means that the P_k deflator carries special relevance. Thus, it may be the case that the P_{yk} ratio ($P_{yk} = P_y/P_k$) could fall, eroding the purchasing power of the surplus generated, especially during crises; or else the comparative evolution of the price deflators may not necessarily be differentiated, but rather the influence of P_k could be channeled through different activities to the whole economy, thus contributing to higher relative inflation compared to developed countries.

On the other hand, the exchange rate (ER) depends fundamentally on the competitiveness of domestic capital (Astarita, 2010; Shaikh, 2016). Given the analytical priority of production, and thus of investment over consumption, the market ER will be used instead of PPP.[3] Consequently, both P_k and ER do acquire a special relevance, qualitatively different in more backward economies.

Review of the Literature

I am unaware of similar studies of surplus generation in Latin America with respect to the United States. Nevertheless, reference can be made to Kilsztajn (1998), who compared several indicators of capital accumulation and profitability between various economies of Latam (Argentina, Brazil, Chile, Colombia, and Mexico) and the developed world (France, Germany, the United Kingdom, Japan, and the United States), observing that the rate of profit in the former was at 40.5% (in net terms) and at 14.4% in developed countries (31.2% vs 13.4% in gross terms) – being higher in Mexico (47% to 67%) and lower in Brazil (23% to 29%). However, these figures refer to the 1980s, with calculations made using the ER at PPP.

Recently, Basu, Huato, Jauregui, and Wasner (2022) have presented measures of a world profit rate drawing from the Extended Penn World Table 7.0 and the Socio Economic Accounts of the World Input-Output Database (SEA-WIOD), for a period from 1950–1960 to 2019, but without specific analysis of underdeveloped economies, or Latam in particular. Methodologically, there is agreement with the present research in that their proposal views the relevant aspect not as GDP but as the capital contributed by each country to total capital. Even so, in this article, the aggregation of profit does not consider the share of each country in total capital; furthermore, I do not use ER at PPP. These authors' results reveal a downward trend in profitability, and they divide the period into two parts (before and after 1980) in which the trend is similar but the rate of decline changes. Thus, the rate of profit using the market ER declines to an average of 0.32% in 1960–2019, to −0.95% in 1960–1980, and to −0.08% since 1981, which allows us to contextualize the ratios calculated in this paper.

International comparisons of the rate of profit in the long run have generally targeted developed economies (Li, Xiao, & Zhu, 2007; Trofimov, 2017), probably because of statistical availability and reliability, although other studies in recent years have incorporated semi-peripheral regions. Using the PWT, Roberts (2020) shows that the profit rate of the semi-peripheral economies belonging to the G20 declined from the second half of the 1960s until the outbreak of the debt crisis in the early 1980s, with some stabilization thereafter. The series with a profile closest to Latam's rate of profit corresponds to a group of eight G20 countries including

Argentina, Brazil, and Mexico, where the rate dropped by half between 1950 and 1989. Subsequently, after a partial recovery by means of neoliberal policies in the following decade, it fell again from the late 1990s until 2017. Drawing from national sources, Maito (2018) makes a comparison of the profit rate in 14 economies, both developed and peripheral, including Argentina, Brazil, Chile, and Mexico. Profitability in these peripheral countries decreased between 1955–1959 and 1980–1984, later stabilizing until 2009. In any case, the fall amounts to 40%, very similar to the results for Latam shown here, although in my estimation the change in trend in this region occurred at the end of the 1980s.

On the other hand, regarding the profit rate in Latam countries, several other studies that do not make a general comparison of the region are based on national sources instead of the PWT and are therefore not conducted in international currency. I will make reference only to the most relevant of these from the perspective of my research objective.

Maito (2015) calculates a long-run series on the rate of profit in Argentina, which fell by 33% between 1951 and 2011, together with the volume of surplus and what I have denominated the labor productivity of surplus, which increased by 86% in this same span. Moreover, between 1955–1959 and 2005–2009, the drop is determined to have been a scant 14% in Maito (2018), while Michelena (2009) points out that in 1960–2007, there was some initial decline in 1970s and then a significant recovery from the mid-1980s, lasting until 2007. In both cases, the results differ from those derived from the PWT.

For the Brazilian economy, there are several papers covering a similar period. Marquetti, Maldonado, and Lautert (2018, 2019) show an overall decline of 56% in the profit rate between 1953 and 2008 – five points more than in the present study, which is similar to the update carried out by Grazziotin, Fornari, and Marquetti (2022) until 2017 –, along with a drop until the early 1990s and stabilization thereafter. For Maito (2018), profitability dropped by 47% between 1955–1959 and 2005–2009. In fact, this trajectory coincides with measures offered in Mateo (2018), where this ratio fell by 58% or 63% between 1950 and 2008, depending on whether the net or the gross capital stock is used, respectively. However, the main decline occurred until 1989–1993, reaching between 70% and 78%, and recovering in the following years; these findings are even higher than the 67% decrease until 1989–1990 found in the present research.

Duque Garcia (2022) addresses the period 1967–2019 in Colombia, but from the perspective of economic cycles. The profit rate is here found to have followed a cyclical behavior, with an increase (1967–1977), a decrease (1978–2000), and a recovery (2001–2019), although with a net drop across the overall period. Examining Chile, Polanco (2019) studies the profit rate from 1900 to 2010 without verifying any downward trend, while in Maito (2018) the profit rate is found to have decreased by 15% between 1960–1964 and 2005–2009, compared to a 16% increase according to the PWT.[4]

Finally, there are numerous studies of the rate of profit in Mexico, but these cover very different periods. Worth mentioning is Mariña and Moseley (2001), who show a decline of 41% (48%) between 1950 (1951) and 1999, reaching a minimum in 1986 – and thus a drop of 52% in 1950–1986 –, before then stabilizing in the 1990s. In turn, Maito (2018) shows a fall of just 7% between 1950–1954 and 2005–2009, far from the 70% figure according to the PWT.

Consequently, a certain coincidence is indeed observed in regional terms, with discrepancies in particular cases and with the notable exception of Brazil.

THE DYNAMICS OF CAPITAL VALORIZATION

Contingent Aspects of Valorization: Prices, Exchange Rates, and the Labor Force

As expected, average inflation – measured as the GDP deflator – has been relatively high in Latin America throughout these recent decades.[5] The United States has experienced both lower inflation and less variability, with an average of 3.1% in 1951–2019 (compared to 3.6% in ECU, 13%–16% in COL, PRY, and MEX, and 30%–70% in the others).

In 1950–1980, inflation in the United States averaged 3.9%, while in Latam it was under 10% per year only in ECU and MEX (at 6.2% and 9.5% on average, respectively). In the following period, average inflation in the United States fell to an average of 2.5% per year; in Ecuador that figure was even lower, while the other countries of Latin America stabilized their prices at below 10% annual inflation, with the exception of Argentina.

However, the inflation gap with the United States has not narrowed as clearly as expected in the group of Latam countries. If the convulsive decade of the 1980s is excluded, and the period 1950–1980 is compared with 1990–2019, then this gap was reduced in ARG, BOL, CHL, and very slightly in URY as well as in BRA if the starting-point is moved to 1995. Meanwhile, the gap has widened compared to COL, ECU, MEX, PER, and PRY. Still, during the first two decades of the twenty-first century, greater price stability was observed in the region along with an ostensible fall in the differential with the United States, again with the exception of Argentina.

Disaggregating in terms of the deflators, the P_{yk} ratio shows a downward trend in Latin America, which reproduces but amplifies the fluctuations in the rate of profit (Fig. 1). Capital became relatively more expensive up by 30% until 1989, except in the 1960s, when P_{yk} increased at an average of 0.42% per year. This decline slowed after 1990, although with cyclical oscillations coinciding with the phases of growth and crisis.

Interestingly, the P_{yk} index in the United States declined in the period at an annual rate of −0.68%, very similar to the rate in Latam, although in the United States, this has intensified since the early 1990s. In this case, there is no clear center/periphery asymmetry.

With regard to the exchange rate, the currencies of the Latam economies depreciated against the dollar throughout the period, as might be expected. Macro depreciations were observed in the 1980s and, in some cases, in the early 1990s, but also in the mid-1970s in ARG and CHL, which began the shift toward neoliberalism in those years. In any case, as a general rule, greater exchange rate stability has been observed in recent decades.[6]

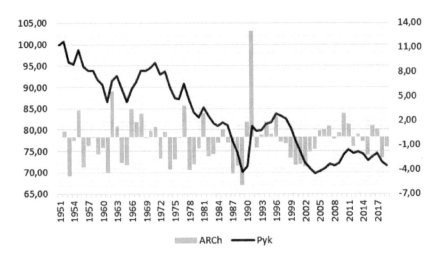

Fig. 1. Output-Capital Price Ratio (P_{yk}) in Latin America. *Source:* See annex. *Note:* Index (1951 = 100, left) and annual rates of change (%, right)

Finally, reference should be made to employment (Fig. 2), which in Latam multiplied by 5.25 in this period – more than double the result in the United States, with a factor of 2.43 – i.e., employment in Latin America has grown at an average of 2.47% per year, compared to 1.32% in the US.

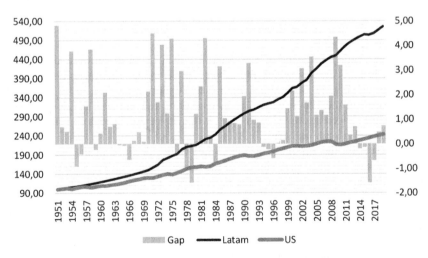

Fig. 2. Dynamics of Employment in Latin America and the United States. *Source:* See annex. *Note:* Index (1951 = 100, left) and gap in annual rates of change (right).

The rate of job creation before the 1980s was higher, increasing until the 1970s; after that, employment slowed in both areas. Nevertheless, most relevant is that the gap intensified after 1980, especially through that decade and during the early 2000s, and this can be associated with the regime of accumulation and with the most dynamic sectors, with implications for the evolution of both productivity and GDP per capita, as will be seen later. Anyway, more labor force employed in no way necessarily lead to more value generated.

The Rate of Profit

The profit rate has been higher in Latin America than in the United States, but with a trend toward convergence (Fig. 3). In the early 1950s, profitability in Latam was at 30.7% and in the United States at 8.4%, meaning 3.65 times higher in the peripheral region. In the decades that followed, this ratio declined by 61% in Latam, reaching its minimum in the final year of the series (2019). In the United States, evolution in the profit rate has been quite the opposite, with no clear downward trend, but a slight drop of 15% overall.

The trajectory of the profit rate in Latam can be divided into several subperiods, with a turning point in 1989–1990:

i. an initial decline of 29% until 1961;
ii. then relatively constant until 1973, with 10% of the total increase;
iii. falling until 1989–1990, when the rate of profit was at 47% of the 1973 level, and as much as 58% below the initial 1951 rate;
iv. but then this decline slowed, with several fluctuations, showing a slight drop of 9% with respect to 1990.

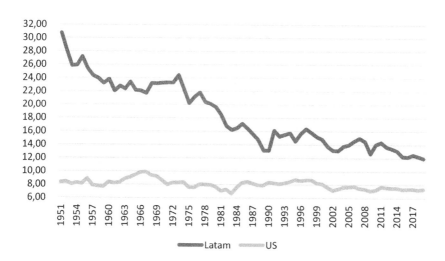

Fig. 3.   Profit Rate in Latin America and the United States (%). *Source:* See annex.

Until 1990, the profit rate in Latam fell to an average of −2.15% per year, especially in the 1950s and 1980s (−2.80% and −3.94% on average, respectively), then moderating to only −0.32% per year. In contrast, this rate in the United States grew until 1966, later falling by 33% until reaching a 1982 low. After this there was partial recovery, with a decline of 18% between 1997 and 2019, and with cyclical minimums appearing in 2001, 2008, and 2019 (Table 1).

The evolution of profitability in Latam has been broadly similar for all the countries in the sample, with the significant exception of Chile. In this economy, the rate of profit almost doubled between 1951 and 1990, then fell, but with an overall increase of 85%.[7] In the other countries, declines in the profit rate ranged from −31% (in Bolivia, itself an exception with regard to the rate increase experienced in the 1980s) to −86% (in Ecuador, where it increased only in the 1970s). In general, declines ranged between −50% and −65%.

The Volume of Surplus

The surplus in constant terms generated in Latin America grew at an annual rate of 2.6% in 1951–2019, or slightly above the United States (at 2.36%). Until 1980, growth amounted to 4.3% per year in Latam, but since 1980 it has remained at 1.3%, although averaging 2.2% from 1990 onward. This slowdown was furthermore accompanied by greater instability: for the 29 years between 1951 and 1980, the volume of profit fell seven times, which was interestingly also the case in the United States. However, the same number of declines occurred in the decade of 1980s (only four in the United States), and then another 12 times in the period 1990–2019 (four more than in the United States), as shown in Fig. 4.

While the average rate of surplus growth moved upward in the 1950s, 1960s, and 1970s, with rates of 2.78%, 4.74%, and 5.17%, respectively, following the collapse of the 1980s the recovery has been downward, with average rates of 3.72% in the 1990s, 2.20% in 2000s, and just 0.54% in the last decade. Therefore, the volume of surplus grew less in Latam than in the United States only in the 1980s and the 2010s, with small differences (at 0.54% vs. 0.59% per year).

The average annual rates of variation of the volume of surplus of each country in local currencies are shown in Fig. 5. With greater or lesser intensity, a contrast in evolution is seen before and after 1980, with the exception of BOL, where it grew by 1.11% in 1950–1980 and by almost 4% annually thereafter. However, certain results should be further scrutinized for the following: (i) ARG, where the real boom occurred in the 1950s (8.5% of average growth), followed by the 1990s (6%), and where the other phases proved rather mediocre; (ii) CHL and URY, both of which reveal anomalies that are difficult to explain due to exceptional growth in the 1960s and the levels and reiteration of annual fluctuations; and (iii) ECU, where the rate has declined on average across all decades since 1980, yielding the lowest overall average rate of increase between 1950 and 2019, at barely 0.63%.

Even when comparing the average growth rate of the surplus in 1950–1980 and then in 1990–2019, the results remain conclusive: in COL, this rate increased by 15% less per year in the second period, while in CHL that difference is almost

Table 1. Comparative Dynamics of the Profit Rate in Latam Countries and the United States.

Period	ARG	BOL	BRA	CHL	COL	ECU	MEX	PER	PRY	URY	US
					Total Variation (%)						
1951–90	-62.51	-48.99	-65.57	92.70	-53.94	-54.78	-65.77	-71.95	-29.18	-33.86	-2.27
1990–19	-9.04	33.89	10.00	-3.70	-1.72	-69.49	-28.23	38.86	-24.05	-29.94	-12.65
1951–19	-65.90	-31.71	-62.13	85.56	-54.73	-86.20	-75.43	-61.05	-46.21	-53.67	-14.63
					Annual Rates of Change (%)						
1950s	2.22	-3.51	-3.39	1.56	-3.46	-2.50	-3.56	-7.37	-2.63	-21.94	-0.20
1960s	-4.39	-5.24	2.37	8.52	-1.26	-3.49	-2.79	3.58	025	19.56	-0.23
1970s	-2.49	0.07	-2.38	-3.31	-0.69	1.05	-1.16	0.88	-0.06	326	-1.23
1980s	-3.02	2.05	-7.27	0.37	-1.89	-2.93	-2.41	-7.87	-1.22	-3.22	1.54
1990s	3.88	-1.44	2.54	0.11	-1.41	-4.36	-1.12	3.91	-7.24	-1.20	-0.77
2000s	-0.79	6.44	0.20	2.42	2.56	-3.85	-1.66	2.23	6.28	0.77	0.09
2010s	-4.31	-2.05	-1.93	-3.16	-1.41	-3.80	-0.58	-3.02	-1.47	-3.40	-0.74
1951–19	-1.57	-0.56	-1.42	0.91	-1.16	-2.87	-2.04	-1.38	-0.91	-1.12	-0.23

Source: See annex.

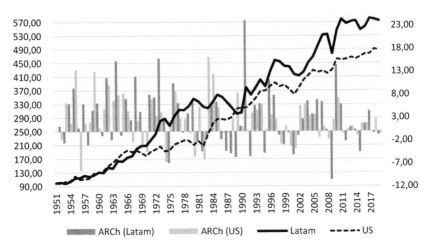

Fig. 4. The Volume of Surplus in Latin America and the United States.
Source: See annex. *Note:* Index (1951 = 100, left) and annual rates of change (%,
right).

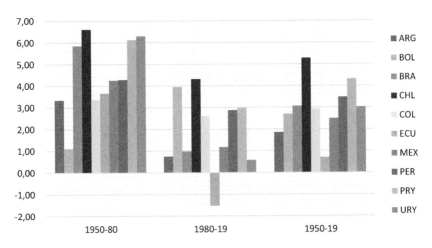

Fig. 5. Variation in the Volume of Surplus for Latam Countries. *Source:* See
annex. *Note:* Average change per year (%) in domestic currency.

double (27% lower). The drops in ARG and BRA amounted to between 50% and
55%, falling by two-thirds in PRY and by as much as 72%–78% in MEX and
URY. In contrast, the average growth rate in PER was 40% higher, and more
than four times higher in ECU.[8]

Investment and Capital

Turning now to consider the denominator of the rate of profit, the volume of net investment follows a trajectory somewhat similar to that of the surplus and, more generally, that of macroeconomic dynamics. In Latin America, this grew faster than in the United States (by 3.18% vs. 2.5% in 1951–2019), multiplying the initial investment volume by 8.42 in Latam, compared to 5.35 times higher in the United States in 2019. In both cases, investment grew more until 1980, but particularly in Latam, by an average of 6.15% in the first sub-period, 6 times greater than since 1980, and 2.6 times greater than in the period after 1990. Consequently, the contrast in sub-periods before and after the early 1980s is clear.[9]

Bearing in mind the dynamics of the volume of profit, and despite the fact that the fundamental causality goes from profit to investment ($P \rightarrow I$), it can be claimed that the flow of investment in Latam has a lower capacity to generate surplus value than in the United States. In other words, in order to produce one unit of surplus in the Latam region, much more investment is required than would be the case in the United States. The indexes shown in Fig. 6 reveal that Latin America increased its surplus by 63.8% of the increase in investment in 1951–2019, compared to 89% in the United States. This divergence was smaller during the pre-1980 phase, when the volume of profit grew less (almost 53%) in Latin America, but at only 13 points below US growth (66.4%).

Something striking occurred in Latam later in the 1980s: both surplus and investment fell in absolute terms, although their ratio was 34.8%, that is, a smaller relative fall in surplus value in the face of a collapse of investment. In the United States, however, the situation was quite the reverse, with this ratio reaching a record 123.9%, meaning a greater increase in profit than in investment

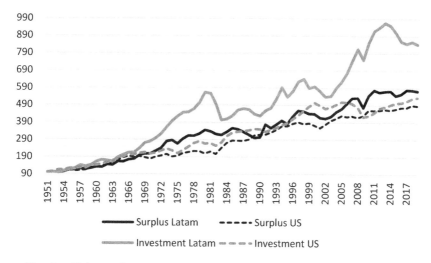

Fig. 6. Volume of Investment and Surplus in Latin America and the United States. *Source:* See annex. *Note:* Index (1951 = 100) at constant prices.

outlay. Even after this sharp divergence, the decades that followed led to a certain dualism. On the one hand, the investment efficiency ratio improved considerably for Latam, approaching two-thirds and thus surpassing the 1950–1980 ratio. On the other hand, the US economy not only improved its ratio but saw a relative widening of the gap with Latam, which reached 90.7%.

Likewise, this greater increase in investment flows has materialized in an even more pronounced divergence in terms of the net capital stock in both areas, since this *stock* variable accumulates the changes in terms of *flows*.[10] In Latam, the volume of capital was multiplied by 17.3 over the period, while in the United States, the factor was 6.3. In this case, the divergence in the trajectories of the capital stock occurred at the end of the 1960s, and this has been reflected in the different dynamics of the rate of profit, offering a clear example of the higher productive efficiency of the US economy.

UNEVEN PRODUCTIVE DEVELOPMENT IN THE UNITED STATES AND LATIN AMERICA

The LPS grew at 1.6% per year in Latam until 1980, but in the following 39 years it fell to an alarming −0.9% on average, an incredibly negative path. Certainly, the 1980s constituted the worst phase, when the fall reached −4.3% per year. But even if that decade is excluded, the average increase for the period 1990–2019 would be at 0.23%. Nonetheless, in the first two decades of the 21st Century, this productivity index fell at −0.20% and −0.90% per year, respectively.

Consequently, the divergence with the US economy has widened, as shown in Fig. 7. Overall, between 1951 and 2019, this productivity index grew almost 8

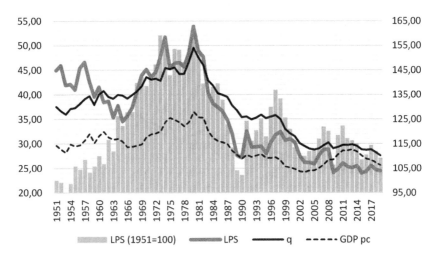

Fig. 7. GDP and Dimensions of Productivity in Latin America. *Source:* See annex. *Note:* Index (1951 = 100, right) and relative path with respect to the United States (%, US = 100, left).

times more in the United States, with an increase of 1.03% per year, while in Latam this figure was at 0.13% per year on average. There was a trend toward convergence with the United States until 1980, when this productivity grew at 0.66 points more each year in Latin America. However, this was followed by a radical change in dynamics, and only in the 1990s did the labor productivity of surplus increase at a higher rate in Latam than in the US.

It should nonetheless be noted that the evolution of the relative LPS (Latam as a percentage of the United States) before 1980 experienced two distinct phases: first, a phase of divergence from 1951 to 1965, when the average fell from an initial 44.9% to a minimum of 34.5%; then a trend toward convergence, reaching a maximum in 1980, when Latam achieved a relative LPS level of 53.9% in relation to the United States. For this reason, the alleged trend toward convergence was in fact limited to just 15 of the 68 years that comprise the period. If five-year averages are considered, then the relative LPS went from 43.7% of the US level in 1951–1954 to 46.5% in the 1970s, that is, an increase of only 6%.

On the other hand, the decade of the 1980s saw a reversal of the relative growth of 1965–1980. In just 10 years, the percentage dropped by half, from the aforementioned 53.9%, it declined to a minimum of 27.1% in 1990. Thus, it can be claimed that the 1965–1980 period represented an "accident" or historical exception. In fact, there is considerable continuity between the divergence of 1951–1965 and the divergence of the last three decades observed. Moreover, in the first phase of divergence, the rate of decline of the relative productivity index was at −1.86% per year, while in the second phase, if starting from the peak of 1991, this fall would be at −1.01% per year, thereby slowing the divergence prior to 1965 to a surprising degree.

The level and evolution of the capacity to generate surplus in Latin America and the United States is embodied in labor productivity (q_L) and, by extension, in GDP per capita, both commonly used macro variables. In the early 1950s, q_L represented 36%–37% of the US level, lower than the LPS index but indicating a slow, steady path toward convergence until 1980. In that year, the relative peak was reached at almost half (49.5%) of the US level, with a jump in 1979 and a sizable drop in the following years.

The period after 1980s shows a divergence that has been broadly maintained in phases of economic growth but that has widened during recessions. In 2019, relative q_L represented 27.6% of the US figure, slightly higher than LPS. This evolution coincides with the relative GDP per capita, which saw a peak of 36.5% in 1980, but suffered a gradual decline thereafter.

In short, the divergence between Latin America and the United States has been growing since 1980, and this provides fundamental clues for the analysis of capital valorization.

CONCLUSION

This study of capital valorization in some representative countries of Latin America has shown evidence of a downward trend in the rate of profit between

1951 and 2019, amounting to a cumulative fall of 61%. This path has not been uniform but was concentrated in the 1950s and 1980s, with a turning point in 1989–1990, after which the rate of decline slowed substantially. It can be claimed that this has been the functional rationale of neoliberal restructuring to overcome the "lost decade" of the 1980s. Compared to this evolution, the profit rate in the United States has been more stable, with a drop of only 15% across the period.

Behind this fall in the rate of profit can be found a trend in the generation of surplus which slows and becomes less stable from 1980 onward, and this makes sense of the turning point in investment and capital accumulation. Thus, as noted, 1980 also constitutes a break with respect to the productive gap with the US economy. For this period as a whole, but especially since 1980, the divergence in the productive capacity to generate surplus has been growing, even though the prior convergence (limited to 1965–1980) can actually be considered an exception within a general trend toward polarization, or the unequal development of capitalism. It is especially revealing that the LPS in the United States grew at almost 8 times that rate in Latin America between 1951 and 2019.

Another finding of this research refers to the fact that the higher inflation in Latam and the gap with respect to the United States, and by extension the exchange rate depreciation, together with the relative fall P_{yk}, did not represent obstacles to capital accumulation or to the rise in surplus productivity in Latin America until 1980. Thus, the main achievement of recent decades appears to one of monetary stabilization. Latin America seems to require a greater amount of investment than the United States – which will materialize in an even higher level of capital stock – in order to generate less surplus in dollars per unit of labor. The paradox is that the neoliberal period, while generating greater efficiency in the actual investment and some stabilization of the price ratio, it could not boost the process of capital accumulation, indeed slowing it down and with an increasing gap in investment with respect to the United States. Furthermore, Latin America seems to unfold an *extensive* way of valorization, with rising amount of labor but without improving its productivity of surplus.

On the other hand, there are certain limitations in this research that should be made explicit. First, the long-term analysis implies the impossibility of disaggregating the surplus and capital series by sector and by assets, and the inclusion of residential stock is perhaps the main drawback. Considering the behavior of employment, which has not decreased since 1980, together with the relationship of investment to capital stock, the need is justified to develop this analysis toward a sectoral and asset disaggregation of the dynamics of capital accumulation, associated in turn with the economic policy of liberalization and external openness.

Second, discrepancies have been encountered as regards national sources. In the case of the rate of profit in the United States, data from the PWT reduce considerably the decline derived from the Bureau of Economic Analysis (BEA) – Carchedi (2018) found a steep decline of −68% between 1950 and 2015. As for Latin American economies, inconsistencies have been detected (especially in the 1960s in URY and PRY), but these do not seem to impact the overall results.

STATISTICAL ANNEX

The source of reference in this paper is the PWT 10.0 (see Feenstra, Inklaar, & Timmer, 2015), which covers the period 1950–2019. However, due to the absence of data in 1950 for CHL and PRY, most of the series refer to 1951–2019. The Extended PWT 7.0 base (EPWT, see Marquetti, Miebach, & Morrone, 2021) was used to measure: (i) the labor share, and thus to calculate the profit share as a residual; and (ii) the number of employed workers (*L*).

Unless otherwise specified, calculations for comparisons are made in dollars. Labor productivity (q_L) takes gross output (GDP*) because of the availability of series in the PWT. For the measure of the output and capital deflators (P_y, P_k), GDP and net capital in 2017 dollars are taken, respectively, according to PWT 10.0. P_k is used for the volume of surplus (profit), capital stock, and investment.

This section presents some complementary series. In Table 2, we can observe the evolution of the rate of profit and its components by decades and by sub-periods. This has been incorporated into the 1990–2019 phase due to distortions introduced by the negative performance in the 1980s, and because it allows for a similar comparison in terms of the number of years contained in the pre-1980 stage.

Table 3 shows the indicators of productivity, employment as a source of valorization, and the most common macroeconomic variables in which the process of value generation ultimately materializes: total and per capita GDP.

On the other hand, and in relation to the labor productivity of surplus (LPS), it should be noted that the widening of the divergence between Latam and the United States is common to all countries in the region, except for the relatively small economies of the Southern Cone (CHL, PRY, and URY). In the cases of

Table 2. Average annual Change of the Profit Rate and Its Determinants in Latin America and the United States

			Volume (Constant Prices)					
	Profit Rate		Surplus		Investment		Capital	
Period	Latam	US	Latam	US	Latam	US	Latam	US
1950s	−2.80	−0.20	3.10	3.04	4.99	4.26	7.09	3.35
1960s	−0.24	−0.23	4.74	3.30	5.59	3.88	5.99	3.82
1970s	−1.68	−1.23	5.17	1.63	7.25	2.47	6.90	3.08
1980s	−3.94	1.54	−1.25	4.24	−2.73	2.75	3.15	2.81
1990s	1.20	−0.77	3.72	1.57	3.42	3.70	2.89	2.59
2000s	−0.55	0.09	2.20	2.16	3.58	−1.59	2.40	2.15
2010s	−1.72	−0.74	0.54	0.59	−0.12	2.49	2.49	1.38
1951–1980	−1.53	−0.55	4.37	2.65	6.15	3.53	6.39	3.42
1980–2019	−1.26	0.05	1.31	2.17	1.03	1.80	2.74	2.25
1990–2019	−0.32	−0.47	2.20	1.47	2.36	1.47	2.60	2.06
1951–2019	−1.37	−0.23	2.60	2.36	3.18	2.50	4.28	2.75

Source: See annex. PWT 10.0 and extended PWT 7.0 base.

Table 3. Productivity, Employment and GDP in Latin America and the United States (Average Annual Rates of Change [%]).

Period	LPS		Productivity		Labor		GDP		GDP pc	
	Latam	US	Latam	US	Latam	US	Latam	US	Latam	US
1950s	1.07	1.79	2.87	2.34	1.80	1.23	4.43	3.59	1.87	1.84
1960s	2.33	1.49	3.31	2.44	2.36	1.79	5.74	4.27	2.90	2.96
1970s	1.44	−0.34	2.45	1.16	3.67	1.98	6.22	3.16	3.76	2.23
1980s	−4.37	2.41	−1.85	1.50	3.27	1.79	1.36	3.32	−0.70	2.35
1990s	1.69	0.36	1.21	2.21	2.00	1.20	3.23	3.44	1.57	2.30
2000s	−0.20	2.00	0.67	1.59	2.41	0.15	3.09	1.74	1.84	0.80
2010s	−0.90	−0.71	0.27	0.94	1.45	1.32	1.72	2.27	0.65	1.56
1950–1980	1.63	0.97	2.88	1.98	2.70	1.66	5.65	3.67	2.94	2.34
1980–2019	−0.97	1.05	0.06	1.57	2.30	1.11	2.37	2.70	0.84	1.75
1990–2019	0.23	0.59	0.73	1.60	1.97	0.87	2.71	2.49	1.37	1.55
1951–2019	0.13	1.03	1.25	1.71	2.47	1.32	3.76	3.05	1.73	1.95

Source: See annex. PWT 10.0 and extended PWT 7.0 base.

CHL and URY, some results are problematic, as (surprisingly) the former had a level of LPS only slightly higher than that of BOL or PRY in the early 1950s, then experienced outstanding growth in the 1960s of 13% per year on average – with less-than-logical variations in some years. In the case of URY, the evolution up to 1980 was absolutely anomalous, with annual oscillations in 1959–1970 that remain difficult to explain, reaching a relative LPS of 82% of the United States in 1980. In any case, it should be noted that the gap with the United States has been reduced by more than half in CHL since the mid-1980s; it has increased slightly in PRY since 1978, while it has remained very similar in URY since 1976.

The most common pattern, however, is that followed by the three main economies of the region: MEX, BRA, and ARG. All showed a rapprochement with respect to the United States in the first three decades of the period − very weak in the case of MEX, at 2.7% in total − and a wide divergence thereafter, with similar magnitudes in percentage terms: ARG at −55%, BRA at −58%, and MEX at −62%. As a result, their overall balance of divergence reaches −42%, − 28%, and −61%, in the same order. Fig. 8 shows the change in LPS in Latin America, with the exception of the above-mentioned small countries of the Southern Cone.

One element to take into account is the P_{yk} price ratio. If analyzed in national currencies for the set of countries, it can again be seen that the small countries of the Southern Cone (CHL, PRY, URY), together with BOL, are the only ones in which this ratio decreased between 1951 and 2019. However, the results for CHL and URY are explained by the surprising relative increase of P_{yk} in the 1960s, at an annual average of 9%–10%, a result radically different from that seen in the rest of these countries.

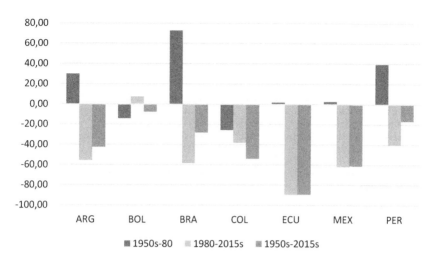

Fig. 8.   Dynamics of the Labor Productivity of Surplus in Some Countries of Latin America (*Total Variation Between 5-Year Periods of Relative LPS [%, US= 100]*). *Source:* PWT 10.0 and extended PWT 7.0 base. *Note:* Total change (%) between 5-year periods (averages of 1950–1954 and 2015–2019), and 1980.

NOTES

1. For a discussion on the implications of inflation in Brazil, see Marquetti et al. (2019).

2. However, the possible faster capital turnover in the core areas makes their level of profitability higher than indicated in the calculations, as claimed by Maito (2016).

3. However, this paper will not address the relationship between the exchange rate and the rate of profit – an issue of great importance around which significant controversies are found in the literature. See Marconi, Magacho, Machado, and De Azevedo (2020) for a review with empirical evidence in the case of Brazil, as well as Ibarra and Ros (2019) for the Mexican economy.

4. More recent work such as Durán and Stanton (2021) likewise reveals no downward trend in the profit rate in 1985–2018, but rather a cyclical trajectory, albeit with methodological differences in the calculations.

5. Worth noting is the sharp contrast between the deflators in local currencies and those corresponding to GDP in dollars, which are even lower in Latam than in the United States.

6. Some cases deserve specific mention: (i) in Mexico, the rate of depreciation has doubled since 1990 (although it is true that the ratio with respect to the dollar is low, at 6.8% per year compared to 3.3% in 1950–1980 and 1990–2019, respectively); (ii) in Brazil, the ER has depreciated since 1995 by only 6.2% annually, compared to 30% in 1950–1980; and (iii) in Peru, the rate of depreciation was the same in 1950–1980 as it has been since 1990. In other countries – the Southern Cone, Bolivia, and Colombia – depreciation since the 1990s has been lower than in 1950–1980.

7. It is nonetheless possible to question these data, since the level of the profit rate up to 1962 was abnormally low. While this ratio was around 25%–35% in all other countries considered, in Chile it was under 15%, and in several years of the 1950s it was even below 10%. Likewise, the data from Uruguay can be questioned; in the first two decades of the period, levels were exceptionally low, beneath even 5% in 1956–1969, as reflected in anomalous annual rates of change.

8. However, in the case of PER, if compared with the period after 1980, then the drop in the average growth rate of the surplus would amount to one-third, as the decline in the 1980s reached −5.7% per year. Furthermore, the drops in the two large South American economies of ARG and BRA would amount to −77% and −83%, respectively.

9. The dynamics of investment in the United States have proven less volatile; although it grew at 3.5% annually until 1980, the fall in the rate of growth since that year has been lower – increasing by slightly more than half of what it was earlier, at 1.8% per year. Even so, the United States also experienced a 'lost decade', with declines amounting to −1.59% annually in the first decade of the 2000s.

10. However, due precisely to the inertia of the stock measure, this does not reveal the contrast between the different periods as clearly as the flow of investment does. The rate of capital accumulation fell in Latam from 1980 onward, from an average of 6.4%–2.7%, while increasing in the 1980s. Something similar occurred in the United States, where the rate of growth of the capital stock went from 3.4% to 2.2% per year on average before and after 1980, respectively.

REFERENCES

Astarita, R. (2010). *Economía política de la dependencia y el subdesarrollo*. Buenos Aires: Universidad Nacional de Quilmes.

Basu, D., Huato, J., Jauregui, J. L., & Wasner, E. (2022, November 12). World profit rates: 1960–2019. *Review of Political Economy*. doi:10.1080/09538259.2022.2140007

Carchedi, G. (2018). The old is dying but the new cannot be born: On the exhaustion of Western capitalism. In G. Carchedi & M. Roberts (Eds.), *World in crisis: A global analysis of Marx's law of profitability* (pp. 36–77). Chicago, IL: Haymarket.

Duque Garcia, C. A. (2022). Economic growth and the rate of profit in Colombia 1967–2019: A VAR time-series analysis. *Review of Radical Political Economics, 46*(2), 162–183.

Durán, G., & Stanton, M. (2021). The Chilean economy, an analysis of the dynamics of profits, investments and production: A Marxist approach. *Capital & Class, 46*(3), 377–400.

Feenstra, R., Inklaar, R., & Timmer, M. (2015). The Next generation of the Penn World Table. *The American Economic Review, 105*(10), 3150–3182. Retrieved from www.ggdc.net/pwt

Grazziotin, H., Fornari, A., & Marquetti, A. (2022). Taxa de lucro e acumulação de capital no Brasil: concepções teóricas, análise histórica e relação de causalidade. *Economia Ensaios, 37*, 176–208.

Ibarra, C., & Ros, J. (2019). Profitability and capital accumulation in Mexico: A first look at tradables and non-tradables based on KLEMS. *International Review of Applied Economics, 33*(3), 426–452.

Kilsztajn, S. (1998). Produto, capital e taxa de lucro: países industrializados e América Latina. *Brazilian Journal of Political Economy, 18*(3), 424–439.

Li, M., Xiao, F., & Zhu, A. (2007). Long waves, institutional changes, and historical trends: A study of the long-term movement of the profit rate in the capitalist world economy. *Journal of World-Systems Research, 13*(1), 33–54.

Maito, E. E. (2015). *Value, periphery and crisis: Argentina 1910–2011*. MPRA Paper. 67560.

Maito, E. E. (2016). Distribución del ingreso, rotación del capital y niveles de rentabilidad. *Economía: Teoría y Práctica, 45*, 169–206.

Maito, E. E. (2018). The Tendency of the rate of profit to fall since the nineteenth century and a world rate of profit. In G. Carchedi, & M. Roberts (Eds.), *World in crisis: A global analysis of Marx's law of profitability* (pp. 129–156). Chicago, IL: Haymarket.

Marconi, N., Magacho, G., Machado, J. G., & De Azevedo, R. (2020). Profit margins, exchange rates and structural change: Empirical evidences for the period 1996–2017. *Brazilian Journal of Political Economy, 40*(2), 285–309.

Mariña, A., & Moseley, F. (2001). La Tasa general de ganancia y sus determinantes en México. *Economía: Teoría y Práctica, 15*, 37–65.

Marquetti, A., Maldonado, E., & Lautert, V. (2018). The profit rate in Brazil, 1953-2008. In G. Carchedi, & M. Roberts (Eds.), *World in crisis: A global analysis of Marx's law of profitability* (pp. 253–278). Chicago, IL: Haymarket.

Marquetti, A., Miebach, A., & Morrone, H. (2021). *The Extended Penn World Tables 7.0*. UFRGS Texto para discussão, 2021/01.

Marquetti, A., Morrone, H., Miebach, A., & Ourique, L. E. (2019). Measuring the profit rate in an inflationary context: The case of Brazil, 1955–2008. *Review of Radical Political Economics, 51*(1), 52–74.

Mateo, J. P. (2018). The accumulation of capital and economic growth in Brazil: A long-term perspective (1950–2008). *Review of Radical Political Economics, 50*(2), 370–391.

Mateo, J. P. (2019). *The theory of crisis and the great recession in Spain*. London: Palgrave Macmillan.

Mateo, J. P. (2020). La Acumulación de capital en la periferia: una propuesta analítica desde la economía política. *Cuadernos de Economía, 42*(122), 119–130.

Michelena, G. (2009). La Evolución de la tasa de ganancia en la Argentina (1960–2007): caída y recuperación. *Realidad Económica, 248*, 83–106.

Polanco, D. (2019). *The profit rate in Chile: 1900–2010* (p. 275). UMass Amherst Economics Working Papers.

Roberts, M. (2020, July 25). *A world rate of profit: A new approach*. The Next Recession.

Shaikh, A. (2016). *Capitalism: Competition, conflict, crises*. New York, NY: Oxford University Press.

Trofimov, I. (2017). Profit rates in developed capitalist economies: A time series investigation. *PSL Quarterly Review, 70*(280), 85–128.

FROM "CRYPTO-ALTERNATIVES" TO A REGIONAL UNIT OF ACCOUNT: MONETARY PROPOSALS IN LATIN AMERICA FOR A GREATER SHARED AUTONOMY

Joaquín Arriola and Juan Barredo-Zuriarrain

ABSTRACT

Weak regional commercial and productive integration and monetary dependence on the economic poles are evidence of the consolidation of Latin America's peripheral position in the world economy. This research analyzes different monetary initiatives launched individually or collectively by countries in the region to alleviate this position, such as the petro, the SUCRE, or El Salvador's bet on the legal acceptance of bitcoin as a payment instrument. After identifying some of their limitations, we propose some basis for monetary coordination with which to advance in the dynamization of productivity and trade complementarity of the countries of the region.

Keywords: Money; monetary policy; monetary integration; cryptocurrencies; unit of account; regionalization; alternatives

INTRODUCTION

Global economic growth by region at a glance reveals a very uneven evolution. East Asia – with China as the main engine – has been taking off for the past three decades with growth rates well above the world average. They are followed far behind by South and Southeast Asia and, further back, by other developing countries. Developed economies, with much higher income levels, show weak growth rates. Plunged into a cycle of stagnation since the 1980s, Latin America

Value, Money, Profit, and Capital Today
Research in Political Economy, Volume 39, 95–114
Copyright © 2024 Joaquín Arriola and Juan Barredo-Zuriarrain
Published under exclusive licence by Emerald Publishing Limited
ISSN: 0161-7230/doi:10.1108/S0161-723020230000039007

has seen its relative importance in the world economy fall to the benefit of the developing regions mentioned above.

This stagnation is largely explained by the difficulties of adapting to the major industrial changes that are continuously reshaping the patterns of capital accumulation worldwide. Latin America has made little progress in the development of technological and high value-added sectors. Moreover, some countries are unable to break out of their role as exporters of raw materials, gradually consolidating their peripheral role in the global economy, with all that this entails in terms of instability.

This is also evident in the monetary sphere: Latin-American countries demonstrate in varying ways a strong dependence in their exchange rate and monetary policies on the central countries, principally the United States. To this dependence must be added the technological subjugation they experience with respect to communication and multilateral financial clearing platforms – such as CHIPS (i.e., Clearing House Interbank Payments System),[1] CIPS (Cross-Border Interbank Payment System), or SWIFT (Society for Worldwide Interbank Financial Telecommunication) –, which are treated as instruments of geopolitical control mainly by the United Kingdom and the United States. Today's open conflicts involving world powers show that these platforms are key levers in the various attempts to isolate and embargo countries (see the cases of Cuba, Venezuela, Iran and, more recently, Russia).

In this highly hierarchical monetary landscape, a wide range of unconventional monetary initiatives have emerged in Latin America in which the countries involved, individually or even collectively, try to gain room to maneuver with regards to their domestic and regional policy. The recent legal acceptance of bitcoin as a payment instrument in El Salvador, the accounting trick in Ecuador to lend the government more dollars than those kept in reserve, the Petro in Venezuela or the SUCRE launched by the countries of the ALBA (Bolivarian Alliance for the Peoples of Our America, or *Alianza Bolivariana para los Pueblos de Nuestra América*) are the clearest examples.

The objective of this research is to use the lessons learned from these initiatives to propose successful forms of monetary integration between countries in the region. We assert that exclusively monetary initiatives – such as clearing systems, the creation of a monetary union, or even a continental digital currency – have, per se, little potential to transform the role played by Latin American countries in the ongoing geographic reconfiguration of the dynamics of global accumulation. On the contrary, to develop its full role in political and economic self-determination, a monetary instrument must incorporate mechanisms of solidarity, trade, and investment coordination among member countries.

This chapter is divided into four sections. First, we describe the framework of dependence and vulnerability in which Latin America has been immersed for the last four decades. A second section reviews the nonconventional monetary initiatives launched at different dates and in different countries in the last two decades. This is achieved by first addressing the national cases and then delving into the experience of the SUCRE. In the third section, we propose possible ways to move toward a framework of greater shared autonomy in Latin America in light of the major changes in the international monetary order. The final section concludes this research.

ECONOMIC INSTABILITY AND DISINTEGRATION IN LATIN AMERICA IN RECENT HISTORY

Regardless of the differences that may exist between countries or even within them, Latin America as a region suffers from stagnation. This is derived from its inability to adapt and take an active part in the continuous and accelerated transformations of global value chains. Its most immediate expression is the low level of economic growth coupled with a relative backwardness in terms of specialization in high-value sectors in addition to the low level of intraregional trade.

But there is also a reflection of this stagnation at the exchange rate and monetary levels in the form of external debt and relatively low levels of reserves in conjunction with episodes of high inflation (or even hyperinflation) and deflation.

A Stagnant and Disintegrated Region

Some basic data show the long cycle of stagnation in Latin America: while its weight in the world population has remained unchanged for 30 years (7.7% of the total), its weight in value added has fallen by 2020 to the levels of the 1980s, i.e., below 5%. In the 1960s and 1970s, during the *Fordist* accumulation regime, per capita income in Latin America was above 90% of the world average, while in the last three decades it has gradually fallen to around 75% of the world average.

The difficulties the region is encountering in participating actively in the development of the new phase of the industrial revolution is undoubtedly an essential component of the explanation for this poor relative performance. Indeed, as Fig. 1 shows, there is a clear correlation between increasing specialization in high-tech products and growth rates. But the graph also tells us that only Asia seems to be taking advantage of its changing role in the international division of labor and its increasing specialization in high-tech products.[2]

In terms of Latin America and the Caribbean's share in world trade, there is little productive dynamism, with no significative changes in the pattern of trade specialization. The export of raw materials, primary products and agrifood manufactures, has remained the same in the first decades of the twenty-first century.

According to data from UnctadStats, out of the 19 points of weight in overall world exports that developed countries have lost between 1995 and 2021, Latin America has gained less than one. Regarding industrial exports, developed countries have lost 21.6 points of weight, while Latin America and the Caribbean (LAC) has only improved by 0.7. In the last 30 years, the pattern of export specialization in LAC has not changed substantially in aggregate terms. The slight fall in labor-intensive and low-skilled industries, especially textile and garments is barely offset by a slight increase in higher value-added

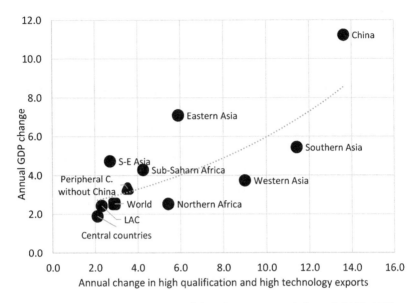

Fig. 1.   Relationship Between High-tech Exports and Growth 2000–2018.
Source: UNCTADStats (https://unctadstat.unctad.org/EN/) and own elaboration.
Note: In current dollars. East-Asia includes China, but not Japan.

manufacturing. That said, a disaggregated analysis would show that this apparent better export position has materialized only in very focalized sectors (automotive) and countries (Mexico), while others, like Argentina or Brazil, show poor trade performance in those sectors.

The region shows symptoms of stagnation and marginalization not only in terms of product specialization, but also in terms of the origin and destination of trade flows. As seen in Table 1, it has the lowest level of real regional integration,

Table 1. Intraregional Trade (in Percentage of Total Exports) in Selected Regions.

	1995	2000	2005	2010	2015	2019	2020
Sub-Saharan Africa	13.8	13.1	12.8	17.5	21.1	19.8	20.0
Latin America and the Caribbean	20.4	17.6	18.3	20.0	17.2	14.9	13.7
South America	25.1	23.4	18.8	20.0	18.7	16.1	14.9
Asia	52.8	51.5	56.2	59.6	59.6	59.4	58.3
Southeastern Asia	23.7	22.2	24.4	24.5	24.1	22.7	20.8
Eastern Asia	34.6	34.6	39.3	38.1	36.2	34.3	34.5
Northern America	35.9	39.7	40.8	32.4	31.1	30.1	29.7
Europe	67.9	72.9	74.1	70.7	66.6	67.8	67.7

Source: UNCTADStats (https://unctadstat.unctad.com/).

slightly slower than those of sub-Saharan Africa and well below Europe or Eastern-Asia.

The flip side of this weak integration is a strong dependence on the United States. According to UNCTADstat data, in 1996–2000, the United States accounted for 46% of Latin America's total merchandise imports, and 53% of the region's exports went to the United States. In 2012–2017, the emergence of trade with China (19% of imports and 12% of exports) did not prevent the United States from remaining the leading trading partner, accounting for 32% of imports and absorbing 43% of Latin American exports.

The COVID-19 pandemic has only aggravated Latin America's trade de-structuring, as the weight of intra-regional trade. This amounted to 21% before and during the Great Recession starting in 2008, but during the pandemic (2020–2021) fell to 15%, the lowest level in the last quarter of a century. As for foreign investment, the Economic Commission for Latin America and the Caribbean (ECLAC) (2021) reports a decline in intra-regional investment, from 12% in the 2010–2014 period, 10% in 2015–2019, and then to 6% in 2020.

The Peripheral Position, on the Monetary Level

In terms of monetary and exchange rate policy, the search for a framework of stability in the above-described context of price volatility and capital inflows and outflows has led the countries of the continent to try different exchange rate regimes in recent decades. However, the various exchange-rate regimes chosen generally reflect two factors that affect the continent not only in strictly monetary terms, but also in its international economic relations: the lack of room to freely manage the different economic policy tools and the dependence on a few global economic poles.

The most extreme manifestation – in monetary terms – of this dependence is dollarization. In some historical cases, such as Puerto Rico or Panama, or more recently in Ecuador (since 1999) or El Salvador (since 2000), dollarization is official. To this must be added the episodes of informal dollarization in Argentina, Bolivia or, currently, Venezuela.

Opposite to these rigid regimes, but far from opting to let their currency fully float, most countries have been trying out formulas in which pegged exchange-rate regimes alternate with short periods of greater volatility. In general, although countries have shown themselves incapable of maintaining the exchange rate stability of their currency against the dollar for long periods, neither do they want to let it float. This is due to the implications of this for the different forms of dependence (Calvo & Reinhart, 2002). In that sense, the International Monetary Fund periodically acknowledges cases such as Honduras, Guyana or Bolivia, in which, in contrast to the supposedly floating *de jure* classification, practice shows more or less rigid de facto anchors to the dollar (e.g. IMF, 2012).

In the last three decades, within the entire range of intermediate and unstable exchange rate regimes, we find strong pegs to anchor currencies, mostly the dollar. It includes examples such as the currency board of Argentina in

1991–2002, or the fixed rate with occasional adjustments of Cuba, Belize, Guyana or Venezuela (the latter until 2018–2019). Close to this extreme we find the crawling peg of Bolivia, Nicaragua, or recently Venezuela (since 2018).

Perhaps the primary novelty in the range of options followed has been the adoption of the so-called "inflation targeting" strategy. This policy was adopted in New Zealand and Canada in the early 1990s, spread to most developed countries after the late 1990s and, since the 2000s, has been applied by at least eight Latin American countries, including Brazil, Colombia, Chile, and Mexico. This shift from an anchor to the US dollar and then to a price targeting strategy cannot be understood without the commercial and financial diversification of some of these countries, with China as an emerging partner in most cases. According to the World Integrated Trade Solution (WITS) of the World Bank – data for 2019 –, China is already the main partner for countries such as Brazil, Chile or Peru.

Inflation targeting implies the direct sacrifice of the interest rate, but also the use of fiscal policy and reserves management for the purpose of price stability. It is, in summary, another exchange rate and monetary policy within the wide range of policies observed across the continent as a clear sign of a relationship of dependence that occurs in various dimensions. The clearest manifestation of this dependence is the necessary but almost impossible task of each country to maintain stability in its cost and price structure with respect to the major international economic poles (historically the United States). Not so obvious but equally important is ideological dependence: inflation targeting, which represents the major exchange rate alternative to traditional regimes, is a strategy imported from developed countries. The adoption of a policy proposed in developed countries, whose currencies and macroeconomic frameworks are in a more comfortable position than Latin America's, reinforces the likelihood that the Latin American continent will continue to disintegrate and play a peripheral role at the service of the old and/or new powers.

It could be justified that monetary submission is the price to be paid by LAC countries in exchange for the price stability required for the circulation of international monetary capital. However, in this aspect too, there has been clear instability for decades. It should be noted that Latin American countries maintain a level of reserves equivalent to 9.5 months, compared to 13.7 months for the world average (WDI data). This relative weakness in the assets backing their own currencies makes Latin America – even the largest countries – particularly sensitive to inflationary processes or political processes of rejection of the national currency and, eventually, of hyperinflation, as seen in Table 2. This phenomenon, that should be described more as political mistrust of the national currency than as a strictly economic phenomenon, was especially evident in the 1980s. It corresponds to the most intense cycle of hyperinflation, with the examples of Nicaragua, between 1985 and 1991 – the peak phase of the US aggression against the Sandinista government – and Bolivia, during the Siles Zuazo government (1982–1985), a period of rapprochement with Cuba and high political instability.

But, as shown in Table 2, instability for money capital also manifests in frequent periods of deflation, such as those observed in the last three decades.

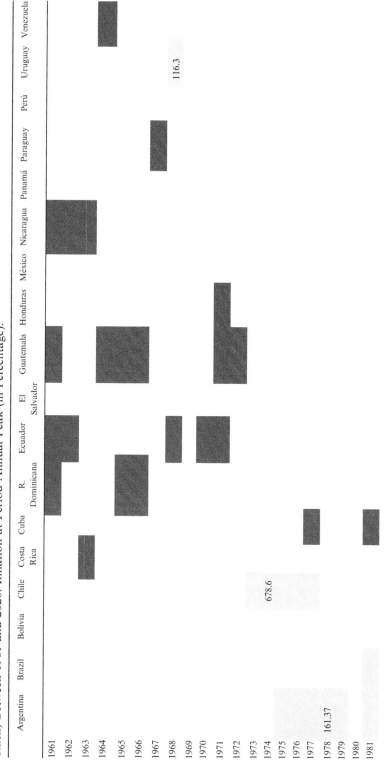

Table 2. Periods of (Hyper)Inflation (annual GDP deflator rate >100%: in grey) and Periods of Deflation (annual GDP deflator rate <0%: in black) Between 1961 and 2020. Inflation at Period Annual Peak (in Percentage).

Table 2. (*Continued*)

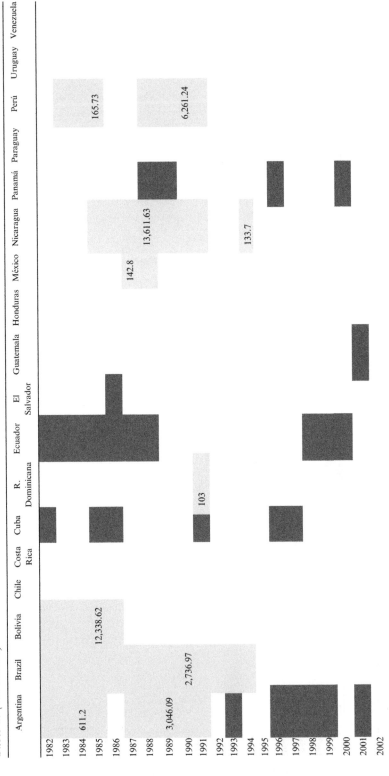

Source: Own Elaboration From World Development Indicators and Banco Central de Venezuela for Data (2015–2020) Concerning This Country.

This last type of phenomenon, moreover, is an added obstacle to the process of valorization of capital. This is insofar as the fall in prices in the middle of the process of production and sale of commodities threatens the return of capital.

In this context of instability and dependence, there is also a list of initiatives that have been launched with a view to alleviating, in various ways, the problems arising from the position these countries occupy in the global dynamics of capital accumulation. The following section deals with the most representative ones.

ALTERNATIVE MONETARY INITIATIVES IN THE RECENT HISTORY OF LATIN AMERICA

Generally speaking, individual monetary initiatives do not have, per se, the potential to substantially alter the "local" characteristics of capital accumulation patterns. If anything, they can, on a case-by-case basis, contribute to questioning the rules and customs of the asymmetrical and hierarchical world monetary system.

Initiatives involving two or more countries do have a greater power to reshape global economic relations insofar as monetary agreements include aspects involving commitments in terms of trade and investment.

National Initiatives Against Dependence on the US Dollar

Curiously, some of the official initiatives have been promoted by governments of countries with the strongest anchors to the US dollar. Without following a chronological order, we will focus on the purpose and scope of some recent initiatives: the recognition of bitcoin as a payment instrument by El Salvador, Ecuador with the so-called "balance sheet expansion" by its Central Bank, Venezuela's petro, or the SUCRE system.

In the case of Ecuador, an officially dollarized country, the so-called "balance sheet expansion" was presented as an innovation of the Central Bank (*Banco Central del Ecuador* [BCE]). It allowed, during the period of President Rafael Correa, to issue credit in dollars to finance the government in excess of the government's dollar reserves. This was done with the foresight that the balances would be virtually locked in and that there would be no effective demand for dollar bills. It must be admitted that this mechanism gave more leeway to fiscal policy than a monetary issue limited to 100% of the reserves. However, this mechanism is not particularly novel; the BCE was, after all, applying the typical credit issuance logic of developed financial systems, by which debt acknowledgments are issued far in excess of existing reserves.

In contrast to the fiscal "leverage" applied in Ecuador, the bet on bitcoin as legal tender in El Salvador from 2021 is undoubtedly more remarkable. With an interest rate that has not fallen significantly since the dollarization of 2001 and capital formation levels falling relative to Central America as a whole, the legal acceptance of bitcoin in the country sought to simultaneously address different challenges.

First, with around 5–6 billion dollars per year of personal remittances inflows (Banco Central de Reserva de El Salvador, 2022), bitcoin aims to drastically reduce the commissions paid to international platforms. This goal seems far from being achieved: in the first year after the approval of the national bitcoin course, only 52 million out of a total of 7,635 (0.06%) had been transferred via bitcoin.

Second, the government has started to issue debt in bitcoins. Having acquired from mid-2021 to July 2022 a total of 2,381 units at an average price of $45,004, it can be said that the rhythm of issuance is not very significant. Beyond the average price per unit, it is worth noting the high volatility of the market price in the different auctions: the maximum price paid for bitcoin was $60,435 per unit in October 2021, and a minimum of $19,000 was reached in July 2022.

Finally, El Salvador has implemented a system of using geothermal energy to "mine" bitcoins. With a closed number of bitcoins that can be generated, a production cost is established which increases as the total number of bitcoins set by the mining algorithm is exhausted. Until the mining cycle is completed, this variable production cost is a reference to the fact that bitcoin has a production price, regardless of the market price that fluctuates with speculation. Due to its geological characteristics, the use of geothermal energy can lower the real cost of mining in El Salvador.

It is difficult to measure whether bitcoin will give the country more autonomy in the long term than the dollarized regime, or whether it will plunge the country into a scenario of strong volatility and uncertainty due to its use at an international level.

What is more certain is that the intention of a dollarized country to resort to a financial asset whose issuance does not depend on the Federal Reserve, but on the availability of technology and cheap energy, poses a challenge to the traditional hegemony of the dollar.

Quite different to this is the launch of the Petro by the Venezuelan government since 2018. It is also presented as an ordinary cryptocurrency, but with the advantage of being backed by oil and the potential to avoid the financial blockade of the United States. Truthfully said, it does not meet the characteristics generally attributed to cryptocurrencies. First, although it may use blockchain technology, the conditions for traceability are not provided; second, the fundamental issuance is not decentralized but controlled by the State according to its financing needs. Third, unlike bitcoin and other cryptocurrencies, the large cryptocurrency exchange houses do not work with the Petro and its market price responds more to the *Banco Central de Venezuela*'s discretion than to the formula announced in its Whitepaper and composed of the price of different goods (mainly raw materials) in dollars. Therefore, although it shares with cryptocurrencies the fact that it is a financial asset, it resembled better one of the forms of financing of a State, only in this instance, backing its debt with its main commodity: oil.

But even as a simple tradable financial asset, although there is great opacity around the traded volumes of this financial asset, it can be said that its scope and transformative capacity are very limited: neither is it widely accepted in the international market, nor has it managed to dodge the extension of sanctions since 2018, and nor does it pose a way out of the mono-exporting scheme of the national economy.

Collective Projects of Monetary Integration: The Case of the SUCRE

Better prospects were opening up for the Unitary Regional Compensation System (SUCRE, for *Sistema Unitario de Compensación Regional de Pagos*), agreed upon in 2008 and launched in 2009 by the ALBA countries plus Ecuador. With a logic similar to that of the European Payments Union or Keynes' bancor proposal – both after World War II –, SUCRE was composed of four elements. A common unit of account called the *sucre* (lower case), the Regional Monetary Council (CMR, Spanish acronym for *Consejo Monetario Regional*), a Central Clearing Compensation Chamber and the FRCC, which stands for the regional Trade and Reserves Convergence Fund (*Fondo de Reservas y Convergencia Comercial* in Spanish). As immediate goals, it aims to improve the member-countries reserve management as well as to reduce their dependence on the US dollar liquidity.

But it was also designed to encourage trade among members. The system recorded in *sucres* a single balance for each country resulting from the multi-lateral clearing of operations between member countries. The total balances were semi-annually settled in dollars. For any surplus or deficit balance that was considered excessive – according to a previous calculation applied to the reality of each country –, a burden was applied in order to promote trade integration and economic growth. An excessive surplus by a country could be reduced in two ways: the surplus country should increase its total demand within the SUCRE system or the excess may be transferred to the FRCC. Then, the CMR could use them in order to finance productive and infrastructure projects in the region. The ultimate objective was to develop, through trade but also through these invest-ments, a zone of "productive complementarity," a term that evokes the devel-opment and relocation of value chains through the coordination of SUCRE member countries.

During the first years, this system channeled a growing volume of operations and gained ground over the numerous agreements and payment platforms in the continent. This boom can be explained in large part by the promotion of the system by the governments of the member countries.

That said, let us bear in mind that the SUCRE was a unitary system but not the only regional integration mechanism. On the contrary, private and public agents could (and still can) opt for different parallel systems to carry out their operations with neighboring countries. In fact, the SUCRE was not even the only system promoted unanimously by each member country.

The coexistence of the SUCRE with other alternative forms of payments between the same partners means that the mechanism that enables symmetrical adjustment between countries becomes meaningless. A country with a deficit close to the limit that makes it excessive will opt to import through different mechanisms; at the same time, a surplus country will diversify instruments so as not to have to reach a surplus to transfer to the FRCC. This makes the symmetrical, expansionary, and systematic adjustment provided by the mechanism impossible (Barredo-Zuriarrain & Cerezal-Callizo, 2019, p. 13).

In the end, like so many other instruments, the SUCRE depended on the political will of its members. Without the initial political impetus, the volumes channeled through the SUCRE started to dwindle since 2013. Since 2016, no annual report has been published that reflects the operations, values, origin and destination of goods traded under this system.

If we go back a few years earlier, we see that something similar happened with the CPCR (Spanish acronym for the Agreement for Reciprocal Credit and Payments) proposed by ALADI (the *Asociación Latinoamericana de Integración*, or Latin American Integration Association) in 1982. This provided for a four-month payment offset. At its peak, in the last two decades of the last century, this payment facility, which included the main Latin American countries, centralized 90% of intra-regional trade. By 2003, however, it had fallen to 1.5%, a level to which it returned in 2016 after a few years of slight recovery.

Again, part of the explanation lies in the existence of different integration platforms. In this case, exporters pressed for a settlement of less than the four months provided; while importers preferred to resort to the six months of the SUCRE.

Nevertheless, there are not only alternatives promoted at the governmental level. There is also evident competition from real-time payment mechanisms that have been widespread for decades and more developed in recent years. The latter may be advantageous at the individual level for the agents involved in the sale and purchase. Fundamentally, however, they help to consolidate the peripheral role in the highly hierarchical world monetary structure.

MONETARY-FINANCIAL WARFARE AND ALTERNATIVES FOR LATIN AMERICA

There is no successful formula for a stable monetary integration with which the continent overcomes its peripheral position and gains a certain degree of autonomy. Proof of this is the SUCRE, seen above, which was born out of very good intentions on the part of its members, but was forgotten a few years later. However, even the Eurozone, which followed the integration steps set by mainstream economics (Balassa, 1962), had already shown signs in its first decade of being an instrument that exacerbated regional divergences in favor of the capitalist class in the central countries, while exacerbating the instability of the Great Recession of 2008.

Nevertheless, members of any regional initiative in LAC must be aware that they require a strong political commitment, with all the short-term sacrifices that this entails. This ranges from the most modest initiatives – diversifying money reserves as well as the use of international payment systems – to those with a more transformative spirit incorporating, for example, a common unit of account and investment mechanisms for the promotion of productive specialization.

Geopolitics of Payments-Systems

The United States has undoubtedly played a hegemonic role, at least in the second half of the Twentieth Century, in the world economy. However, some indicators show a certain decline in favor of China. In terms of purchasing power parity, its GDP has been surpassed by the Asian country. It is also surpassed by the same country in international trade (15% of exports, 20% excluding intra-European trade), and is already the European Union's leading partner.

In terms of foreign direct investment, the long-term trend shows an export of productive capital from China, which is compared with a certain stagnation in the United States. Particularly noteworthy is the expansion of Chinese capital into areas such as Asia, Africa and even Latin America, some of which were considered to be under the historical influence of the United States or European countries.

Yet, in the monetary and financial sphere, the United States continues to hold a clearly dominant position. World dollar reserves represent 55% of the total in 2021, standing much higher than the ratio of any other currency. Moreover, according to the Triennial Central Bank Survey of the Bank for International Settlements (2019), the dollar still accounts for 88.3% of foreign exchange market turnover, a far cry from the 32.3% of the euro, which is in second place.

However, as mentioned above, for a country's influence in the international monetary and financial sphere, it is also essential to master the payment platforms, private or public, that both channel and clear international transactions. This is a very powerful political weapon in the hands of the countries that manage these systems (Labonte & Murphy, 2017; Nelson & Rosen, 2019), since the exclusion of an entity of a national financial system from the automatic payment clearing system implies high transaction costs and the actual exclusion of the possibility of making international payments on a regular and continuous basis.

In this area we also see the United States in a clearly dominant position. It exerts control not only over institutions within its own financial regulatory structure – such as Fedwire[3] – but also over private payment systems such as CHIPS. The latter is cheaper than Fedwire, with fewer participating entities but more spread throughout the world, or over multinationals specializing in payments between individuals and based in the United States. This includes PayPal, Mastercard, VISA, etc. This control gives the US government ample possibilities to impose financial sanctions unilaterally or to exclude governments, institutions or individuals from using US dollars in international financing. This means that they cannot receive payments for exports, pay for the purchase of goods or hold US dollar-denominated assets. In recent years, the United States has even demonstrated the ability to control or even block payments made through SWIFT (Carter & Farha, 2013, p. 1257; Wong, 2022), which, based in Belgium, is the most widespread messaging system between banks around the world for making payments.

A different case is that of China. Despite its clear rise as a new world engine and its commercial and investment expansion, it continues to play a discreet role in the international monetary system. More than a reserve currency issuer, in recent decades it has been the major supporter of the US dollar: the country holds 25% of world reserves (COFER,[4] IMF), half of which are estimated to be in dollars.

As of March 2022, the renminbi (RMB) accounted for only 2.7% of international reserves, far behind the positions of the dollar, the euro, the pound sterling and the Japanese yen. However, since the end of the 2000s, the Chinese currency has shown a growing international influence at different levels. First, it has signed agreements with heterogeneous international institutions for the use of the RMB (World Bank, BRICS [Brazil, Russia, India, China, and South Africa] New Development Bank, European Bank for Reconstruction and Development, etc.), being especially relevant is the inclusion of the currency in the Special Drawing Rights (SDRs) tray. Moreover, in recent years, it has intensified the combination of its regional expansion projects at the trade and investment level with the promotion of the RMB: Association of Southeast Asian Nations (ASEAN) agreements in 2009, swap lines with 36 countries including the Chiang Mai Initiative (International Monetary Institute, 2017), and the Belt and Road Initiative extending over the Asian continent to Africa, Europe and Oceania (Kamel, 2018), etc.

Finally, with the promotion of large liberalized markets and the launch of its own payment system – the Cross-Border Interbank Payment System, or CIPS – (Faudot, 2016), it aspires to consolidate an institutional framework that challenges the dominance of the United States in the centralization – and eventual blocking – of international financial operations. In the framework of geopolitical confrontation aggravated since the beginning of 2022, with Russia existing as a target of Western sanctions, the CIPS system may be reinforced to the extent that Russia – which has its own "System for Transfer of Financial Messages"[5] – must orient itself toward the Asian giant.

It would not be surprising if the reorientation of Latin American trade and investment toward China – as seen above – were to be followed by a serious commitment by the region toward the renminbi and its entire infrastructure. Although this implies a reconfiguration of monetary relations in the region, it is likely that, in the absence of a regional integration project that transcends the purely monetary dimension, economic relations with the emerging Chinese pole will continue to be, for Latin America, as they have been up to now, from a peripheral position. Therefore, without losing sight of the windows of opportunity that are opening up in the new context, Latin America must propose formulas that will enable it to move toward a scenario of greater autonomy shared by the member countries.

A Latin-American Cryptocurrency?

In light of the increasing use of institutional financial exclusion as part of trade and political warfare (Frebowitz, 2018), significant expectations have been raised about the feasibility of organizing nonproprietary payment systems with blockchain technology, and about the possibility of using cryptocurrencies as global money not tied to the US dollar (Nelson, 2019; Nelson & Rosen, 2019).

Blockchain systems allow so-called cryptocurrencies to fulfill a very relevant function as alternative electronic payment systems (Perkins, 2018). However, this function as a means of payment is only exercised for goods for which it is explicitly stated that they can be paid for in a particular cryptocurrency.

Cryptocurrencies do not fulfill the requirements of a monetary unit in capitalism; in addition to the functions that mainstream economics assign to money – means of payment, store of value, unit of account –, currency in capitalism is the social sign that validates the general system of exchanges, which dominates production, distribution, and consumption, i.e., currency is a sign of value. In order to fulfill this function, it has to express (and be exchanged for) the source of value, which is labor power converted into a commodity. In other words, a currency that is not used to pay wage earners is not a capitalist currency.

Apart from that, it must be recognized that, seen as financial assets or as means of payment, cryptocurrencies that use blockchain technology are relevant for our topic. That is because of the very system of circulation, in which the relationship is only bilateral, between the one who pays and the one who collects, without the intervention of any authority or central institution that registers the transaction or those who carry it out. Unlike what happens with other electronic payment systems, whether or not they use their own monetary tokens, in the management of blockchain flows there is no central institution that sells or buys the cryptocurrencies.

Rather, it is moved directly by their owners who have obtained them in their work as "miners" or because they have previously obtained them from one of these. The system's algorithm guarantees that no one can use cryptocurrencies they do not have, or use them to make two simultaneous payments, because every movement is recorded on all computers in the network in general, but none in particular (Su, 2018).

Only in the case of extreme and extensive political attempts of financial exclusion, as has happened with the sanctions against Venezuela, can the development of a global Latin American cryptocurrency make sense. It is the communal, horizontal nature of the cryptocurrency system – rather than the anonymity of transactions – what worries global financial authorities (see Houben & Snyers, 2018). In the event of an open confrontation with the operators of the global payment system, the possibility of establishing a regional means of payment of this kind is always open. Excluding this situation, a well-organized and trustworthy regional payment system based on a weighted unit of account is the best option for now.

Strengthening Regional Finance to Promote Industrialization

Latin America needs to increase its margin of economic and political autonomy in order to reposition itself in the changing landscape of the global division of labor. This implies adopting a set of measures that, based on its own experience and that of other regions, can also articulate a framework of shared autonomy in the monetary and financial spheres.

One of the possibilities for collaboration, apparently not very transformative but certainly complex, would consist in moving, as has been done in recent years, toward a reduction of the dependence on national currencies in relation to one or a few international currencies. This can be done simultaneously on at least three levels.

In the first instance, by discontinuing the use of the SWIFT system as the sole system for clearing and settlement services. This involves linking the international payment system of the countries in the region with, for example, the Chinese CIPS and the Russian PESA system, as well as to the various proposals launched in recent years to integrate both initiatives or even to extend them to countries such as Turkey or Iran.

Secondly, Latin American national currencies should move toward a scenario where, in the event that the exchange rate of national currencies is anchored, it is not anchored to a single currency, but rather to a basket of currencies, with the Special Drawing Rights (SDR) being a reference basket that is already established.

Thirdly, it is advisable to continue with the diversification of central bank reserves that were already begun at the beginning of this century. Here, the ideal would be a swap program between Central Banks so that each one's reserves would include an increasing share of the currencies of the continent's neighboring countries. However, we cannot ignore the objective difficulties for its implementation, among others, the lack of trade links between neighboring countries and the instability that periodically plagues the region's currencies and pushes central banks to seek refuge in safer assets.

Given these difficulties and the lack of incentives for each country to accept neighboring currencies as reserve assets, it is more viable to opt for a common, shared unit of account – such as the SUCRE – which implies different commitments for national governments depending on the challenges posed.

This unit of account can serve as a common reference to achieve exchange rate stability in the region, anchoring it to a basket of currencies – or directly to the SDR – and, at the same time, fixing a value for each national currency with respect to the unit of account. That said, the exchange rate stability of this unit requires at least two conditions: (1) the assignment of part of the reserves of each central bank to a pool for the common defense of the exchange rate in the foreign exchange market, as well as (2) the periodic revision of its exchange rate with respect to the currencies issued by these central banks.

From the SUCRE we can also retain the mechanism of symmetrical and periodic multilateral compensation in order to improve the national management of foreign currency liquidity, as well as to promote intra-regional trade. That said, unlike the failed initiative of the ALBA countries, the necessary periodic settlement of balances between countries should be executed in currencies other than the US dollar.

Nonetheless, this new monetary architecture should also serve to achieve greater economic integration in LAC and achieve an international division of labor more favorable to the development of higher value-added activities. This may include the processing of raw materials and primary products and the development of industrial sectors, regional transport and logistics. Strengthening the LAC industrial base by means of supporting key areas such as next generation information technology (IT), high-end equipment and new materials (or other specific content for action that may be considered) requires joint actions in various fields, from research to the establishment of regional energy networks. However, all efforts in this direction will be futile in the absence of coherent and articulated financial planning and reform among the nations of the subcontinent.

For all these reasons, the regional monetary project should incorporate, in addition to the unit of account, a supranational entity that would be both a debt issuer and a productive investment bank. Bond issues or other debt securities should be backed jointly by all the countries, or at least by the countries participating in a specific investment project. The possibility of issuing it in the unit of account backed in turn by the reserves of the member countries would reduce the cost of financing as well as the exchange rate risk associated with debt issues in foreign currencies.

For its part, the supranational bank should avoid the institutional and political limitations of European institutions, with a European Central Bank (ECB) controlled by banking capital and isolated from the direct needs of economic policy, and a European Investment Bank with little access to European liquidity.

Having said all this, we do not ignore the series of difficulties associated with a reform of this type that makes it politically improbable compared to alternatives that consolidate the status quo. They bear greater advantages in the short term, such as bilateral trade agreements with old and new world powers, recourse to the IMF or the World Bank as sources of financing, or compliance with the different embargoes applied by the United States.

In this sense, there are valuable lessons to be learned from the SUCRE. Not only because of the successful – but temporary – implementation of some of the mechanisms described here, but also because the fundamental conditions for its full effectiveness and sustainability were not met. As a final point, we believe it is important to mention two of them. Firstly, a multilateral compensation mechanism, especially if it incorporates a symmetrical adjustment clause, cannot be optional but must channel all the trade flows of the member countries in order to make sense. Secondly, the project must include, from the first steps, countries that already have important trade and financial links between them. SUCRE was promoted by and for countries with ideologically connected governments – mainly ALBA – but not with intense bilateral relations. In this sense, the Southern Common Market (MERCOSUR in Spanish, acronym of *Mercado Común del Sur*, and MERCOSUL in Portuguese, for Mercado Comum do Sul) presents a greater cohesion and is, therefore, a relevant institution from which to germinate a monetary project with potential for the development of an innovative and high value-added industrial base for the region.

CONCLUSION

Several lessons can be drawn from the various monetary initiatives launched or supported by different governments in Latin America and the Caribbean over the last two decades. The most obvious is the realization that the governments of the region are aware of the framework of dependence and instability in which they develop their international economic relations and are furthermore pressing to find ways to alter this position. The second lesson, and that of a more general nature, is given to us by Marx (1993, p. 122), when he points out that it is impossible to revolutionize the relations of production and distribution by means of a mere transformation of the instrument of circulation. Related to the first two, the third point argues that, even within the framework of the fundamental laws governing the capitalist mode of production, joint monetary experiences between countries can be effective tools for dealing with the vulnerability inherent in their peripheral condition. But for this, beyond sharing a unit of account, a clearing house or a common reserve fund (among other possibilities), monetary integration must be associated with measures involving commitments to relocation in terms of trade and investment.

Without the need or even the convenience of going to extreme formulas such as the creation of a single currency or a cryptocurrency, the countries of LAC can work around a common unit of account from which to advance from immediate challenges – management of foreign exchange reserves – to more ambitious ones, such as making collective progress in the production of high value-added goods and services and achieving a fairer distribution. Nonetheless, all this implies putting bilateral relations with the different world poles - with their obvious short-term advantages – onto the backburner, in favor of a long-term commitment to Latin America.

NOTES

1. The Clearing House Interbank Payments System is the largest system of payments between private agents.

2. Industries considered high-tech and high-skill by UNCTAD include electronics and their components, chemical and pharmaceutical manufacturing, medical, optical and precision instrument manufacturing, cinematographic products, art manufacturing, musical instruments, and arms manufacturing.

3. The Fedwire Funds Service, owned by the Federal Reserve Board, is a real-time gross settlement system. Together with CHIPS, they have a dominant position in domestic and international large payments in US dollar.

4. IMF database on currency composition of official foreign exchange reserves.

5. Also known as SPFS (*Система передачи финансовых сообщений* (СПФС), romanized by Sistema Peredachi Finansovykh Soobscheniy) or by PESA, acronym for Peredachi Soobscheniy Sistema.

REFERENCES

Balassa, B. (1962). *The theory of economic integration.* London: Allen Unwin.

Banco Central de Reserva de El Salvador. (2022). *Informe estadístico de remesas familiares.* El Salvador.

Bank for International Settlements. (2019). *Triennial Central Bank Survey of foreign exchange and Over-the-counter (OTC) derivatives markets in 2019.* Available on: https://www.bis.org/statistics/rpfx19.htm

Barredo-Zuriarrain, J., & Cerezal-Callizo, M. (2019). Lessons from the SUCRE and TARGET2 systems for a sound international monetary system in a financialized economy. *Journal of Post Keynesian Economics, 42*(1), 39–58.

Calvo, G. A., & Reinhart, C. M. (2002). Fear of floating. *Quarterly Journal of Economics, 117*(2), 379–408.

Carter, B. E., & Farha, R. (2013). *Overview and operation of US financial sanctions, including the example of Iran* (p. 1257). Georgetown Law Faculty Publications.

ECLAC. (2021). *La Inversión extranjera directa en América Latina y el Caribe.* Santiago de Chile: Economic Commission for Latin America and the Caribbean (ECLAC) – Comisión Económica para América Latina (CEPAL).

Faudot, A. (2016). Internationalisation du renminbi: enjeux et limites des réformes institutionnelles. *Revue d'Economie Financiere, 121*, 305–326.

Frebowitz, R. L. (2018). *Cryptocurrency and state sovereignty.* MA Thesis. Monterey, CA: Naval Postgraduate School.

Houben, R. & Snyers, A. (2018). *Cryptocurrencies and blockchain: Legal context and implications for financial crime, money laundering and tax evasion.* Policy Department for Economic, Scientific and Quality of Life Policies. Directorate-General for Internal Policies. PE 619.024.

International Monetary Fund. (2012). *Annual report on exchange arrangements and exchange restrictions.* Washington, DC.

International Monetary Institute. (2017). *RMB internationalization report.* Research Report, 1702, Renmin University of China.

Kamel, M. S. (2018). China's belt and road initiative: Implications for the Middle East. *Cambridge Review of International Affairs, 31*(1), 76–95.

Labonte, M., & Murphy, E. (2017, August 12). *Who regulates whom? An overview of the U.S. financial regulatory framework CRS report R44918.* Washington, DC.

Marx, K. (1993). *Grundrisse: Foundations of the critique of political economy.* London: Penguin Books.

Nelson, R. M. (2019). *Examining regulatory frameworks for digital currencies and blockchain.* Statement before the Committee on Banking, Housing and Urban Affairs, US Senate. Congressional Research Service. Hearing on July 30. 7-5700. Available on: https://www.banking.senate.gov/hearings

Nelson, R. M., & Rosen, L. W. (2019, February 8). *Digital currencies: Sanctions evasion risks. Congressional Research Service, IF10825.* Washington, DC.

Perkins, D. W. (2018, December 7). *Cryptocurrency: The economics of money and selected policy issues Congressional Research Service, R45427.* Washington, DC.

Su, E. (2018, October 17). *Financial innovation: Digital assets and initial coin offerings. Congressional Research Service IF11004.* Washington, DC.

Wong, R. (2022). What is SWIFT, and could sanctions impact the US dollar's dominance? *Federal Reserve Bank of Richmond Economic Brief*, 9.

PART III

PROFIT TODAY

MULTINATIONAL FIRMS' PRACTICES: AN ATTEMPT AT A MARXIST THEORIZATION

Christian Palloix

ABSTRACT

This chapter presents a critical analysis of the wealth current practices of multinational firms as wealth predators; and relevant references from the theory of multinational corporations and globalization from a Marxist perspective. The Marxist approach has also contributed to a theory of the self-expansion of capital (internationalization of the circuits of capital) on a global scale, within an analysis of the differentiation and of inequality.

Keywords: Multinational firms; oligopolies; international trade; organization; industry; theory

INTRODUCTION

Multinational firms (MNFs), a major actor of capitalism today, (or, better said, multinational groups), prove to be a predator of wealth fueling the disorders of the capitalist economy on the global and national levels. Many of the dysfunctions that the current COVID-19 pandemic has accentuated can be attributed to the MNFs: the leveling off of GDP growth in advanced countries; the marked slowdown in GDP growth in emerging countries; the sharp contraction in foreign direct investment; the slowdown in world trade; the slowdown in productivity growth; the threats of financial crisis (or crises) like the one in 2008; growing distribution inequalities, etc.

We propose the following:

- a presentation and initial critical analysis of the current practices of multinational firms,[1] which are predators of wealth,

Value, Money, Profit, and Capital Today
Research in Political Economy, Volume 39, 117–143
Copyright © 2024 Christian Palloix
Published under exclusive licence by Emerald Publishing Limited
ISSN: 0161-7230/doi:10.1108/S0161-723020230000039008

• a presentation of the contributions of the theory of multinational firms according to a Marxist approach.

MULTINATIONAL FIRMS' PRACTICES: PREDATORS OF WEALTH

The new practices of multinational firms over the period 1990–2022: the disconnection brought about by the supply chains between, on the one hand, the flows of manufactured goods' values and use values and, on the other, the flows of commodities' valorization in prices.

During the period beginning in the early 1990s through to the present, it is possible to identify three successive new institutional and organizational configurations of multinational firms, referred to as institutional and organizational arrangements,[2] in the agri-food and chemical industries:[3]

• a first arrangement that consisted of the separation of MNFs' profit centers (holdings and commercial subsidiaries) from their cost centers (industrial subsidiaries) with what is called a "rake" organization;
• a second arrangement, which emerged in the early 2000s, where the organizational arrangement takes precedence over the institutional arrangement through the rise of "supply chains" (not to be confused with "global value chains"), notably in Europe, and which operates a disconnection between, on the one hand, the flows of value and use of manufactured products and, on the other, the flows of these products' valorization in price terms, leading to a significant transfer of the wealth created (by labor) from the MNFs to tax havens (under the guise of a "profit split");
• a third arrangement, which started in the early 2010s, once again in the context of a disconnection of flows operated by "supply chains," where the intangible asset called a "brand" is the keystone of a new institutional and organizational arrangement that is even more predatory regarding the riches created and their massive transfers to tax havens.

Over the course of these three institutional and organizational mutations, the multinational firm (more multinational group than multinational firm,[4] in fact) will more than reinforce:

• a "market power,"
• a "productive power," and
• a "financial/rentier power,"

which it can deploy all over the world as its presence expands through a succession of subsidiaries.

- The first "arrangement" of the 1990s–2000s with the separation of operating companies (commercial and support functions) from industrial companies (see Fig. 1):

The 1990s are marked by the strong expansion of multinational firms (and which, of course, will continue well beyond). The expansion of these MNFs is based both on their internal growth and on their external growth thanks to the acquisition here and there of a number of national/regional/local companies, which are then integrated into the regional/global holding company.[5] Thus, for instance, in the 1990s–2000s, the Unilever Group would acquire the companies Fralib (teas, chocolate drinks), Miko (ice cream), Bestfoods (soups), Amora Maille (mustard, condiments), and Puget (oil) in France, drastically restructuring these acquisitions (with a number of site closures). The same is true for the large multinational groups operating in Europe at that time.

During the years 1990–2000, we observe a first institutional/organizational arrangement of MNFs with, on the one hand, (global/regional) "holding" companies, profit centers that collect the dividends, and, on the other, subsidiary companies (restructured as soon as they are acquired), grouped by country and split into two:

- an operating company (OC), which comprises the head office activities (with their support functions) and the commercial activity,[6] that heads the various industrial companies; and

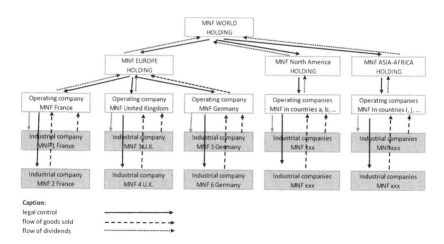

Fig. 1 First Institutional and Organizational Arrangement of the MNF: The "Cost" Factories (Separation of the Operating Company and the Industrial Company).

- industrial companies (ICs) that group together the production activities (the IC may have several establishments), but are *stripped* of their former support functions and their commercial activity.

The industrial companies are reduced to "cost" factories that transfer their production to the operating company at "cost plus,"[7] with a remuneration based on a margin rate (residual "mark-up") so as to perhaps grant employees a profit-sharing incentive.

The creation of value appears solely at the level of the OC, which is a profit center, the IC now being only a cost center.

The (commercial) operating companies deliver dividends to the regional holdings, which pass them on the world holding. The assets are still massively physical (tangible assets), while contributing to the rise of intangible assets (brands, patents, licenses, etc.).

- The second "arrangement" of the years 2000–2010 with the irruption of supply chains in a regime of price transfers (cost plus, profit split): the disconnection between, on the one hand, the flows of manufactured goods' values and use values and, on the other, the valorization flows of these goods as commodities in prices (see Fig. 2):

Domiciled in a tax haven, the holding company operates a separation between:

- on the one hand, the process of manufacturing the products from the raw materials through to the finished product leaving the factories, and which is where the creation of values comes about, with a flow of use-values that goes via the industrial companies to the warehouses (more often than not out-sourced) and supplies the mass-market retail sector (hyper-/super-markets),

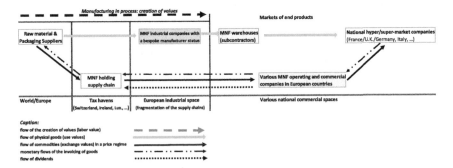

Fig. 2.   Second Institutional and Organizational Arrangement – The Irruption of Supply Chains in a Cost Plus/Profit Split Regime.

- on the other, a flow of valorization of the products delivered by the circuit above in the form of goods invoiced in a price system (at cost plus/profit split[8]) to the operating companies, which in turn invoice the mass-market retail sector, with the flows of payment in return associated to this valorization flow.

The "supply chain"[9] owns both the "inputs" (raw materials, packaging, etc.) made available to the IC and its "outputs" (the goods produced). The ICs are reduced to a status of "façonnier" or bespoke manufacturer, a service of supplying custom-made goods (only their turnover[10] is attributed to them) that produce material use-values, which are made available to the "supply chain" that owns them. In *accounting terms*, the ICs no longer appear as the place where "wealth" is created (and that is, precisely, the aim of the new organization). Furthermore, their spatial inscription appears deterritorialized – except for the use of the labor force!

The "supply chain" (SC) sells the goods (produced by the ICs) to the MNF's different commercial companies (CCs) in each European national space at "cost plus" (full costs = raw material and other costs + supply costs + ICs' controllable costs[11]).

The commercial company, which markets the goods coming from the "supply chain," pays back to it a part of its operating profit (EBIT) made with the mass-market retail sector: profit split at x% of this (25/50%), its legitimation being the coverage of risks. In appearance, it is the "market" that creates the "value," and this, too, is one of the new organization's objectives, independently of the transfer of a large part of the creation of wealth to a tax haven.

To do this, the MNF mobilizes two different types of accounting for the creation of wealth:

- traditional social accounting (tax returns) to pay the corresponding tax and where the creation of wealth has already partly disappeared,[12] and
- confidential accounting called P&L,[13] which traces the creation of value (it does have to be measured) so as to share it in a "profit split."

And the model is spreading to both the so-called developed countries and to emerging countries.

This supply chain, according to the Marxist theory of value and prices,[14] is structured as follows according to the differentiation of its main vectors:

- the production process under the regime of labor-value (creation of wealth);
- the course of production and circulation under the regime of use-value;
- the course of the commodities' materialization (overall process) under the regime of market prices.

In the liberal economic theory, the supply chain, as an institution and an organization, borrows its rationale and ideological foundations from both the value chain of Michael Porter (1999) and the theory of agency of Michael Jensen and William Meckling (1976)[15]; in accordance with the agency theory, the supply chain is referred to as the "principal" that

- ensures the governance of the "agents" (i.e., the industrial and commercial firms in both France and Europe with a contractual link to the "supply chain"), and
- bears the "risks" (?) (legitimization of the "profit split").

Moreover, the focus on "global value chains" (GVCs) – a different concept to that of "supply chain" – has the merit of targeting the fragmentation of the world production of goods, especially regarding intermediate goods, a fragmentation that, on the contrary, encourage the various international institutions (IMF, OECD, World Bank, WTO) to further liberalize the world economy, the anticipated weight of the GVCs in world exports standing at 60% in 2030 according to WTO forecasts.

- The third "arrangement" of the years 2010–2020 when the "brand" asset and the "supply chain" mutually reinforce each other in the levying of wealth: the model called "limited risk distributor" (LRD) (see Fig. 3):

Here, the operating and commercial company (OC) is limited to the function of a distributor with limited liability. This means that the remuneration of the work of commercializing and marketing the "branded" products will be done through the payment of a margin fixed at x% (between 2% and 5%) of the turnover (triple net) realized by the OC's "brands." If the OC thus remunerates the "brands" it distributes, brands that are "housed" in a tax haven, the IC is also often asked to pay a fee linked to the brands' maintenance (there is no stopping the MNFs' unbridled imagination to pay their shareholders and boost their share price).

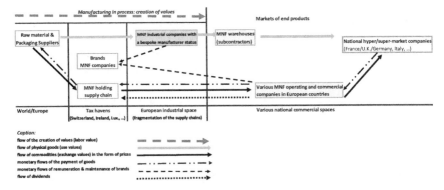

Fig. 3.   Third Institutional and Organizational Arrangement – The Rise of the Intangible Assets "Brands."

On the one hand, the new LRD model does not change anything in the upstream supply chain at "cost plus," but it does change the downstream wealth creation chain, where the operating company is emptied of its previous apparent creation of wealth (profit split) by the "market": it is the "brand" that takes precedence over the other institutions, and that creates wealth! And the "brand" is obviously domiciled in a tax haven, where it is paid for the creation of the wealth that is supposedly associated with it.

The MNFs' assets are now focused on intangible assets (brands, patents, licenses, etc.) which are at the center of the MNFs' preoccupation with governance in view of the "goodwill" or "badwill" that affects the valuation of these intangible assets on their balance sheets, in particular due to the evolution of their share prices on stock markets.

Within the supply chain, the disconnection between, on the one hand, the materiality of the flow of physical goods as use values resulting from the manufacturing processes within the ICs and, on the other hand, the flow of commodities invoiced in market-price and transfer-price systems becomes more pronounced.

- *Over the course of arrangements 2 and 3, the MNFs delocalize and break up the operating companies' support functions* (accounts receivable and payable, human resources, supplies, IT, etc.) *to low-wage countries, as well as the industrial companies* (see Fig. 4):

Once the industrial companies have been stripped of their support functions, it is the turn of operating companies to be partially stripped of their support functions, relocated to Eastern European countries (accounts receivable and accounts payable, payroll and other human resource services, supply chain management, etc.) or to Asia (information technology, etc.). Similarly, the MNFs delocalize the industrial companies of their supply chain to low-wage countries. For example, Unilever Group, which had more than 10 industrial companies in France in the 2000s, has only three left today, after relocating massively to

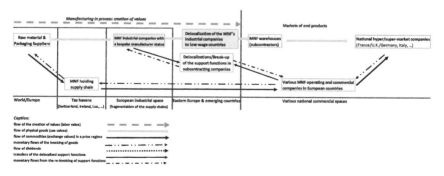

Fig. 4. Delocalization of Support Functions and of Industrial Companies in the Context of Arrangements 2 and 3.

Eastern European countries. And the same is true for a number of multinational firms in the agri-food and chemical industries.

In terms of jobs, the importance of the support functions' delocalizations is just as great as that of the industrial delocalizations.

Multinational Firms' Increasingly Important Place in World Economic Activity

Based on the ratio between the combined turnover of the multinational firms' sales and world GDP, which fell from 35.6% in 2010 to 34.8% in 2015, the internationalization of production has since tended to increase, reaching 35.8% in 2019 (no UNCTAD data are available for 2020 and 2021). At the same time, there is a slight slowdown in GDP growth, from 3.3% per year over the period 2010–2015 to an average of 3.2% in the years 2015–2020.

A similar trend can be observed in the weight of the MNFs' added value in world GDP, which declines from 9.0% in 2010 to 8.0% in 2015 and rebounds to 9.2% in 2019 (no UNCTAD data are available for 2020 and 2021) (Fig. 5).

Employment by MNFs rose from 63.0 million people in 2010 to 69.5 million in 2015 (+2.0% per year) and 82.4 million in 2019 (+4.3% per year) (no UNCTAD data are available for 2020 and 2021).

However, during the pandemic, we note a sharp contraction of foreign direct investment (FDI) inflows from USD 1,480 billion in 2019 to USD 963 billion in 2020 (−34.9%), and this especially in developed economies, where it fell from USD 764 billion to USD 319 billion (−58.2%), while the amount of FDI to developing economies remained relatively unchanged at USD 645 billion (−9.9%), i.e., an amount higher than that of the developed economies (increasing FDI to Asia).

According to consulting company Trendeo, the drop in world investments in 2020 and 2021 stood at around 43% (Fig. 6).[16]

The MNFs' cross-border merger and acquisition operations do not slow down during the COVID-19 health crisis, their amount declining only slightly, from USD 491 billions in 2019 to USD 475 billions in 2020 (−3.3%), while the amount corresponding to new (greenfield) investments in 2020 and 2021 is not available (Fig. 7).

Multinational Firms and the Predation of Wealth: The Growing Revenues of Multinationals via Tax Havens[17]

Gérard De Bernis (1978) conducted a critical analysis of the impact of trans-national firms on economic activity that remains highly relevant to this day, including:

- "the unification of techniques within branches," which replaces old techniques (and technologies) with new ones, leads to a dislocation of the national inter-industry matrix;

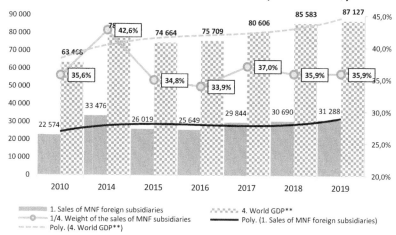

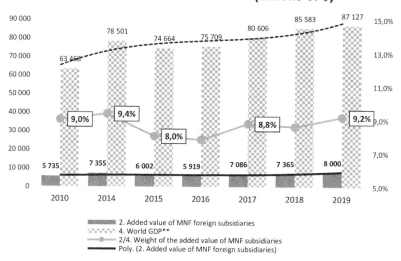

Fig. 5. Internationalization of Production. *Source:* UNCTAD (various years).

- "the branches' internationalization" calls into question the autonomy of the autonomous national accumulation, with cumulative international inequalities of development;

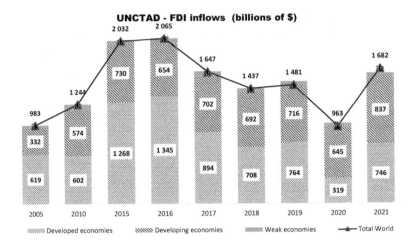

UNCTAD - FDI inflows (billions of $)

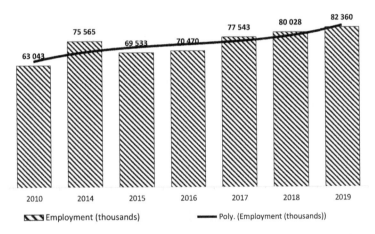

Employment by MNFs (in thousands)

Fig. 6. Inflows of FDI & Employment by MNFs. *Source:* UNCTAD (various years).

- "the transnationalization of capital" modifies here and there the conditions of income distribution, and allows us to denounce the practice of price transfer that introduces a break between the place where the surplus value is created and the place where the profits are paid out;
- the intervention of the MNFs in the various national spaces modifies the usual economic rules and behaviors within the framework of national economic processes,
- all of which leads to rising unemployment.

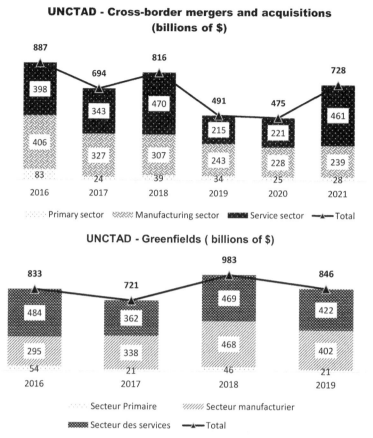

Fig. 7. Cross-Border Mergers and Acquisitions and New Investment Projects. *Source:* UNCTAD (various years).

Today, FDI revenues via tax havens tend to be on the rise. A NBER study on profit transfers[18] estimates that 40% of multinationals' profits are transferred to tax havens each year, i.e., USD 900 billion (or € 765 billion), resulting in a loss of USD 200 billion (or € 170 billion) in corporate tax revenues in 2018, or 10% of their income; and this with two characteristics:

- profits are for the greater part generated by the intangible rather than the tangible assets;
- the US is the main winner and the EU the main loser.

According to the example cited for Spain, this country loses 13% of its corporate tax revenues, i.e., USD 3.72 billion of tax revenues on USD 14.9 billion of profits transferred to tax havens.

In the case of France, the undeclared profits of USD 46.7 billion (€ 39.7 billion) represent a shortfall of USD 15.4 billion (€ 13.1 billion) in corporate taxes per year.[19]

Moreover, the profits of MNFs differ between tax havens and non-tax havens:

- in tax havens, foreign companies are distinctly more profitable than local firms;
- in the other countries, foreign firms are less profitable than local companies.

Admittedly, in July 2021, 132 countries agreed to a minimum tax rate of at least 15% on the profits of their MNFs – in the face of a 25% tax requested by NGOs –; however, in the light of the transfer prices according to the supply chains, there is still a long way to go to obtain these multinationals' P&L sheets before profit transfers.

We should also note that, during the current slowdown of world GDP growth, and especially of emerging countries' GDP, during the current development of income inequalities, shareholders' incomes are doing well given that world dividends should exceed USD 2,000 billion in 2022,[20] a sum above their pre-COVID-19 pandemic crisis level.

A Specific Reinforced Organization of the MNF During the 2020–2021 Public Health Crisis

In France, the public health crisis provided MNFs with opportunities to improve their EBIT rate. Far from reviewing their organizational model, MNFs further strengthened it by generalizing the supply chains and the "brands" model in accordance with the three vectors designated in the previous point, and this with announcements of site closures or restructuring to improve the course of the valuation of their balance-sheet assets.

A first way is to manipulate the first vector of the upstream supply chain by closing down or selling the industrial companies whose production costs are deemed too high compared to the expected performance of the "principal:"

- the Unilever Group sold the Saint-Vulbas site (cleaning products) to the Spanish group Persán in 2020, and announced in 2021 the closure of its site at Duppigheim (dehydrated soup and liquid soup)[21];
- the Dutch group Refresco (fruit juices) announced the closure of the Château-Thébaud site in 2021[22];
- the German group HeidelbergCement (with its French subsidiary Ciments Calcia) shut down the cement plant at Cruas and restructured that of Gargenville in France in 2021[23];
- the Cargill group stopped the upstream activity (wet-starch plant) of the Haubourdin site in 2020 (over 150 layoffs)...[24]

A second way is to manipulate all or some of the vectors of retroceding profit to the "principal" of both the "brands" and the "supply chain:"

- the General Mills group sold back to the French dairy cooperative Sodiaal Union its stake in Yoplait France in 2021, due to a profitability considered insufficient;
- the Heineken group, in 2021, laid off a number of employees of its Food-Away-From-Home sales force (cafés/restaurants/hotels) and its headquarter support functions;
- the Danone group, after the ousting of its chairman and CEO Emmanuel Faber in 2021, is questioned by its shareholders about the profitability of its "water" and "ultra-fresh" assets.

At the same time, after the decline observed in 2020 to € 28.6 billion (−42%), the amount distributed as dividends by the French CAC 40 companies recovered sharply in 2021: the amount to be distributed was announced as standing at € 41 billion (+44%),[25] thus expunging the decline observed in 2020 as a result of the public health crisis.

The focus on GVCs during the public health crisis[26] highlights the supply risks associated with them, namely breakdowns, and in particular regarding pharmaceutical and medical goods. Can we talk then of de-globalization?

In brief, during the public health crisis, MNFs appear to be little affected in their activities by relying on the organization of their supply chains (well beyond the "Global Value Chains"). On the contrary, they seize the opportunities that the difficulties of globalization offer them – which, in their view, justify their site closures, restructuring and divestments/acquisitions – to increase their profitability, distribute more dividends and improve the course of the valuation of their assets.

Multinational Firms and the Surge in Share Prices on Financial Markets

The graph below (Fig. 8), taken from R.J. Shiller (2000), with updated data on his website through to 2013, regarding the parallel evolutions of the share price of large firms on the US financial markets and of the price of dividends distributed by large firms on these same stock markets underlines their disconnection with the surge in share prices: it is the share price (in relation to the intangible assets of "brands") that matters and which soars. It is clear that updated data through to 2021 would further accentuate the disconnection, with a strong progression of both share prices and dividends, in a context of growing social inequality.

The issuance of credit money by the central banks, and which is followed by the banking systems here and there, no longer contributes to financing the expansion of tangible assets and the creation of wealth but, rather, feeds the MNFs' speculative practices by supporting the price of shares pledged on fictitious assets, the "brands." The financial activity is in turn disconnected from the productive economy, with the risks of crises that ensue.

To conclude this first part: are multinational groups' "national" subsidiaries still "companies" in the traditional sense of the term, i.e., with an entrepreneurial capacity?

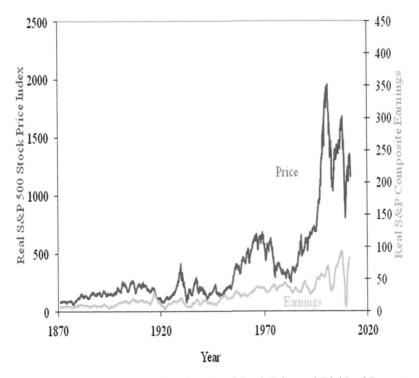

Fig. 8.   Evolution of the Deflated Index of Stock Price and Dividend Present
Value on US Stock Markets (1870–2013). *Source:* Shiller (2000). Updated data on his
website through to 2013.

Apparently not, because these subsidiaries do nothing more than apply the
strategies (sales and marketing, industrial, financial) defined by the multinational
group. For instance, a US group, which had acquired a French sub-group producing ultra-fresh dairy products as a joint-venture, resold this stake despite the
sub-group's turnaround over recent financial years, the grounds being that the
brand of its ultra-fresh dairy products did not have an audience that the US
group could develop at a global level. Yet it is the second largest group worldwide
in ultra-fresh dairy products in terms of turnover.

And even for liberal authors, these multinational groups are no longer firms in
the sense of oligopolistic competition itself: for Teppar and Hearn (2019), duly
referring to the fundamentals of liberal economics, these groups have dispensed
with the obligation of "competition" seen as being at the heart of the functioning
of capitalism; in the case of the United States, the authors indicate that, in terms
of market share in different branches, the four largest firms have a concentration
rate ranging between 70% and 95%.[27]

Even more: in view of the disconnection within the supply chain between, on
the one hand, the flow of invoiced goods associated with the remuneration of

assets including "brands" (transfer prices) and, on the other, the flow of production both in labor-value and in use-value, in view also of the disconnection between the share prices on the stock markets and the course of the distribution of dividends (which reflects more or less the evolution of the so-called real economy), *the MNFs disconnect the economy's price from its reality*, with the risks of crises that accompany this global disconnection.

THE CONTRIBUTIONS OF THE THEORY OF MULTINATIONAL FIRMS ACCORDING TO THE MARXIST APPROACH

• A recent theory of multinational firms confined to mainstream economics?

Rainelli (2003) maintains that multinational firms have long been a blind spot in international trade theory, for a number of reasons related to the hypotheses of mainstream economics concerning the construction of an international equilibrium linked to the non-mobility of the factors of production[28]: thus immobility of factors, no MNFs possible. It was not until the 1970s and 1980s that some hypotheses of mainstream economics (monopolistic competition, internalization of transaction costs, etc.) were lifted and, as a result, an efflorescence of theoretical analyses of international firms appeared, which, to a lesser or greater extent, strayed away from mainstream economics.

These remarks by Rainelli disregard the contributions of the Marxist theory, a lack all the more glaring since the latter preceded them with a number of superbly ignored contributions, and especially since this theory comprises a critical dimension that is absent from the mainstream theory and the other renewed approaches.

• Avowedly renewed approaches to the multinational firm (within both mainstream and heterodox economics)

Among the other approaches marking the course of the theory of MNFs, the theorization moves away somewhat from mainstream economics, notably in the cases of Stephen Hymer (1960, 1968, 1970) and Charles-Albert Michalet (1976, 2002, 2007), in our eyes the two most rigorous and innovative proponents of the renewed approach to the multinational firm who draw on the contributions outlined above by Rainelli: contributions inherited from J.S. Bain's theory of "barriers" (1956), from E.H. Chamberlin's theory of "monopolistic competition" (1933) and that of J. Robinson (1933), from R.H. Coase's theory of transaction costs (1937)... except that many of these contributions are found in Marxist theory long before those of the authors mentioned.

• Contributions toward a Marxist theory of multinational firms

Rudolf Hilferding (1910) would be the first to approach in a new way – unfortunately all too often ignored – the analysis of monopolies, and hence of multinational firms and imperialism.

It is worth recalling that the 1960s and 1970s brought about a renewal of Marxist theory centered on globalization (Samir Amin, Andre Gunder Frank, Giovanni Arrighi, Christian Palloix, etc.), and hence on multinational firms in terms of the internationalization of capital, based on Marx's cycle of capital and on a number of R. Hilferding's contributions.

Furthermore, it should be noted that the previous presentation of MNFs' practices was based on the fundamentals of Marxism in terms of labor-value, use-value, and market price.

Hilferding's Surprising and Little-Known Contributions to a Theory of Monopolies and by Extension of Multinational Firms[29]

Hilferding (1910) developed a theory of monopolies – and hence of multinational firms – based on an analysis of the restrictions/barriers to entry (long before J.S. Bain, 1956) and oligopolistic competition (well before Chamberlin, 1933; & Robinson, 1933), these famous contributions that supposedly allowed the approaches' renewal that Rainelli talks about (including Hymer and the Reading School with J. Dunning).

Admittedly, it should be said that a number of the Marxist foundations of Hilferding's analysis (value, price, money, capital...)[30] in his 1910 book diverge noticeably from Marx's analysis in the form of a depleting legacy based more on Books 1 and 2 of *Capital* and with an almost absolute lack of references to Book 3, and whose main weaknesses are:

- the return to a Ricardian conception of labor-value, reduced to a quantum of social labor that is self-declared and incorporated into the commodity,
- a seamless crossing from labor-value to price of production, while at the same time referring to the three laws of capitalism (tendency toward the maximization of the rate of profit, tendency toward an equalization of the rate of profit, tendency of the rate of profit to fall),
- a curtailment of the theory of prices to that of prices of production by ignoring the formation of market prices,
- a reductive use of the capital cycle, of its functional forms and of the fractions of capital, by giving priority to the cycle of money capital M-C-M'.

And yet Hilferding innovates by showcasing the irresistible march of monopolies, for which he delivers new foundations of analysis by introducing new analytical tools: barriers to entry, oligopolistic competition, tendency to a differentiation of the rates of profit, credit money as a money specific to capitalism.

Hilferding's contributions are as follows:

(1) The monopolies' irresistible march forward: an (erroneous?) history of the economic facts on the concentration and centralization of capital:

  ⸰ The core of Hilferding's book is full of empirical observations and statistical data on the concentration and centralization of bank capital and industrial capital. The movement of the monopolies' formation, of their generalization and of their power appears as a tidal wave of great magnitude emanating from the European nations and the United States, to which nothing resists and which is self-evident, without any critical reading.

  The excess of Hilferding's thesis, which is somewhat disputed by historians of economic facts, is nonetheless the lever of a new representation of capitalism.

(2) Toward an analysis of monopolistic competition (before J. Robinson and E.H. Chamberlin):

  The joint-stock company brings about a separation between the capital's ownership and the use of this capital (valorization, accumulation) and develops a superior institutional and organizational form in terms of the "assets" efficiency. We encounter here the forerunners of both:

  – the distinction between the power of shareholders and the power of managers, as developed much later by A.D. Chandler (1977);
  – the analysis of property rights by the "New Institutionalist School."

The analysis developed by Hilferding on cartels and trusts essentially focuses on highlighting a very strong increase of the value of the assets invested in the form of productive capital, of the extent of the invested capital's mobilization, which necessarily refers to an increase in the organic composition of capital with its risks in view of the tendency of the rate of profit to fall (TRPF).[31]

The probing of the organization of cartels and leads our author to make them the new instruments of a capitalist planning, which supplants the unconscious regulation by the market:

> The whole of capitalist production would then be consciously regulated by a single body [the cartelization, C.P.] which would determine the volume of production in all branches of industry. Price determination would become a purely nominal matter, involving only the distribution of the total product (...) Money would have no role. In fact, it could well disappear completely, since the task to be accomplished would be the allocation of things, not the distribution of values.[32]

(3) A new approach to credit money as a new mode of financing productive capital due to the scale of capital mobilization

  Hilferding abandons the limited viewpoint previously reserved to credit money to make of it the new generalized mode of financing capitalist production:

> We have seen earlier how credit money originates in circulation. (...) As capitalist credit, however, it puts money [whether cash or credit money, C.P.] into circulation only in order to withdraw more money. It puts money into circulation as money capital in order to convert it into productive capital. Thus it expands the scale of production, and this expansion

presupposes the expansion of circulation (...). Capital (investment) credit (...) transfers money
and converts it from idle into active money capital.[33]

The transformations deriving from a credit money hitherto tagging behind
the dynamics of capitalism are now ripe to bring forth a credit money that
ensures, leads the dynamics of capitalism, but it is necessary to go through a
new law in the making, the tendency to a differentiation of the rates of profit
(TDRP).

(4) The new dynamics of capitalism: the tendency to a differentiation of the rates
of profit[34] between the monopoly sector and the competitive sector, due to
industrial barriers:

Hilferding turns here to the behaviors of the monopolies' private agents, in
search of maximum profit rate (MPR) in the context of an irreducible fixation
of an ever-increasing invested fixed capital, i.e., in the context of the TRPF:

Thus we see how, for entirely different reasons, the rate of profit tends to be depressed below the
average at both poles [monopolies and competition, C.P.] of capitalist development. Where
capital is sufficiently powerful a counter tendency emerges in order to overcome this trend. The
final outcome is the abolition of free competition, and a trend towards the maintenance of a
lasting inequality of rates of profit...[35]

with some stylistic precautions about the return to the tendency toward
equality of profit (TTEP).

This new law of TDRP is based on the existence of *barriers* to the mobility of
capital – a theory of barriers developed before that of Bain (1956). The
industrial system is therefore divided into branches, with (commercial and
technical) barriers[36] that appear as obstacles to the TTEP:

In place of the old legal restrictions imposed by medieval tutelage, new economic restrictions
have emerged (...). A second limitation consists in the fact that technical progress expands the
scale of production, and that the increasing volume of constant capital, especially fixed capital,
requires an ever-greater absolute sum of capital in order to expand production itself on a
corresponding scale or to establish new enterprises.[37]

but barriers that are immediately reintroduced as a means of returning to the
TTEP as a stylistic precaution:

Since the tendency toward equality of profit is identical with the striving of the individual
capitalist to maximize his profit, the removal of this limitation must also begin with the
individual. This occurs through the mobilization of capital.[38]

The way is open for credit money to be the one to ensure both the maintenance of technical and commercial barriers and the removal of these barriers,
while producing new ones, i.e.: financial barriers.

Hilferding persists and signs about the TDRP, which also stems from the way
that the cartel firms set prices:

Cartelization involves a change in the average rate of profit. The rate of profit rises in the
cartelized industries and falls in the non-cartelized ones (...). For those industries which remain
non-cartelized the rate of profit continues to fall. The cartel price will rise by the same amount
above the price of production as it has fallen below the price of production in the non-cartelized

industries (…). Thus the increase in the cartel price is limited by the extent to which it is possible to reduce the rate of profit in the non-cartelized industries.[39]

always with this viewpoint, which is theoretically fixed on the transfers of profit (here in the form of excess profit of some to the detriment of the others) in the context of the fixing of the production prices within the industrial system's branches, with a mode of setting prices by the cartel's industries (companies).

Lastly, we believe it is needful to recognize Hilferding's authorship of the theory of barriers in industrial economics.

(5) Credit money as a dynamic of the new regime of accumulation based on the TDRP:

A new derivation of credit money emerges as the money supply of finance capital (and not only of bank capital) that ensures, on the one hand, the financing of the monopoly sector on the basis of a regime of accumulation that rests on the TDRP and, on the other one, the export of capital as a return to the TTEP.

Credit money therefore acquires a new status, as the money – and the supply of money (De Brunhoff, 1971, 1973, 1979) – peculiar to capitalism for the financing of the monopoly sector, while simultaneously subjecting the monopolistic industrial sector to… finance capital:

…present-day industry is carried on with an amount of capital far exceeding that which is owned by the industrial capitalists. With the development of capitalism there is also a continual increase in the amount of money which the non-productive classes place at the disposal of the banks, who in turn convey it to the industrialists. … [W]ith the development of capitalism and of the machinery of credit, the dependence of industry upon the banks increases.[40]

It is up to credit money to ensure an exit from the impasse in which the competitive sector with a lower rate of profit finds itself, by financing the export of capital[41]: removal of the exit barriers for the competitive sector's capital.

(6) Finance capital,[42] a new fraction of capital?

Let us leave to Hilferding the responsibility of defining it (repeated in an even more linear way by Lenin, 1916):

I call bank capital, that is, capital in money form which is actually transformed in this way into industrial capital, finance capital (…). An ever-increasing proportion of the capital used in industry is finance capital, capital at the disposition of the banks which is used by the industrialists.[43]

Finance capital is the *moment* when bank capital also becomes industrial capital during the functional cycle of capital, which throughout the conceptual chain is only notional capital. Can we make of it, in Hilferding's mind, a new fraction of capital,[44] which sits alongside and dominates the other fractions of capital (bank, commercial, industrial) as Lenin would later do?

A Theory of the Multinational Firm Correlated to the Analysis of Marx's Cycle of
Social Capital and to Globalization

The Marxist analysis of the multinational firm in the 1960s–1980s was carried out jointly to the analysis of the worldwide expansions of capitalism and imperialism.[45]

In the 1970s, along with a number of other authors (e.g., Aglietta, 1974; Poulantzas, 1973...), I used Marx's cycle of social capital to describe a process of internationalization – corresponding to successive phases of market globalization, industrial globalization, and financial globalization – out of which emerged the fractions of capital that the MNFs represent during industrial globalization first and then during financial globalization (Palloix, 1973, 1975) (Fig. 9).

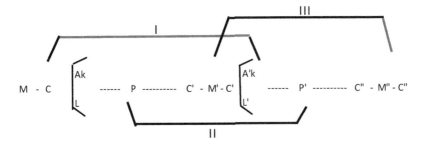

Fig. 9.   The Cycle of Social Capital and the Phases of Globalization.

The symbols used are:

M: money, where $M' > M$;
C: commodity, where $C' > C$;
Ak: capital advance, where $A'k > Ak$;
L: work advance (labor power), where $L' > L$;
P: production process, where $P' > P$.

Therefore, we can distinguish three cycles of social capital that combine in the course of these globalizations:

I. – the cycle of commodity-capital – trade globalization
II. – the cycle of productive capital – industrial globalization
III. – the cycle of money-capital – financial globalization.

As an example, we can inscribe as follows the Smithian and Ricardian theories of foreign trade in the world cycle of commodity-capital (Palloix, 1973), recalling Ricardo's oft-ignored statement (Fig. 10):

> Foreign trade, then, (...) has no tendency to raise the profits of stock, unless the commodities imported be of that description on which the wages of labour are expended [English original].[46]

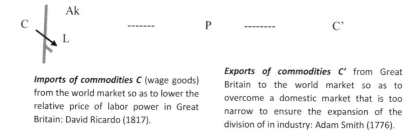

Imports of commodities C (wage goods) from the world market so as to lower the relative price of labor power in Great Britain: David Ricardo (1817).

Exports of commodities C' from Great Britain to the world market so as to overcome a domestic market that is too narrow to ensure the expansion of the division of in industry: Adam Smith (1776).

Fig. 10.   Inserting the Smithian and Ricardian Theories of Foreign Trade in the World Cycle of Commodity-Capital.

Each type of globalization – furthermore differentiated in the world space – does not erase the previous one: industrial globalization feeds on market globalization; financial globalization today relies on trade globalization and industrial globalization, which are renewed by it.

New Elements for a Marxist Analysis of the Multinational Firm

In spite of the underestimation in terms of barriers (technological, industrial, commercial, etc.) or of oligopolistic competition at the time of Hilferding's contributions, later Marxist research in industrial economics used the elements available to advance an analysis of the firms' engagement in terms of producer competition and capital competition (Borrely, 1975; Palloix, 1977, p. 51, 1978).

The capital advances Ak engaged in cycles I, II and III represent the segmented fractions of individual capital ventures – which is what the multinational firms are – during their process of valorization and accumulation according to both the different branches and the different countries in which they are involved.

The engagement of the MNFs' capital Ak, at market prices, is carried out:

• in the form of intangible assets (brands, patents, licenses, goodwill, etc.);
• in the form of tangible assets (factory, supply chain, etc.);
• in the form of financial assets.

This engagement of Ak is carried out in relation to the establishment of commercial and marketing barriers (differentiation and innovations of products, brands, patents, and licenses), of industrial barriers (differentiation of required technologies and according to the innovations in progress), of financial barriers within each internationalized branch (producer competition) and from internationalized branch to internationalized branch (capital competition), that is to say, an inscription of the international firm in an international industrial economy.[47]

The multinational firms present any product innovation as a unique product inserted in a new protected branch (with its new barriers), as can be seen below

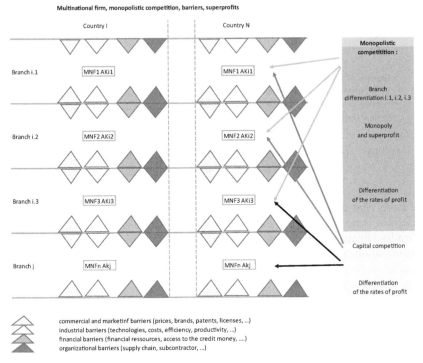

Fig. 11.   Multinational Firm and International Industrial Economy.

(Fig. 11): a monopoly price allowing it to escape price competition, and thus increase the rate of profit. Each MNF of the branch *i* will present its product as a product both unique and different from all the others of branch *i*, contributing to build barriers between the sub-branches *i*1, *i*2, . . ., *i*n.

The forms of intra-branch competition, called producer competition, are to some extent limited to the competition of national producers in their so-called national branches, provided these have escaped the grip of MNFs.

Besides, in monopolistic competition and the competition among the different kinds of capital, this engagement of Ak is linked according to the branches and the country to a labor force L, whose price and skills differ from country to country.

CONCLUSION

The contributions of the Marxist theory on the multinational firm have nothing to hide from the contributions of the authors claiming to adhere to those of Bain, Coase, and the theory of monopolistic competition with imperfect information;

quite the contrary, especially since the Marxist contributions are accompanied by a critical reflection on multinational firms' negative impacts on economic activity.

This paper has presented: a critical analysis of the wealth current practices of multinational firms as wealth predators; and relevant references from the theory of multinational corporations and globalization from a Marxist perspective.

The practices of multinational corporations show an evolution of their "supply chain" arrangements (not to be confused with "global value chain") with new features that have been developing over the period 1990–2022, with a particular a disconnection between, on the one hand, the value of manufactured goods and, on the other hand, the valorization of commodities, which has led to massive transfers of wealth through the supply chain, ending up in tax havens. This new model changes the downstream wealth creation chain, where the nationally operating company (subsidiary company) is emptied of its previous apparent creation of wealth (profit split) by the "market:" it is the "brand" that takes precedence over the other actors, and it is the "brand" that creates wealth! And the "brand" appears to be domiciled in a tax haven, where it is paid for the creation of the wealth that it is supposedly associated with. The multinational corporations' assets are now focused on intangible assets (brands, patents, licenses, etc.) which are at the center of the multinational corporations' governance concerns with the "goodwill" or "badwill" that affects the valuation of these intangible assets on their balance sheets.

Among the approaches marking the course of the theory of multinational corporations, the theorization moves away somewhat from mainstream economics, notably in the cases of Hymer and Michalet, who draw on the contributions inherited from Bain's theory of "barriers", from Chamberlin's theory of "monopolistic competition" and that of Robinson, from Coase's theory of transaction costs – except that many of these contributions are found in Marxist theory long before those of the authors mentioned. Hilferding was the first to approach in a new way (unfortunately all too often ignored) the analysis of monopolies, and hence of multinational corporations and imperialism.

The Marxist approach has also contributed to a theory of the self-expansion of capital (internationalization of the circuits of capital) on a global scale, within an analysis of the differentiation and of inequality.

NOTES

1. See also the joint research on multinational firms carried out with my colleague Lyazid Kichou: Kichou and Palloix (2003, 2016).

2. For the sake of convenience, we adopt here an institutionalist approach to designate the practices of multinational firms based on North's (1990) distinction between the rules of the game that define the institutions and the players that represent the organizations. The institutional arrangement defines the rules of the firm, of the MNF (property rights, wage rules, commercial rules...), whereas the organizational arrangement defines the "government" (commercial, industrial, financial...) of the firm, of the MNF.

3. These arrangements are found at General Mills/Yoplait, Unilever, Kraft/Mondelez, Continental Foods, Cargill, Carlsberg, ... and copy, in their own ways, the arrangements developed in a more sophisticated way (no factories of their own, but instead

subcontracting factories) by Apple, Nike, and others. But the same is true, for example, albeit in less sophisticated forms, in the automobile industry (Renault and other operators).

4. Today, the multinational firm often takes on the form of a conglomerate group – holder of a basket of so-called "global brands" – therefore encompassing several sectors of activity (ranging, for instance, from chemicals to the agri-food industry), and also covering several branches within a sector (for example, within the agri-food industry, branches such as water, ice cream, chocolate, etc.).

5. The multinational firm's global space is divided into regions (also called "clusters"): North America, Latin America, Europe, Asia, Africa, sometimes with groupings of the type "Europe-Asia," etc.

6. The operating company will gradually lose its support functions during the subsequent arrangements, from then on being reduced to a commercial company.

7. Cost plus: full costs (raw material costs + controllable costs + supply costs) + residual rate of remuneration (as a percentage of full costs).

8. It was left to the OECD to draw up a manual on the proper conduct of cost plus and split profit transfer pricing.

9. The "supply chain" is a distinct concept from the "global value chain" found in the analyses of UNCTAD, the OECD, the IMF and others.

10. A turnover that essentially concerns the payment of the cost of the employees, and also the costs of energy, site maintenance, etc., and which covers the cost of supplying the bespoke manufacturing services (in the form of what, in analytical accounting, are called controllable costs), a cost guaranteed and taken over by the supply chain in the calculation of its costs.

11. The conversion costs (CC) or controllable costs are the industrial company's own internal costs (excluding the costs of raw materials, packaging, etc.) with: CC = variable costs (operating personnel + energy + other variable costs) + fixed costs (maintenance personnel + maintenance + other fixed costs) + depreciation costs.

12. The concept of value loses all meaning as regards the creation of wealth, firstly since the latter, as far as the ICs are concerned, has flown to the CC (the pseudo added value, here, only depends on the mark-up rate allocated as a percentage of the IC's "costs plus" between 2% and 5% in order to best achieve the legal obligations toward employees in terms of participation and profit sharing), and secondly as far as the OC is concerned since the added value has been levied via the transfer prices to the supply chain's holding company.

13. P&L: acronym of Profit and Loss. This Anglo-Saxon accounting internal to the firm, which is spreading rapidly, distinguishes on a consolidated basis (IC + CC + others costs) by brand, by sector of activity, and globally: the margin on variable costs, the margin on fixed costs, the margin after marketing and advertising costs, and EBITDA.

14. Benetti (1974) and Dostaler (1978a, 1978b).

15. The starting point of the agency theory: any exchange between agents, any relationship of any kind, can be analyzed as an exchange of property rights (C.P.). Moreover, the nature of the firm depends on a node of contracts (C.P). Definition of the agency relationship by Jensen and Meckling (1976):

> We define an agency relationship as a contract under which one or more persons (the principal(s)) engage another person (the agent) to perform some service on their behalf which involves delegating some decision making authority to the agent (p. 5).

16. See: *Usine Nouvelle* (French weekly business magazine), December 8, 2021.

17. On multinationals' income in tax havens, see: Nyman and Vicard (2018).

18. Tørsløv, Wier, and Zucman (2020).

19. ATTAC (Association for the Taxation of financial Transactions and Citizen's Action), October 2, 2021.

20. See: *Les Echos* (French financial daily), January 12, 2022.

21. *Les Echos*, April 14, 2021. The site of Saint-Vulbas is located near Lyon, France; and that of Duppigheim near Strasbourg, France.
22. *Usine Nouvelle*, April 6, 2021. The site of Château-Thébaud is located near Nantes, France.
23. *Usine Nouvelle*, November 28, 2020. The site of Cruas is located between Montélimar and Valence in France, and that of Gargenville near Paris.
24. *Le Monde* (French daily newspaper), August 18, 2020. The site of Haubourdin is located near Lille, France.
25. *Le Revenu* (French weekly business magazine), March 19, 2021.
26. OECD (2021).
27. Teppar and Hearn (2019, p. 33).
28. Rainelli (2003, p. 17).
29. Palloix (2006).
30. On the Marxist value-price discussion, renewed in the 1970s and 1980s: Benetti (1974) and Dostaler (1978a, 1978b). On the Marxist discussion about money: De Brunhoff (1967, 1971, 1979).
31. Hilferding (1970/1910, p. 265) *et seq.*
32. *Idem*, p. 329. The author anticipates here the notion of fictitious price that would be used in the USSR's planning with the "objectively determined valuations" (ODV) of price determination by Kantorovitch.
33. Hilferding (1970/1910, p. 136).
34. We find the thesis of the TDRP in the writings of the SIFI group (Andreff, Deleplace, Gillard, Lespès, Sardais...) (1974), but in relation to the emergence of a sector of dual-purpose goods (capital goods and wage goods) that is juxtaposed to the traditional sectors of capital goods on the one hand and wage goods on the other.
35. Hilferding (1970/1910, p. 270).
36. Industrial economics tends to attribute the authorship of the theory of barriers (to entry, to exit) in both "producer competition" and "capital competition" to J.S. Bain (1956). *Cf.*, for instance, Borrely (1975) andArena et al. (1988).
37. Hilferding (1970/1910, p. 265).
38. *Idem*, p. 266.
39. *Idem*, pp. 324–325.
40. *Idem*, p. 317.
41. *Idem*, p. 328.
42. As De Brunhoff (1979, p. 41) points out, the concept of "finance capital is formulated by Hilferding, who uses the expression *Finanzkapital* there where K. Marx uses that of *Geldhandlungskapital* or money-trade capital".
43. Hilferding (1970/1910, p. 318).
44. *Cf.* the critique developed by De Brunhoff (1973), who contrasts the concept of financial capital in Marx and Hilferding:

In *Capital*, Marx considers finance capital as a particular branch, distinct from industrial capital. The entire function of finance capital is located in the relation M-M′, i.e. in the management of the means of financing, without involving transformations that include the movement of commodities and the means of production according to the formula M-C-C′-M′. The place of finance capital is determined, then, at the intersection of two different relations, on the one hand, the technical dependence of this capital on industrial capital and, on the other, its relative autonomy, which means that, despite its functional character, finance capital remains out of step with industrial capital. The two relations intersect, but do not merge. (...) Whatever the subsequent historical modifications of the relations between the two types of capital, one should not confound their articulation in the mode of production in general, where one can distinguish production structures and financing structures, with the particular forms taken by this articulation at any particular stage of capitalism. Unfortunately, the synthetic notion of finance capital financier used by Hilferding comprises one such confusion. It confers a structural reach to what is only of transitory importance. It commingles different realms, that of the organization of the different structures within capitalism with that of the concrete, historically dated modalities of this organization. (Hilferding, 1970/1910, pp. 91–92)

45. Read here the analyses conducted at that time by Samir Amin, Giovanni Arrighi, Andre Gunder Frank, Christian Palloix....
46. Ricardo (2001/1817, p. 89).
47. Dearly wished by Rainelli (1991).

REFERENCES

Aglietta, M. (1974). *Les Principaux traits contemporains de l'internationalisation du capital.* Paris: INSEE (Institut National de la Statistique et des Études économiques) *mimeo.*

Arena, R., Benzoni, L., De Bandt, J., & Romani, L. (1988). *Traité d'économie industrielle.* Paris: Economica.

Bain, J. S. (1956). *Barriers to new competition.* Cambridge, MA: Harvard University Press.

Benetti, C. (1974). *Valeur et répartition.* Paris: Grenobre: François Maspéro and Presses Universitaires de Grenoble.

Borrely, R. (1975). *Les Disparités sectorielles des taux de profit.* Grenoble: Presses Universitaires de Grenoble.

Chamberlin, E. H. (1953/1933). *Théorie de la concurrence monopolistique.* Paris: Presses Universitaires de France.

Chandler, A. D. (1977). *The visible hand: The managerial revolution in American business.* Cambridge, MA: Harvard University Press.

Coase, R. H. (1937). The nature of the firm. *Economica.* New Series, *IV*, 386–405.

De Bernis, G. (1978). Les Firmes transnationales et la crise. In X. Greffe & J. L. Reiffers (Eds.), *L'Occident en désarroi.* Paris: Dunod.

De Brunhoff, S. (1967). *La Monnaie chez Marx.* Paris: Éditions Sociales.

De Brunhoff, S. (1971). *L'Offre de monnaie: Critique d'un concept.* Paris: François Maspéro.

De Brunhoff, S. (1973). *La politique monétaire: Un essai d'interprétation marxiste.* Paris: Presses Universitaires de France.

De Brunhoff, S. (1979). *Les Rapports d'argent.* Paris/Grenoble: François Maspéro and Presses Universitaires de Grenoble.

Dostaler, G. (1978a). *Marx, la valeur et l'économie politique.* Paris: Anthropos.

Dostaler, G. (1978b). *Valeur et prix: Histoire d'un débat.* Paris/Grenoble: François Maspéro and Presses Universitaires de Grenoble.

Hilferding, R. (1970/1910). *Le Capital financier: Étude sur le développement récent du capitalisme.* Paris: Éditions de Minuit.

Hymer, S. (1960). *The international operations of national firms: A study of direct foreign investment.* Ph.D. dissertation, Cambridge, MA: Massachusetts Institute of Technology.

Hymer, S. (1968). La Grande "Corporation" multinationale: Analyse de certaines raisons qui poussent à l'intégration internationale des affaires. *Revue Économique, XIX*(6), 949–973.

Hymer, S. (1970). The efficiency (contradictions) of multinational corporations. *The American Economic Review, 60*(2), 441–448.

Jensen, M., & Meckling, W. (1976). Theory of the firm: Managerial behavior, agency costs and ownership structure. *Journal of Financial Economics, 3–4,* 305–360.

Kichou, L., & Palloix, C. (2003). Économie institutionnelle des groupes multinationaux de l'agroalimentaire en ce début de XXIe siècle. *Economie Appliquée, LVI*(1), 93–123.

Kichou, L., & Palloix, C. (2016). Gouvernance et gouvernements des firmes multinationales : Fondements théoriques et pratiques. In *Économie et Institutions.* Université d'Amiens, 7–9 December, p. 26.

Lenin, V. I. (1966/1916). *L'Impérialisme, stade suprême du capitalisme.* Paris: Éditions Sociales.

Michalet, C. A. (1976). *Le Capitalisme mondial.* Paris: Presses Universitaires de France.

Michalet, C. A. (2002). *Qu'est-ce que la mondialisation?* Paris: La Découverte.

Michalet, C. A. (2007). *Mondialisation, la grande rupture.* Paris: La Découverte.

North, D. C. (1990). *Institutional change and economic performance*. Cambridge: Cambridge University Press.

Nyman, L., & Vicard, V. (2018, September 14). Les Revenus des multinationales dans les paradis fiscaux. *Blog CEPII*.

OECD. (2021, February 11). *Global value chains: Efficiency and risks in the context of COVID-19*.

Palloix, C. (1973). *Les Firmes multinationales et le procès d'internationalisation*. Paris: François Maspéro.

Palloix, C. (1975). *L'Internationalisation du capital: Éléments critiques*. Paris: François Maspéro.

Palloix, C. (1977). *Procès de production et crise du capitalisme*. Paris: François Maspéro.

Palloix, C. (1978). *Travail et production*. Paris: François Maspéro.

Palloix, C. (2006). Monnaie de crédit et capital financier chez Hilferding. *Cahiers d'Economie Politique, 51*, 265–285.

Porter, M. (1999). *Choix stratégiques et concurrence: Techniques d'analyse des secteurs et de la concurrence dans l'industrie*. Paris: Economica.

Poulantzas, N. (1973). L'Internationalisation des rapports capitalistes et l'État-nation. *Les Temps Modernes, 319*, 1479–1485.

Rainelli, M. (1991). L'Économie industrielle internationale : Une discipline en construction. *Revue d'Économie Industrielle, 55*, 5–11.

Rainelli, M. (2003). *La Nouvelle Théorie du commerce international*. Paris: La Découverte.

Ricardo, D. (2001/1817). *On the principles of political economy and taxation*. Kitchener: Batoche Books.

Robinson, J. (1933). *The economics of imperfect competition*. London: Macmillan.

Shiller, R. J. (2000). *Exubérance irrationnelle*. Hendaye: Valor.

SIFI. (1974). Internationalisation du capital et processus productif: Une approche critique. *Cahiers d'Economie Politique, 1*, 9–121.

Teppar, J., & Hearn, D. (2019). *The myth of capitalism: Monopolies and the death of competition*. Hoboken, NJ: Wiley.

Tørsløv, L., Wier, L., & Zucman, G. (2020, April). *The missing profits of nations*. NBER Working Paper.

UNCTAD (various years). World Investment Report. Geneva.

TURNOVER TIME AND MARX'S DECOMPOSITION OF PROFIT ADJUSTMENT IN THE PROCESS OF EQUALIZATION

Guido De Marco

ABSTRACT

The welcomed introduction of Fred Moseley to a 27-page excerpt from Marx's Economic Manuscript of 1867–1868 *draws attention to the influence of turnover times on the formation of prices of production. This chapter discusses the profit-adjustment decomposition outlined by Marx in these pages where he tries to distinguish the influences of turnover time and capital composition on the formation of the prices of production. It provides an alternative decomposition based on Marx's analysis in the second volume of* Capital *and argues that these pages do not support Moseley's claim that prices of production are intended only to describe a long-run equilibrium condition. It therefore suggests considering the profit adjustment in relation to the dynamic formation of the general rate of profit throughout the equalization process.*

Keywords: Turnover of capital; real rate of surplus value; general rate of profit; prices of production; transformation of surplus value; process of capital reproduction; equalization process

Capital, as self-valorizing value, [...] can only be grasped as a movement, and not as a static thing. Marx (1978/1893, p. 185)

INTRODUCTION[1]

For over a century, the circulation time of capital and the related phenomenon of turnover time have slipped into oblivion with harmful consequences for the

Value, Money, Profit, and Capital Today
Research in Political Economy, Volume 39, 145–165
Copyright © 2024 Guido De Marco
Published under exclusive licence by Emerald Publishing Limited
ISSN: 0161-7230/doi:10.1108/S0161-723020230000039009

correct understanding both of Marx's theory of prices of production and of the relationships between industrial capital and merchant's capital (commodity capital and money-dealing capital), also limiting the understanding of the dynamics of the recent crisis.

It is not surprising, therefore, that the English translation of a very interesting excerpt of 27 pages from Marx's *Economic Manuscript of 1867–1868* (2019) has gone almost unnoticed, even though it has been presented by a very useful introduction by Moseley (2019). This excerpt shows Marx's interest in the study of the influence exerted by the divergences between turnover times and between compositions of capital on the adjustment of profit rates, which is characteristic of the equalization process of the industries' average rates of profits and of the formation of prices of production. The importance of developing the analysis of turnover was still in Marx's thoughts in the 1870s, an analysis which he had not been able to take into account in the first and second parts of *his Economic Manuscript of 1864–1865* ((Marx 2015/1864–1865); henceforth MMV3) for the third volume of *Capital* (Marx [1894] 1981; henceforth KV3), where he discusses "The Transformation of Surplus-Value into Profit" and "The Transformation of Profit into Average Profit."

In what follows, I discuss a limitation present in Marx's attempt to analyze the profit-adjustment decomposition and suggest an alternative decomposition that explicitly identifies the key role of turnover time of variable capital advanced by industrial capitalists in the formation of prices of production. In the section "A Reminder on Turnover Time," after a discussion on the meaning and importance of turnover time, I recall the difference between the *real* rate and the *annual* rate of surplus-value which is a key consequence of considering turnover times. In the section "Marx's Profit-Adjustment Decomposition," I shortly summarize the main content of the 27-page excerpt. I then point out in the section "Limitations of Marx's Formulas" some limitations of the formula sketched out by Marx for the profit-adjustment decomposition and provide in the section "Profit-Adjustment Decomposition after *Capital* Volume II" an alternative formulation, based on Marx's analysis developed in the second volume of *Capital* (Marx (1978/1893), henceforth KV2). In the section "Moseley's Interpretation of Marx's Profit Adjustment," I argue that the excerpt does not provide evidence to support Moseley's (2019) long-run *equilibrium* interpretation in which the equalization of profit rates is achieved through the simple fluctuation of market prices. In the section "A Dynamic Interpretation of Marx's Profit Adjustment," I suggest considering the profit adjustment in relation to the dynamic formation of the general rate of profit throughout the process of equalization during the business cycle. A short final section "Conclusion" summarizes my main conclusions. An appendix presents the definitions and equations that support some of the arguments developed in the main body of the article.

A REMINDER ON TURNOVER TIME

Apart from very few studies, the treatment of turnover times is almost absent from the literature on Marxian economic theory.[2] Thanks to Fred Moseley's editing work and translator Herbert Panzler, Marx's first attempt to explain the profit adjustment related to the formation of prices of production is now available in English (Marx (2019)/(1867–1868)). These pages show Marx's efforts to elaborate his analysis of turnover, subsequently developed in the manuscripts for KV2.

Why Is Turnover So Important?

Marx was well aware of the importance of developing the analysis of turnover. In Manuscript II for KV2, he remarked that since the early 1820s, the lack of adequate consideration of turnover had led "to the complete destruction of the Ricardian school" (KV2, p. 373). He considered the differences in turnover times and the differences in organic compositions of capital *at the same level of abstraction* and explicitly stated that they both influence the process of formation of the rate of profit (KV2, p. 294). He stressed again this point in MMV3. From the very first page of this manuscript, Marx warns that "the production process, considered as a whole, is a unity of the processes of production and circulation" (MMV3, p. 49), and this unity cannot be considered a mere abstraction, with no reciprocal impact. If the circulation process contributes "to mystify the origin of surplus-value which has been transformed into profit," (MMV3, p. 92) this does not imply that it plays no role in the general process of reproduction of capital and above all in the tendency to the equalization of the industries' average profit rates; on the contrary, it means that if the circulation process is not fully understood, the transformation cannot be grasped:

> The way the immediate production process is entwined with the circulation process – and the transformation of surplus-value into profit proceeds from the concrete unity of both processes – also contributes in many respects [...] to mystifying the surplus-value which has been transformed into profit.[3]

Indeed, this mystifying role should not be used as a justification for considering only the production process (forgetting that, actually, there is no surplus-value without production *and* without circulation). In this way, the richness of Marx's analysis is lost and the way through which "the transformation of surplus-value into profit proceeds from the concrete unity of both processes" disappears. The most severe outcome due to the removal of turnover analysis is the disappearance of the concrete, temporal – not merely logical – dimension of the reproduction process. Naturally, the scholars who do not recognize the importance of turnover time cannot appreciate an analysis that describes its influence on the formation of prices of production.

Unfortunately, Marx did not follow through on his intention to examine the influence of turnover times on the rate of profit in his manuscript for KV3, "since Book Two, which is devoted to discussing this, has not yet been written" (MMV3, p. 261). Engels had to write the full Chapter 4 by himself ("The Effect of the Turnover on the Rate of Profit"), based on what Marx had elaborated in the manuscripts for KV2. These latter manuscripts were mostly drafted *after* the writing of the second chapter of MMV3 (Part Two of Engels's edition of KV3) where Marx discusses the transformation of surplus-value into average profit. This explains why Marx did not use his analysis of turnover in MMV3.

Accounting Definitions Of Turnover Time

In the discussions on the formation of prices of production, the common practice is to assume the same turnover time for all individual capitals. In fact, somehow most scholars see no reason why the length of capital circuit of each industry cannot be assumed to be equal to the same standardized (conventional) period. Indeed, the only obstacle is that this standardized period does not actually exist and does not correspond to the actual average period of reproduction of money-capital advanced in various industries. These scholars dismiss too easily the theoretical implications of the 11 chapters of KV2 (from 7 to 17) dedicated by Marx to the phenomenon of turnover and his in-depth criticisms of the definitions of the categories of fixed and circulating capital attempted by Smith and Ricardo (see Chapters 10 and 11 of KV2), as well as the distinction between the different functional forms of industrial capital, represented by productive capital and capital of circulation [*Cirkulationskapital*] (commodity capital and money-dealing capital).

Unfortunately, most Marxist scholars have continued to stick with the mainstream accountancy practice whereby the different forms of productive capital are defined as fixed or circulating if they participate in the production phase for more than or less than one year, a choice that blurs their fundamental differences. For example, according to Napoleoni, the distinction between *fixed* capital and *circulating* capital is not "important" exactly because "it comes about not on the grounds of economic principles, but on the simple grounds of accountancy" (Napoleoni (1972), pp. 133–134). Similar approach in Pasinetti (1977/1975):

> ...the means of production are of two kinds: those constituting the so-called "circulating capital," which are completely used up in the production process within the year and must therefore be replaced in full, and those constituting the so-called "fixed capital," which are used up only partially during the year, and for which only the used-up part need be replaced.[4]

These are still the commonly accepted definitions. Moreover, in this way, the categories of commodity capital and money capital are blurred together with that of circulating capital (for Marx only productive capital can be fixed or circulating).

In these definitions, there is no trace of the theoretical questions raised by Marx against the analysis carried out by classical economists on the different forms of capital circulation. The difficulties of those economists stemmed mainly from their inability to distinguish "the social, economic character that things are stamped with in the process of social production" because they based their analysis on the "natural character arising from the material nature of these things" (KV2: 303). As recalled by Murray ((1998), p. 47), "Quesnay, Smith and Ricardo [...] never did succeed in properly drawing the distinction [between fixed and circulating capital]," and another mistake of political economists "is to confuse *circulating capital*, which is a form of productive capital, with *capital of circulation* (commodity capital and money capital)..."

For Marx, circulating capital in Smith "is rather lumped together with the shapes that the capital assumes on its transition from the sphere of production to that of circulation, as commodity capital and money capital" (KV2, p. 278). This passage continues and Marx specifies that these latter two forms "are bearers of both the fixed and the fluid components of the value of productive capital. Both are capital of circulation, in contrast to productive capital, but not circulating (fluid) capital in contrast to fixed." All these errors facilitated the blurring of the distinction Marx cared most about, equating variable capital with constant circulating capital.

Marx's Determination of Turnover Time

In his analysis of the three general forms taken by the circuit of capital – commodity capital, production capital, and money capital – Marx singles out the latter circuit as the only one which allows us to consider the value in process in its repeated turnover (KV2, p. 263). For Marx, when circuits of capital repeat, *what is in process is the value advanced*. By turnover time Marx thus means the average length of time taken by the money-capital advanced to complete its circuit, with its three different stages (purchase, production, and sale) (KV2, pp. 234–236). The money-capital that has completed its turnover is that part of the money-capital advanced and returned to its original form (clearly, its value form, not its physical form), i.e. that part of capital advanced which has been used up productively and it has transferred its value to the commodities which have completed the circuit of money-capital with their sale. The number of turnovers is therefore given by the ratio between the amount of value that has completed its turnover in the considered period (the cost of production of commodities sold) and the money-capital advanced at the beginning of the same period (KV3, p. 335). The average length of turnover is given by the ratio between the unit of time chosen as conventional reference (usually a year) and the number of turnovers (KV2, p. 236). This unit of time can also be used to measure the overall time of circulation of a given capital.

The difference between fixed capital and circulating capital hinges upon the different ways their value circulates (KV2, pp. 246–247). A productive capital can be considered "fixed capital" if it circulates "gradually, bit by bit" (KV2, p. 238). Therefore, fixed capitals are not fixed for their physical characteristic or because they participate to the production stage for a period longer than a conventional unit of time (say one year). They are fixed because "perform the same functions over a shorter or longer period, in a series of repeated labour processes" (KV2, p. 237). Conversely, the value of circulating capital is completely transferred to the product each time it participates to the production stage. The difference between fixed capital and circulating capital is due to the difference in the circulation of their values. The circulating capital must be replaced after each production period has been completed, while the fixed capital is replaced only after several production periods have occurred and its value has been gradually transferred to the commodities produced.

Total circulation time is thus made up of production time *and* circulation time (purchase and sale) properly understood. Naturally, the shortening (or lengthening) of circulation time in the phases of purchase and sale does not create value by itself, however, it does affect turnover times and consequently the *annual* surplus-value that can be created in a period of production by the industrial workforce.

Real Rate and Annual Rate of Surplus Value

For the analysis of the rate of profit, the decisive part of capital turnover is that of the variable capital advanced (the money wage of the workforce applied in every single circuit).[5] The annual rate of profit for an individual capital is affected by the relationship between the variable capital advanced v and the number n of its turnovers accomplished during the period considered. This number is determined following the general rule as suggested by Engels (KV3, p. 335): the number of turnovers is the number of times in which the *same* variable capital advanced repeats its circuit during a given period (usually a year).[6] If n is the number of turnovers of the variable capital v advanced at the beginning of the period and V the total variable capital applied or turned over in the period, we have:

$$n = \frac{V}{v} \tag{1}$$

Breaking down the surplus-value S into V and s', where $s' \equiv S/V$ is the *real* rate of surplus-value (on average) for each turnover, it follows $S = s'V = s'nv$. Based on this breakdown of total surplus-value (KV2, pp. 378–383), Marx's formula for the rate of profit reported by Engels is pretty straightforward (KV3, pp. 167–169):

$$r = \frac{s'nv}{k + v} \tag{2}$$

where k is the constant capital advanced (both in terms of fixed constant capital and circulating constant capital).

The *annual* rate of surplus-value (S/v) is affected by the *total* variable capital turned over during the year $S/v = s'V/v = s'n$, thus it depends not only on the *real* rate of surplus-value s' but also on the number of turnovers accomplished by the variable capital advanced.

Scholars who do not take into account the phenomenon of turnover of variable capital do not distinguish between the *real* and the *annual* rate of surplus-value. In the standard approach to turnover times, these scholars either ignore this problem or choose a theoretical unit of time and assume that all flow variables complete their turnover during this period. Sometimes, this period is chosen long enough for the fixed capital to turn over completely and then the analysis is supposed to be feasible in terms of circulating capital. Clearly, this choice makes it impossible to consider the role played by fixed capital in the social reproduction (Moseley, 2016, pp. 231–233). These limits are similar to those attributed by Marx to classical economists, as Murray (1998, pp. 46–51) has reminded us. An important consequence of the dismissal of this difference between V and v is that with it the possibility of fully appreciating the influence exerted by the capital operating in the sphere of circulation disappears.

Unfortunately, in the debate on the formation of prices of production, most scholars, following a long tradition started by Sweezy (1968/1942, pp. 67–68), continue to focus only on the organic composition or the rate of surplus-value, leaving aside the category of turnover time as if it were only a further "complication" or another minor source of unequal rates of profit. A "complication" that Marx introduced to explain the role played by capital in the sphere of circulation and its impact on the conditions of production of industrial capital.

MARX'S PROFIT-ADJUSTMENT DECOMPOSITION

Marx's theory of prices of production holds that the general (average) rate of profit of the social capital is generally different from the average (value) rate of profit r_i of any individual industry "i" with a different organic composition of capital and/or a different turnover time, as well as a different real rate of surplus value. This difference is reduced on average either through the changes that occur in the conditions of production *and* circulation throughout the economic cycle or through a series of profit supplements (reductions) that each individual industry should obtain (bear). This adjustment process is partially discussed by Marx in the second chapter of MMV3 and earlier in several passages of his *Manuscript of 1861–1863*. The whole matter that concerns the formation of prices of production consists in understanding *how* this process operates and unfolds its effects.

The welcomed introduction of Fred Moseley (2019) to the 27-page excerpt from Marx's *Economic Manuscript of 1867–1868* (Marx, 2019) draws attention to the important issue of the influence of turnover times on the formation of prices of production. In these pages Marx analyses the difference between the rate of profit of a given capital advanced and the rate of profit of an average capital (a capital of average composition), determining to what extent this difference derives from the different composition of the annual production costs or from the different turnover times. On the whole, he provisionally assumes that the *real* rate of surplus-value is the same for all industries.[7] Differently from the choice successively made in *Capital*, in these pages Marx always refers to the composition of the annual production costs, even when he utilizes the term "organic composition" of capital.

As recalled by Moseley, the price of production P_i of the annual product of industry "i" is determined by adding the annual cost of production K_i and the profit proportional both to the capital advanced in that industry C_i and to the general rate of profit r:

$$P_i \equiv K_i + rC_i \tag{3}$$

The total value W_i is determined by adding the annual cost of production K_i and the annual surplus-value S_i produced by the annual variable capital applied in that industry:

$$W_i \equiv K_i + S_i \tag{4}$$

Considering that, by definition, $r_i \equiv S_i/C_i$:

$$W_i = K_i + S_i = K_i + r_iC_i \tag{5}$$

The *total profit-adjustment* A_i is given by the difference between the prices of production P_i and the value W_i of commodities sold:

$$A_i \equiv P_i - W_i \tag{6}$$

$$A_i = (r - r_i)C_i \tag{7}$$

Marx's decomposition of eq. (7) ascribes the differences $(r - r_i)$ to three factors: unequal turnover times of capital advanced, unequal compositions of annual production costs, and their combined effect (the real rates of surplus-value are assumed equal). Each of these factors generates the need for the corresponding adjustments A_i^t, A_i^c, and A_i^{tc}, necessary to compensate for the deviation of the value rate of profit r_i from the general rate of profit r, so that:

$$A_i \equiv A_i^t + A_i^c + A_i^{tc} \tag{8}$$

After a series of cumbersome examples, Marx determines these adjustments as follows:

$$A_i = (C_i - K_i)\pi_i + (r - \pi_i)K_i + (r - \pi_i)(C_i - K_i) \tag{9}$$

where $\pi_i = S_i/K_i$ is the ratio between surplus-value and production costs (or profit margin) of the industry "i", called by Marx the "rate of profit related to the cost prices."

When $r_i \neq r$, the compensation or curtailment determined by the *profit-adjustments* A*s should* allow the movement toward equalizing the industry "i" average "price" rate of profit to the general rate of profit, because $W_i + A_i = P_i$.

LIMITATIONS OF MARX'S FORMULAS

The *very simplifying assumptions* used in these pages and their messy form show that they were not ready for publication. Indeed, once these assumptions are relaxed, the profit-adjustment decomposition formulated in the excerpt is no longer adequate, as I show in the *Appendix*.

The years 1867–1868 were certainly not the first or the last period during which Marx dealt with turnover time. Part II of KV2, "The Turnover of Capital," encompasses Chapters 7–17. For the edition of these chapters Engels used only Manuscript II, written between the end of 1868 and the middle of 1870,[8] except for the first 10 pages (pp. 156–165) related to Chapter 7 and the beginning of Chapter 8, based on the end of Manuscript IV (written between June and August 1867). Successively, in the years 1877–1878, other shorter manuscripts were added (see Engels' Preface to the edition of KV2 (pp. 84–85)). I have briefly mentioned these few editorial facts to recall the appropriate context for the drafting of these pages from the 1867–1868 manuscript.

Contrary to the attempts developed in this *Economic Manuscript of 1867–1868*, Marx develops a much deeper analysis in the manuscript used by Engels for Part II of KV2. Especially, in Chapters 10 and 11, Marx reaches important conclusions on the difficulties encountered by Smith and Ricardo who focus their attention on the similarities of form that circulating constant capital and variable capital have in their turnover without distinguishing the specific role played by the turnover of variable capital. In fact, for a given composition of capital advanced and a given real rate of surplus value, *it is only the turnover of variable capital advanced that affects the formation of the rate of profit*. Not surprisingly, then, Marx utilizes a decomposition of the rate of profit that places the valorization process at the center of his analysis. Unfortunately, Marx did not use this formulation of the rate of profit to develop a new profit-adjustment decomposition.

PROFIT-ADJUSTMENT DECOMPOSITION AFTER *CAPITAL* VOLUME II

Starting from eq. (2) it is possible to overcome the limits of the profit-adjustment decomposition sketched out in the 1867–1868 manuscript. Defining the organic composition of capital[9] $q \equiv k/v$, we have:

$$r \equiv \frac{s' \, n}{q + 1} \tag{10}$$

Following a similar reasoning to that sketched out by Marx in the excerpt and assuming an equal real rate of surplus-value s' to focus the attention on the comparison with eq. (9), the difference between the general rate of profit r and the individual industry's average (value) rate of profit r_i is:

$$r - r_i = \frac{s'n}{q + 1} - \frac{s'n_i}{q_i + 1} = s' \left(\frac{n}{q + 1} - \frac{n_i}{q_i + 1} \right) \tag{11}$$

The *total profit-adjustment A_i^** for an individual industry becomes:

$$A_i^* = s'\left(\frac{n}{q+1} - \frac{n_i}{q_i+1}\right)C_i \tag{12}$$

Labeling Q the ratio $1/(q+1)$ and Q_i the ratio $1/(q_i+1)$,

$$A_i^* = s'(nQ - n_iQ_i)C_i \tag{13}$$

This total profit adjustment can be easily decomposed. We can write n in terms of n_i and Δn_i, so that $n = (n_i + \Delta n_i)$. Doing the same for Q, the formula above can be rewritten as follows:

$$A_i^* = s'[(n_i + \Delta n_i)(Q_i + \Delta Q_i) - n_iQ_i]C_i \tag{14}$$

Therefore:

$$A_i^* = s'[Q_in_i + Q_i\Delta n_i + n_i\Delta Q_i + \Delta Q_i\Delta n_i - n_iQ_i]C_i \tag{15}$$

$$A_i^* = s'[(n - n_i)Q_i + (Q - Q_i)n_i + (n - n_i)(Q - Q_i)]C_i \tag{16}$$

The first term in the square brackets of eq. (16) explains the adjustment due to the differences between the overall average turnover time of the variable capital advanced by all industries and the turnover time of the variable capital advanced by industry "i," the second term explains the adjustment due to the differences between their organic compositions and, finally, the third term explains the adjustment due to their combined effect.

Clearly, the definitions of the A*s now change:

$$A_i^{*t} \equiv s'(n - n_i)Q_iC_i \tag{17}$$

$$A_i^{*c} \equiv s'(Q - Q_i)n_iC_i \tag{18}$$

$$A_i^{*tc} \equiv s'(n - n_i)(Q - Q_i)C_i \tag{19}$$

Some results that can be derived from equation (16) are straightforward. There are two limit situations. The first one is when an industry's organic composition of capital is different from that of the average capital and this difference is compensated by different turnover times (increased mechanization implies a shorter period of production and possibly a shorter period of circulation), so that in eq. (16) we have $A_i^* = 0$, because:

$$nQ = n_iQ_i \tag{20}$$

The other limit situation is when the average organic compositions are equal and the turnover times are different, so that $A_i^* \neq 0$ even though $Q = Q_i$. Apparently, these two situations could be easily dismissed considering them as unrealistic conditions that are not worth considering (anyway, no more unrealistic than a stable condition of general equilibrium based only on prices adjustments). *These two situations cannot be explained, of course, by the scholars who do not take into account the theoretical analysis of turnover.* In any case, the key issue for these scholars is that if they want to use the turnover time analysis in empirical research, they will have to develop this analysis without a theoretical foundation. On the other hand, if they will not take into account the turnover time in their researches because they do not include this phenomenon in their theoretical approach, they will miss out on a powerful tool of analysis.

Veronese Passarella and Baron (2015) convincingly argued the decisive role played by capital of circulation in the formation of the rates of profit. More recently, Jones (2021) uses the analysis of turnover in his book *The Falling Rate of Profit and the Great Recession of 2007–2009*. Lately, Jefferies (2022) provides estimates of the turnover of US circulating capital and the profit rate of private corporations from 1964 to 2017.

MOSELEY'S INTERPRETATION OF MARX'S PROFIT ADJUSTMENT

According to Moseley (2019, p. 152), the excerpt (Marx, 2019) "provides additional textual evidence" to support his "macro-monetary" interpretation of Marx's theory. To back up this claim, the first point of his conclusions emphasizes that even in the excerpt "*the general rate of profit is taken as given*, as determined by the prior theory of the total surplus-value in Volumes 1 and 2 of *Capital*" (Moseley, 2019, p. 153). This is a controversial claim with which I disagree (for a more general critique see De Marco (2021), IJPE (2017)). As long as Moseley suggests his interpretation limiting himself to analyzing the so-called transformation problem as opposed to scholars who have discussed this problem in terms of general equilibrium, his willingness to refer to some sort of equilibrium may be understandable though not agreeable. However, the interpretation of Marx's attempt to develop a profit-adjustment decomposition should not be based on a merely logical and one-sided condition of *equilibrium*.

Moseley can legitimately claim that Marx takes the general rate of profit as given, because this is what it is written in the excerpt (although, unlike Moseley, Marx does not add "as determined by the prior theory of the total surplus-value in Volumes 1 and 2 of *Capital*"). On the other hand, there is no theory without the essential interplay of its several components, choosing only one piece of a complex theory can be literally correct but theoretically wrong.

Considering in isolation the analysis developed by Marx in some sections of Chapter 17 of KV1, "Changes of Magnitude in the Price of Labour-Power and in Surplus-Value," one might wrongly conclude that Marx *always* assumes as given the intensity of labor, or the productivity of labor, or even the length of the working day. In fact, in each one of these sections, Marx applies only *provisionally* the *ceteris paribus* condition so he can analyze the factors that contribute to changing the price of labor-power one at a time, while the other factors are assumed to be given. In KV2, Marx presents the schemes of reproduction without considering the rates of profit and, of course, this does not mean that in the social reproduction, in the relations between the departments, these rates do not matter. A similar approach is followed in the first chapter of MMV3 devoted to the analysis of "The Transformation of Surplus-Value into Profit."

To determine the profit-adjustment decomposition, the excerpt *must* assume both a given general rate of profit and the rate of profit of a given industry because this is literally what its definition requires, but that does not imply that for Marx this decomposition is not intended to describe the changes that occur in profit adjustments during the equalization process. Does Marx take into account in this excerpt the process of accumulation? Does he take into account the transfer of capital from less profitable industries to more profitable ones? Should we say that since he does not take into consideration these processes, they are not involved in the adjustment process? If it is true that in Chapter 9 of KV3, Marx *provisionally* provides a description of the formation of prices of production assuming as given the total surplus value produced (to show its redistribution in the example built in its famous tables), nowhere does he present these prices as an *equilibrium* condition.

The methodological remark of my previous examples applies as well to the relations between productive capital and capital of circulation. The analysis of the sphere of production, with its results, can be considered theoretically posited before the analysis developed in the second volume, so that surplus value can be considered as given before its circulation, *leaving aside the changes that could occur in the turnover periods of capital.* However, for a complete understanding of the overall process of social reproduction, it is then necessary to take into account the intertwining of production and circulation processes. Capital invested in the sphere of circulation not only facilitates the realization and redistribution of previously produced surplus value, but also facilitates the acquisition of the conditions of production of new surplus value:

> The expansion and contraction of the circulation time hence acts as a negative limit on the contraction or expansion of the production time, or *of the scale on which a capital of a given magnitude can function* [my emphasis]. The more that the circulation metamorphoses of capital are only ideal, i.e. the closer the circulation time comes to zero, the more the capital functions, and the greater is its productivity and self-valorization.[10]

If we drop the assumption of uniform turnover times, *we can no longer assume that the redistribution of surplus value occurs for all capitals during the last stage of the social reproduction of capital* (as Moseley does). *In fact, it takes place throughout the entire period of reproduction* considered and the interplay between the phases of production and circulation of different but connected parts of capital advanced cannot help but affect the amount of surplus-value produced. If we want to understand the formation of the general rate of profit, we can consider it as given before the start of the process of redistribution of surplus value only as a provisional assumption.

Moseley undervalues Chapter 10 of KV3 (third section of Chapter 2 of MMV3), where Marx addresses the formation of the prices of production and raises the crucial question, in the following terms:

> The really difficult question here is this: how does this equalisation of profits or this establishment of a general rate of profit take place, since it is evidently a result and cannot be a point of departure?[11]

Moseley simply obliterates this question. He emphasizes the messy condition of the 27-page excerpt and nonetheless is ready to mention it in support of his interpretation; however, at the same time, he deems that Chapter 10 of KV3 is not sufficiently developed to be relevant to his interpretation. Indeed, this chapter is clearly at odds with the idea of a given general rate of profit, *definitively* predetermined at the level of abstraction of the first two volumes of *Capital*.

Capitalists cannot simply keep their capitals in the same industries applying the average rate of profit as a mark-up to their money-capital advanced. Indeed, the whole analysis of the redistribution of capital across the various spheres of production developed by Marx in this chapter (and elsewhere) would not make sense if in his view the individual capitalist could simply apply the general rate of profit to his capital advanced, or if Marx had been interested to the long run *equilibrium* prices of production, as suggested by Moseley. In Moseley's interpretation the only factor used to explain the equalization of profit rates is the fluctuation of market prices. Is this factor sufficient or even the only factor considered by Marx? Clearly, it is not so:

> Mere fluctuations – *below* and *above* [prices of production] – if they do not exceed the average extent and do not assume extraordinary forms, *are therefore not sufficient* [my emphasis] to bring about a TRANSFER OF CAPITAL…"[12]

Marx repeatedly refers to the migration of capital from less profitable spheres of production to spheres with higher average rates of profit (MMV3, pp. 305–306; KV3, pp. 297–298). Same reasoning in Marx (MMV3, p. 469; KV3, pp. 488–489). Above all, market prices fluctuations are mainly a *consequence* both of capital transfer and of the attempts of capitalists to change the conditions of accumulation of their capital to achieve the best possible rate of profit. These fluctuations are only one of the secondary ways through which changes occur in the general conditions of social reproduction, including the average productivity of industries, as the equalization process unfolds its effects.

A DYNAMIC INTERPRETATION OF MARX'S PROFIT ADJUSTMENT

Moseley writes that "in order to equalize the rate of profit of [a given industry] with the general rate of profit, a 'profit adjustment' *must* [my emphasis] be added to the surplus-value produced by [this industry]" (Moseley (2019) pp. 150–151). In my view, it is exactly the qualification of this necessity that constitutes a decisive divide with Moseley's interpretation. How does this "must" become effective?

The general rate of profit effectively realized in the long run is unknown, it can be determined only at the end of this period (Marx [2010] (1861–1863), volume 32: pp. 459–460). Capitalists always pursue the best possible rate of profit and in doing so modify the conditions of reproduction of their capital. It is not therefore an accident that Marx refers to the "continual transfer of capital from one sphere to another, where profit stands above the average for the time being" (KV3, p. 310; MMV3, pp. 313–314; see also KV3, pp. 895–896; MMV3, p. 749). The possibilities to realize this continuous emigration and migration of capital hinge upon the capital tied up in the sphere of production and the different composition of capitals (Marx [2010] (1861–1863), Volume 32, pp. 460–461).

Precisely because of the limiting factor represented by the money already invested in fixed capital, Marx stresses the importance of credit and of the accumulation process for the equalization process to take place. Marx attributes to the new capital an even more important role for the equalization process, compared to the role played by the transfer of already existing capitals. Another decisive aspect taken up by Marx is the temporal dimension of this process ("the cycle of fat and lean years" (KV3, p. 300, 310; MMV3, pp. 307–308, 313–314; see also Marx [2010] (1861–1863), Volume 32, pp. 459–460)). The length of the industrial cycle can be different for the various spheres of production. Marx mentions a cycle of 7 years, and considers even 13 or 10 years (2010, Volume 32, p. 461; Volume 40, pp. 277–282; MMV3, p. 278, note 10); however, what matters is not only the reference to the duration of the business cycle, but also the reference to different average annual profit rates achieved in the different stages of the cycle.

Marx's sketchy notes on the profit-adjustment decomposition can thus be rightly explained on the base of his lifelong research project of describing the economic law of motion of capital. The formation of the general rate of profit is the result of conflicting forces generating a persistent imbalance that could possibly equalize the averages of the different industries' rates of profit annually achieved over the long run (the business cycle). The centripetal force exerted by competition pushes the capitals with different rates of profit *within* the same industry and *across* the other industries toward more profitable opportunities (KV3, Chapter 10). As far as the composition of capital already invested allows, there is a capital migration toward more profitable spheres of production. In more profitable spheres new competitors and higher accumulation growth rates flood the market with additional commodities, in less profitable spheres supply shrinks (Shaikh (2016), pp. 295–296).

These changes affect the turnover times, decreasing (increasing) them in the spheres that receive (originate) the inflow (outflow) of new capitals and *consequently* market prices fluctuate toward lower (higher) levels in the spheres with increasing (decreasing) supply. Furthermore, with the changing distribution of capitals across the spheres of production, the levels of average productivity change (even in the case of constant technology (De Marco, 2021)) as well as the levels of capacity utilization. These modified conditions change in turn the industries' average value profit rates, as well as the general rate of profit (KV3, p. 269;

MMV3, p. 281). *At the same time*, the drive toward the best possible rate of profit determines the centrifugal force that feeds the introduction of new technologies; these latter modify and revolutionize the process of production and circulation of capital, as well as the process of valorization and the determination of socially necessary labor, so that the differences between profit rates are ceaselessly renewed.

The equalization process, therefore, will not leave unchanged the key components of the rate of profit, namely the turnover time, the composition of capital, and the real rate of surplus-value. My interpretation of Marx's profit-adjustment decomposition is that the breakdown in eq. (16) describes the changes that *might* occur *during the long-run equalization process* as a consequence of the different organic compositions and the different number of turnovers of variable capital advanced, as well as of the different real rates of surplus value (on the changes of the real rate of surplus value throughout the business cycle see Chapter 25 of KV1, "The General Law of Capitalist Accumulation," especially Section 3, devoted to the industrial reserve army [KV1, pp. 771–772, 781–785]).

In this interpretation of Marx's theory of prices of production, the equalization process may compensate the imbalances of a given industry's average rates of profit compared to the changing general rate of profit, so that the overall sum of profit adjustments may be close to zero (as long as the general rate of profit is determined only for those industries where there are not artificial or natural monopoly [MMV3, p. 749, 925; KV3, pp. 895–896, 1001]).

For a given industry "i," if we consider the sum of the annual profit adjustments of a business cycle (let us assume it lasts T years), eq. (13) can be rewritten as follows:

$$A_{iT}^* \equiv \sum_{t=1}^{T} A_{it}^* = \sum_{t=1}^{T} (s_t' n_t Q_t - s_{it}' n_{it} Q_{it}) C_{it} \tag{21}$$

If we write n_t in terms of n_i and Δn_i, Q_t in terms of Q_{it} and ΔQ_{it}, s_t' in terms of s_{it}' and $\Delta s_{it}'$, so that $n_t = (n_{it} + \Delta n_{it})$ and so on, we have:

$$A_{iT}^* = \sum_{t=1}^{T} \left[(s_{it}' + \Delta s_{it}')(n_{it} + \Delta n_{it})(Q_{it} + \Delta Q_{it}) - s_{it}' n_{it} Q_{it} \right] C_{it} \tag{22}$$

Developing eq. (22) we have:

$$A_{iT}^* = \sum_{t=1}^{T} \left(\Delta Q_{it} n_{it} s_i' + \Delta n_{it} Q_{it} s_{it}' + \Delta s_{it}' n_{it} Q_{it} + \Delta Q_{it} \Delta n_{it} s_{it}' \right.$$
$$\left. + \Delta Q_{it} \Delta s_{it}' n_{it} + \Delta n_{it} \Delta s_{it}' Q_{it} + \Delta Q_{it} \Delta n_{it} \Delta s_{it}' \right) C_{it} \tag{23}$$

Finally:

$$A_{iT}^* = \sum_{t=1}^{T} \left[(Q_t - Q_{it}) n_{it} s_{it}' + (n_t - n_{it}) Q_{it} s_{it}' + \left(s_t' - s_{it}' \right) n_{it} Q_{it} \right.$$
$$+ (Q_t - Q_{it})(n_t - n_{it}) s_{it}' + (Q_t - Q_{it}) \left(s_t' - s_{it}' \right) n_{it} + (n_t - n_{it}) \left(s_t' - s_{it}' \right) Q_{it}$$
$$\left. + (Q_t - Q_{it})(n_t - n_{it}) \left(s_t' - s_{it}' \right) \right] C_{it} \tag{24}$$

The development represented by eq. (24) provides a contribution to a more adequate description of the process of formation of prices of production in Marx's theory of value. Even though several scholars have already demonstrated the consistency of Marx's theory of value with a non-equilibrium interpretation (Freeman & Carchedi (1996)), I suggest that the role of turnover time should be explicitly included in their description of the social reproduction of capital.[13]

CONCLUSION

The profit-adjustment decomposition sketched out in Marx's *Economic Manuscript of 1867–1868* is an attempt to distinguish the influences of the different components that intervene in the formation of industries' average profit rates. I showed the limits of this attempt and provided an alternative decomposition based on the analysis developed in KV2. I have also argued against Moseley's claim that the excerpt supports his long-run *equilibrium* interpretation of prices of production and I suggested a long-run non-equilibrium interpretation.

Besides Marx's theory of prices of production, the oblivion of the analysis of the turnover of capital has been detrimental to the understanding of the relationship between industrial capital, commercial capital and money-dealing capital. Commodity capital or money-dealing capital cannot create value, however, to the extent that their activities reduce (or increase) the circulation time of industrial capital, they allow a shorter (longer) period of reproduction for the money-capital advanced by industrial capitalists. In this respect, the forms assumed by capital in the process of circulation interact decisively with the results that can be obtained by industrial capital and capital at large.

NOTES

1. I am very much indebted to Alan Freeman, José Tapia, Paul Zarembka, and my friends from the Association for the Redistribution of Labor (ARELA) Giovanni Mazzetti, Gabriele Serafini, Mauro Parretti, for their helpful comments. I am grateful for Shanmathi Priya Sampath's patience and excellent editing work. I also am grateful to Fred Moseley for our lengthy correspondence on the issues discussed in the article. The usual disclaimers apply.
2. Besides some early works at the end of the nineteenth century (Hourwich, 1894; Lexis, 1895; Schmidt, 1889), only a few authors in the last century (Alemi & Foley, 1997; Bertrand & Fauqueur, 1978; Fichtenbaum, 1988; Foley, 1982, 1986; Kotz, 1991; Murray, 1998; Rosdolsky, 1977/1968; Senchak, 1983; Tombazos, 2013/1994; Webber & Rigby, 1986) emphasize the role of turnover. Among the most recent studies see: Bryer (2017), Dos Santos (2011), Jefferies (2022), Jones (2021), Saros (2008, 2014), Veronese Passarella and Baron (2015) and Zarembka (2021).
3. Marx (MMV3, p. 92).
4. Pasinetti (1977/1975), pp. 43–44.
5. Sometimes confusion can arise from ignoring Marx's basic assumption that every sale is considered to be made against money as a means of purchase, to distinguish the pure form of commodity exchange from the complications introduced by the use of credit (Marx (1976/1990), henceforth KV1, pp. 278–279; KV2, p. 295). For Marx, the amount of variable capital advanced corresponds to the amount of variable capital applied in every single turnover (KV2, pp. 300, 382). Whenever he gives numerical examples of the variable capital advanced at the start of a repeated circuit of money capital, the figure used for this variable capital advanced coincides with the figure used for the variable capital actually

applied in every single turnover. As the other form of circulating capital advanced (the circulating *constant* capital), the variable capital advanced "goes into the commodity completely, and is therefore completely replaced by its sale. [...] What is involved in both cases is a transfer of given, previously advanced values to the product, and their replacement when the product is sold" (KV2, p. 296).

6. This is actually true only in the case of simple reproduction; when expanded reproduction is taken into account, the determination of the number of turnovers and the formula of the rate of profit is more complex because the variable capital advanced is not necessarily the same during the period considered (see De Marco, 2023).

7. Indeed, Marx argues that "an increased rate of surplus-value may compensate the lesser turnover" (Marx [2019] (1867–1868), p. 168). Unequal rates of surplus-value are considered in the short section B of the excerpt (Marx [2019] (1867–1868), pp. 173–175).

8. Heinrich (2016, p. 108), Veronese Passarella and Baron (2014, p. 1418, note 5).

9. There is a large debate on the correct definition of organic composition, here I prefer to keep its traditional meaning and also not to use the value composition not to insert a further complication. For the definition of the organic composition of capital used in *Capital* see Marx (Marx [2010] (1861–1863), Volume 33, pp. 305–310; KV1, pp. 762–763; MMV3, pp. 252–253, 753–754). Moseley (2016, pp. 333–361) criticizes the interpretation of organic composition of capital presented by Ben Fine and Alfredo Saad-Filho in their works. See also Chapter 8 in Zarembka (2021), I cannot discuss this matter here. I thank Paul Zarembka for raising this issue.

10. KV2, p. 203.

11. MMV3, p. 285.

12. Marx (2010/(1861–1863), Volume 32, p. 460).

13. For a reconstruction of the debate on the formation of prices of production see Howard and King (1987, 1989, 1992), Kliman (2007), and Moseley (2016).

REFERENCES

Alemi, P., & Foley, D. (1997). *The circuit of capital, U.S. manufacturing and non-financial corporate business sectors: 1947–1993*. Retrieved from https://www.researchgate.net

Bertrand, H., & Fauqueur, A. (1978). Rotation du capital circulant et rentabilité. *Revue Économique, 29*(2), 291–331.

Bryer, R. (2017). *Accounting for value in Marx's Capital: The invisible hand*. Lanham, MD: Lexington Books.

De Marco, G. (2021). A critique of Moseley's *Money and Totality*. *World Review of Political Economy, 12*(1), 106–132.

De Marco, G. (2023). *Marx's general rate of profit: how turnover time, accumulation, and rate of surplus value affect the formation of prices of production. Capital & Class*, forthcoming.

Dos Santos, P. L. (2011). Production and consumption credit in a continuous-time model of the circuit of capital, Research on Money and Finance Discussion Paper, 28, School of Oriental and African Studies (SOAS). Department of Economics, University of London.

Fichtenbaum, R. (1988). "Business cycles," turnover and the rate of profit: an empirical test of Marxian crisis theory. *Eastern Economic Journal, 13*(3), 221–228.

Foley, D. (1982). Realization and accumulation in a Marxian model of the circuit of capital. *Journal of Economic Theory, 28*(2), 300–319.

Foley, D. (1986). *Understanding capital: Marx's economic theory*. Cambridge, MA: Harvard University Press.

Freeman, A., & Carchedi, G. (Eds.). (1996). *Marx and non-equilibrium economics*. Cheltenham: Edward Elgar.

Heinrich, M. (2016). Capital after MEGA: discontinuities, interruptions, and new beginnings. *Crisis & Critique, 3*(3), 92–138.

Hourwich, I. A. (1894). The rate of profits under the law of labour-value. *Journal of Political Economy, 2*(2), 235–250.

Howard, M. C., & King, J. E. (1987). Doctor Muhlpfort, Professor von Bortkiewicz and the 'transformation problem. *Cambridge Journal of Economics*, 11, 265–268.

Howard, M. C., & King, J. E. (1989). *A history of Marxian economics* (Vol. I, pp. 1883–1929). Princeton, NJ: Princeton University Press.

Howard, M. C., & King, J. E. (1992). *A history of Marxian economics: Volume II, 1929–1990*. Princeton, NJ: Princeton University Press.

International Journal of Political Economy (IJPE). (2017, January). Mini-symposium on Fred Moseley's *Money and Totality. International Journal of Political Economy, 46*, 1–49.

Jefferies, W. (2022). The U.S. rate of profit 1964–2017 and the turnover of fixed and circulating capital. *Capital & Class*, 1–23. Retrieved from https://thenextrecession.files.wordpress.com/2022/11/03098168221084110.pdf

Jones, P. (2021). The falling rate of profit and the great recession of 2007–2009. *Historical materialism book series* (Vol. 191). Leiden: Brill.

Kliman, A. (2007). *Reclaiming Marx's Capital: A refutation of the myth of inconsistency*. Lanham, MD: Lexington Books.

Kotz, D. (1991). Accumulation, money, and credit in the circuit of capital. *Rethinking Marxism, 4*(2), 119–133.

Lexis, W. (1895). The concluding volume of Marx's *Capital. Quarterly Journal of Economics, 10*(1), 1–33.

Marx, K. (1976/1890). *Capital: A critique of political economy* (Vol. I). London: Penguin Books.

Marx, K. (1978/1893). *Capital: A critique of political economy* (Vol. II). London: Penguin Books.

Marx, K. (1981/1894). *Capital: A critique of political economy* (Vol. III). London: Penguin Books.

Marx, K. (2010/1861–1863). *Marx & Engels collected works* (Vols. 32, 33, and 34). London: Digital Edition, Lawrence and Wishart.

Marx, K. (2015/1864–1865). Marx's economic manuscript of 1864-1865. *Historical materialism book series* (Vol. 100). Leiden: Brill.

Marx, K. (2019/1867–1868). Marx's economic manuscript of 1867-1868 (excerpt). *Historical Materialism, 27*(4), 162–192.

Moseley, F. (2016). *Money and totality. A macro-monetary interpretation of Marx's logic in Capital and the end of the "transformation problem"*. Leiden: Brill.

Moseley, F. (2019). Marx's economic manuscript of 1867-1868 (excerpt) editor's introduction. *Historical Materialism, 27*(4), 145–156.

Murray, P. (1998). Beyond the 'commerce and industry' picture of capital. In C. J. Arthur & G. Reuten (Eds.), *The circulation of capital - essays on volume II of Marx's Capital* (pp. 33–66). London: Macmillan.

Napoleoni, C. (1972). *Lezioni sul capitolo sesto inedito di Marx*. Torino: Boringhieri.

Pasinetti, L. (1977/1975). *Lectures on the theory of production*. New York, NY: Columbia University Press.

Rosdolsky, R. (1977/1968). *The making of Marx's Capital*. London: Pluto Press.

Saros, D. E. (2008). The turnover continuum: A Marxist analysis of capital fluctuations. *Review of Radical Political Economics, 14*(2), 189–211.

Saros, D. E. (2014). Interlocking turnover continua and the structure of capital. *Review of Radical Political Economics, 46*(3), 380–401.

Schmidt, C. (1889). *Die Durchschnittsprofitrate auf Grundlage des Marx'schen Werthgesetzes [The average rate of profit, based on Marx's theory of value]*. Stuttgart: Dietz.

Senchak, A. (1983). *United States capital accumulation: 1963–1977*. Ph.D. thesis. Columbia University.

Shaikh, A. (2016). *Capitalism. Competition, conflict, crises*. New York: Oxford University Press.

Sweezy, P. M. (1968/1942). *The theory of the capitalist development*. New York: Monthly Review Press.

Tombazos, S. (2013/1994). *Time in Marx - The categories of time in Marx's Capital* (Vol. 61). *Historical materialism book series*. Leiden: Brill.

Veronese Passarella, M., & Baron, H. (2015). Capital's humpback bridge: 'financialisation' and the rate of turnover in Marx's economic theory. *Cambridge Journal of Economics, 39*, 1415–1441.

Webber, M. J., & Rigby, D. L. (1986). The rate of profit in Canadian manufacturing, 1950–1981. *Review of Radical Political Economics, 18*(1–2), 33–55.

Zarembka, P. (2021). *Key elements of social theory revolutionized by Marx*. Leiden: Brill.

APPENDIX

I will focus on the more general case considered by Marx ([2019] (1867–1868), pp. 174–190). In summarizing Marx's equations, I closely follow the very useful presentation made by Moseley (2019) in his introduction. I list below the assumptions and definitions used by Marx in the excerpt:

A. The capital advanced in a given industry "i" and an average capital (capital of average composition), whose value rate of profit is, therefore, equal to the general rate of profit, are assumed to be equal $(C_i = C)$.

B. The turnover time of capital advanced, given by the weighted average of the turnover time of fixed capital and circulating capital, is equivalent to the ratio of capital consumed during the year (the annual cost price K_i) to capital advanced (C_i), therefore, given by K_i/C_i. In his examples, Marx assumes that the turnover of the average capital is equal to one year, $K/C = 1$.

C. The rate of surplus-value is the same for the individual capital and the average capital and is equal to 1.

D. The composition of annual cost price is determined by the ratio $(K_i - V_i)/V_i$ (fixed and circulating constant capital consumed during the year $(K_i - V_i)$ over the variable capital V_i applied or turned over during the year).

E. The rate of profit related to cost price (or profit margin) π_i is defined by the ratio of surplus-value to industry production costs, $\pi_i \equiv S_i/K_i$; for the average capital this rate is equal to the general rate of profit: $\pi \equiv S/K = S/C = r$ (since $K = C$ from assumption (B)).

The *total profit-adjustment* A_i is given by the difference between the prices of production P_i and the value of commodities sold W_i:

$$A_i \equiv P_i - W_i$$

$$= K_i + rC_i - K_i - r_iC_i$$

$$= (r - r_i)C_i \tag{A.1}$$

For a given real rate of surplus-value, the total profit-adjustment in (A.1) is decomposed by Marx into three subcomponents, the adjustments due to the differences between the turnovers of capital advanced, to the different compositions of the annual cost prices, and to their combined effect: A_i^t, A_i^c, and A_i^{tc}. The rationale behind this decomposition is the attempt to distinguish between the independent factors that explain the difference in (A.1).

$$A_i \equiv A_i^t + A_i^c + A_i^{tc} \tag{A.2}$$

How are these adjustments determined? For unequal turnovers of capital advanced, Marx assumes the *ceteris paribus* conditions of equal rates of surplus-value and annual cost price composition of a given industrial capital equal to that of the average capital, so that A_i^t is determined as follows:

$$A_i^t = (C_i - K_i)\pi_i \tag{A.3}$$

If the average turnover time of the industry "i" is equal to the turnover time of the average capital, it will be $K_i/C_i = 1$ (see assumption [B]) and there will be no need for a profit adjustment, in fact, in this case, $A_i^t = 0$. If the turnover of the industry is faster-than-average (greater than 1, for assumption [B]) it will be $K_i > C_i$ and, therefore, $K_i > K$ (since $C_i = C = K$ for assumptions [A] and [B]), this means that this individual industry produces, on average, more surplus-value than the average capital (with, of course, a higher-than-average value rate of profit) and the profit-adjustment A_i^t will be negative.

For the adjustment related to unequal compositions of the annual cost prices, Marx assumes equal rates of surplus-value and average turnover time of the individual capital equal to that of the average capital, so A_c is determined as follows:

$$A_i^c = (r - \pi_i)K_i \tag{A.4}$$

At first sight, this formula might appear awkward, because it compares the general rate of profit r with the profit margin π_i, however, taking into account definition [E] and assumption [B], $r = \pi$, therefore, under this assumption, formula (A.4) compares the profit margin of the average capital π and that of industry "i." To better see the relationship between the profit margin π and the composition of the annual cost price of capital $(K - V)/V$, it suffices to consider that we can write:

$$\pi = \frac{S}{K} = s'\frac{V}{K} = s'\frac{V}{K - V + V} = \frac{s'}{(K - V)/V + 1} \tag{A.5}$$

From assumption [C] $s' = 1$, therefore, the profit margin π depends only on the composition of the annual cost price $(K - V)/V$. If the industry's composition of the annual cost price is equal to that of the average capital, then π_i will be equal to π and to the general rate of profit (from [E], $\pi = r$) r so that $A_i^c = 0$. If the composition of the annual cost price of a given industry is higher-than-average ($\pi_i < \pi = r$), this industry produces less surplus-value than the average capital (with a lower-than-average value rate of profit) and the profit-adjustment A_i^c will be positive.

The adjustment A_i^{tc}, necessary to compensate for the combined effect of unequal compositions of the annual cost prices and unequal turnover times of the capital advanced, is determined as follows:

$$A_i^{tc} = (r - \pi_i)(C_i - K_i) \tag{A.6}$$

If the partial adjustments due to the difference in turnover times and to the difference in compositions of the annual cost prices have the same sign, eq. (A.6) will also be positive and will increase the total adjustment; otherwise, if the two differences partially compensate each other, their combined effect will have a negative sign.

Finally, from eqs. (A.2)–(A.6) the *total profit-adjustment* A_i is:

$$A_i = (C_i - K_i)\pi_i + (r - \pi_i)K_i + (r - \pi_i)(C_i - K_i) \tag{A.7}$$

Unfortunately, this decomposition is based on some very simplifying assumptions. Once these assumptions are relaxed, the decomposition is no longer adequate. It suffices to consider formula (A.3) when $K/C \neq 1$ (relaxing assumption [B]). If, for example, $C_i = K_i$ the industry's turnover time is equal to 1 and the adjustment for the industry's turnover is equal to zero (from eq. (A.3)), this does not imply that the turnover of capital of average composition is equal to 1 (since assumption [B] no longer holds).

On the other hand, considering formula (A.4) and relaxing again assumption (B), so that C can be different from K, it follows that the profit margin π is not necessarily equal to the rate of profit r (since $K \neq C$); this means that formula (A.4) no longer compares the annual composition of the cost price of the industry with that of the average capital (since $\pi \neq r$).

It is possible that Marx realized the origin of these problems and did not complete the drafting of the excerpt just because he preferred to work on the manuscripts subsequently used by Engels for editing KV2, where he deepens his analysis of the circulation time of capital and refers to a different definition of the composition of capital (and today better known as organic composition).

PROFIT RATES: THEIR DISPERSION AND LONG-TERM DETERMINATION

William Paul Cockshott

ABSTRACT

This chapter introduces Marx's theory of the determination of profit rates. It contrasts this theory with what happened in the late nineteenth century to British profit rates with a detailed statistical account. It identifies missing features in the standard presentation and contrasts these with the over-accumulation hypothesis that he presents elsewhere. A formal mathematical model using the overaccumulation hypothesis is then given and tested against modern empirical data.

Keywords: Profit rate; tendency for the rate of profit to fall; organic composition of capital; overproduction of capital; accumulation; United Kingdom

MARX'S ACCOUNT

The concept of a tendency for the rate of profit to fall (TRPF) was a common theme in classical political economy. Smith, Ricardo, and Marx all held such a theory. However, their grounds for believing in this tendency were quite various. Smith thought in terms of accumulation leading to an increase in competition between capitals, hence driving down prices and profits. Ricardo dismissed this as a confusion – competition between capitalists influenced the distribution of profit, not its overall amount – and held a theory whose motor lay in the confrontation between rising population and diminishing returns in agriculture. Marx's theory was in a sense more akin to Smith's – at least insofar as it had nothing to do with diminishing returns.

Value, Money, Profit, and Capital Today
Research in Political Economy, Volume 39, 167–187
Copyright © 2024 William Paul Cockshott
Published under exclusive licence by Emerald Publishing Limited
ISSN: 0161-7230/doi:10.1108/S0161-723020230000039010

I shall distinguish two elements in Marx's writings that are particularly relevant to our topic. The main argument which Marx set out at length (and which appears in *Capital I*, his notebooks of the 1860s, and *Capital III*) to the effect that the rate of profit must tend to fall due to an increase in the organic composition of capital, an increase itself driven by the search for maximum profit on the part of capitalists. The second is what Marx calls "absolute overproduction of capital": this element forms the basis for the revised TRPF theory that we defend below.

Marx starts off with a simple numerical example (Marx, 1971, Chapter 13). He assumes that the level of wages and the length of the working day are fixed. Under these circumstances, a given sum of money being paid in wages each week can stand as an index for the number of workers employed. Thus if the wage is £1 per week then £100 represents a workforce of 100 people.

He goes on to make the simplifying assumption that the value created by labor will be divided equally between labor and capital so the total value created per week is £200.

In his terminology, the rate of surplus value $s' = s/v = 100/100 = 100\%$.

This rate of surplus value could however express itself in very different rates of profit depending on the total amount of capital employed. This he designates with a capital C, such that $C = c + v$, the components being variable capital or wages designated by the variable v, with the variable c being what he calls constant capital: raw materials, machinery, buildings, etc. He gives the rate of profit p' as the surplus divided by total capital so $p' = s/C$.

He illustrates this with a table of examples. In all cases he assumes $s = 100$.

c	v	C	p'
50	100	150	67%
100	100	200	50%
200	100	300	33%
300	100	400	25%
400	100	500	20%

Note that in real terms these are unrealistically high profit rates.

You might say "yes 50% is unrealistic, but 20% is within the bounds of possibility." But Marx has assumed that the £100 represent a week of expenditure on labor power. A profit rate of 20% a week is an astronomical annual profit rate of 1,310,363%.[1]

These unrealistic figures are an effect of the ambiguous definitions that Marx uses when discussing profit rates. He is starting out from simple explanatory examples where he tells a story of capitalists advancing constant and variable capital, carrying out production, and then selling the product within a fixed time period. In this sort of example, there is a deliberate ambiguity about the time period within which this all takes place. If he had assumed a production period of a year, and variable capital of £1 million, constant capital of one, two or three millions then his example would be more credible. But the ambiguity over the difference between stock and flow measures of capital does pose an obstacle to students of Marx's writings understanding what is actually implied by these examples.

What he has done so far is give a numerical example that illustrates that the rate of profit will be lower if c rises in relation to v, that is to say that the rate of profit will vary inversely with c/v.

There is nothing in his example that explicitly depends on time. It could as easily be used to show that industries with a high organic composition of capital must experience a lower rate of profit – which is in fact the case as shown in Fig. 1. Marx himself was blocked from making this interpretation of his table because he had, in an earlier chapter (Marx, 1971, Chapter 10), hypothesized that profit rates in different industries would equalize. This was the famous "transformation" argument according to which labor values would be transformed in profit equalizing "production prices."

It is worth going into both how Fig. 1 was computed and the implication of this for Marxian theorization of profit rates and prices.

Recall that the justification for his transformation process was that it appeared to him *obvious* that profit rates would tend to equalize. If actual profit rates do not equalize, it is evident that the production price theory is redundant. It is an attempted answer to an imagined problem. Fig. 1 confirms what previous studies for other countries[2] have shown:

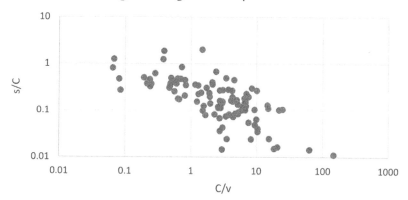

Fig. 1. Profit Rates for UK Industries Show the Inverse Relationship Between Capital Composition and Rate of Return that Marx's Worked Example Predicts. *Source:* Calculated from 2015 United Kingdom Input-Output Analytical Tables, Office of National Statistics, Published 2018. *Note:* Both axes are given a log scales.

- profit rates are significantly dispersed;
- there is a systematic inverse relationship between organic composition of capitals in any given year and their rate of profit.

Studies[3] have shown that for many countries, simple labor values are as good or better than production prices when used to predict the structure of market values of industrial output.

A possible weakness of previous studies lies them carrying over the ambiguity in Marx about what the variable c should actually mean. In Volume I of *Capital* it is clear that c is being used as a flow quantity. It designates the flow of value into the final product from the means of production. It thus includes both the value of raw materials and the value of wear on the machinery used – what we would now call depreciation. This is fine for a theory of the component parts of output values, but not really for a theory of the rate of profit. The rate of profit has to be calculated on the whole value of the stock of machinery and equipment used, only a small part of which will be depreciated in a given year.

This has practical implications when one comes to calculate what the rates of profit in different industries are. The most common approach in the literature is to work from input-output (IO) tables and sum down the columns for each industry, adding up all the different means of production used. This gives a value for c at market prices. To obtain labor values, the c at market price is converted to c in labor by first multiplying the columns of the table with a market price to value conversion vector. A similar procedure is used when computing prices of production, except that in this case the initial multiplication is done using a market price to production price conversion vector.

This approach amounts to using c as defined in Volume I, and ignoring fixed capital stocks. But to include fixed capital stocks in a test of production price theory one should not simply take fixed capital stocks at current market price. Instead one should apply a similar pre-multiplication process to that used for constant capital flows. The stocks of industrial equipment should be pre-multiplied by a market price to production price vector to accurately mimic what the supposed profit equalizing process would produce.[4]

The problem with applying this test empirically is that standard IO tables do not provide capital stock data. For this chapter I have attempted to construct dis-aggregated capital stock tables for the United Kingdom that allow the pre-multiplication process to be applied to test production price theory. The method of calculation are described in the Appendix.

From the data thus derived it was possible to plot the relationship between s/C in Marx's original terminology and c/v that was shown in Fig. 1. As I mentioned earlier, this shows a very strong inverse relationship between organic composition and profitability.

Since this data so strongly contradicts the assumptions of Chapter 10 of *Capital III*, it is worth doing a detailed calculation of the relative accuracy of labor values and fully transformed prices of production in predicting the market value of different industries.

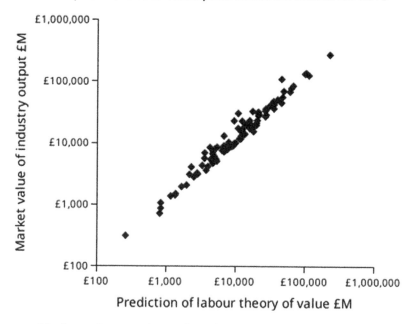

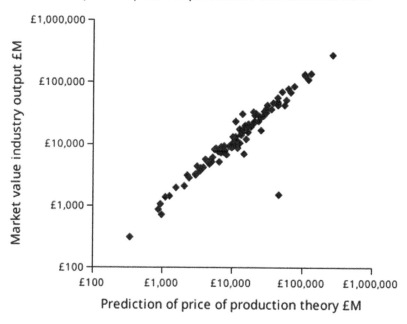

Fig. 2.   The Relationship Between Output Prices, and Two Sorts of Marxian Prices for the UK Industrial Sectors in 2015. *Source:* Calculated from 2015 United Kingdom Input-Output Analytical Tables, Office of National Statistics, Published 2018.

The results are presented graphically in Fig. 2. It is evident to the eye that the labor values are clustered more closely to the diagonal than the prices of production. This is born out by the respective R^2 for the two trend lines. Fig. 2 plots the logs of money values of sector outputs against logs of labor values and logs of prices of production. This is done to spread out the plot.

Correlations[5] of the logs and Mean Absolute Deviations (MAD) were found to be:

Correlation log labor value against log market value	98.4%
Correlation price of production against log market value	94.5%
Mean absolute deviation market value/labor value	18.7%
Mean absolute deviation market value/price of production	44.5%

Discussion

Clearly, for the United Kingdom in 2015 market prices were better predicted by labor values than by prices of production. The MAD for labor values is only slightly greater than the average value given for the China years in Cheng and Li (2020) of 0.168 and well within the range of variations (0.103–0.219). The MAD for price of production is much greater than the average given for China (0.086) and outside the range of variation (0.063–0.120).

A contributory factor to the poor performance of the prices of production must certainly be the very dispersed rate of profit shown in Fig. 1. Correlating profit rate against organic composition reveals an inverse relationship (correlation coefficient −35%) like the data for the USA in Cockshott and Cottrell (1998).

It is unclear whether the difference between this result and that obtained by Han Cheng and Minqi Li for China reflects real differences between the two economies or differences in methodology. This could only be determined by repeating their work with a calculation procedure that excluded taxes from their measure of price of production.

TIME TRENDS

Marx, as we mentioned earlier, saw the differences in profit rate caused by varying organic compositions as something that occurred over time, not something that occurred simultaneously in different industries. Marx followed up his examples with saying:

> This is how the same rate of surplus-value would express itself under the same degree of labour exploitation in a falling rate of profit, because the material growth of the constant capital implies also a growth – albeit not in the same proportion – in its value, and consequently in that of the total capital. If it is further assumed that this gradual change in the composition of capital is not confined only to individual spheres of production, but that it occurs more or less in all, or at least in the key spheres of production, so that it involves changes in the average

organic composition of the total capital of a certain society, then the gradual growth of constant capital in relation to variable capital must necessarily lead to a gradual fall of the general rate of profit, so long as the rate of surplus-value, or the intensity of exploitation of labour by capital, remain the same. Now we have seen that it is a law of capitalist production that its development is attended by a relative decrease of variable in relation to constant capital, and consequently to the total capital set in motion. This is just another way of saying that owing to the distinctive methods of production developing in the capitalist system the same number of labourers, i.e., the same quantity of labour-power set in motion by a variable capital of a given value, operate, work up and productively consume in the same time span an ever-increasing quantity of means of labour, machinery and fixed capital of all sorts, raw and auxiliary materials-and consequently a constant capital of an ever-increasing value.[6]

The argument above rests on the following assumptions:

- A material growth in the means of production implies an increase in the value of the means of production, even if the growth in value is slower.
- The rate of surplus value remains roughly the same.

The first premise is highly questionable, and we will discuss this lower down.

The second premise is fairly safe. Although the rate of surplus value does move, it tends to close to the range assumed by Marx. In 1863 when he was writing this 64% was the British rate of surplus value.[7] One does see situations where the split of income between labor and capital is roughly a 50%/50% split. You do not see situations where the split is 90%/10%. This means that his initial argument to the effect that the total wage bill will act as a rough index of total value created is sound.

On the other hand the fluctuations in constant capital to labor ratios over time and between industries can be much greater. So we can expect profit rates to be negatively correlated with organic composition, as in Marx's argument.

Marx was writing in the 1860s. Fig. 3 shows, taking British data from the period 1855 to 1910, that the rate of profit was indeed negatively correlated with the organic composition of capital. His basic argument that the organic composition would be a strong determinant of changes in profit rates is born out by this data.

If we look at the time trend in Fig. 3 of the organic composition, we see that the expected rise in organic composition was not occurring, and from 1880 to 1900 the trend was downwards.

This must mean that either the physical mass of machinery put in motion by UK workers must have declined, or what Marx called cheapening of the elements of constant capital must have been in operation.

It was certainly the case that the physical mass of basic power machines underwent drastic shrinking during the period in question. The adoption of higher pressure steam first allowed the construction of small high speed triple expansion engines and then of steam turbines (Fig. 4). This means that in some areas the actual mass of machinery declined while its ability to perform work increased.

In other economic areas, the mass of machines certainly did increase. Take shipping as an example, steamships were becoming bigger and more powerful over the period. The issues, however, when looking at the organic composition of capital would be things like:

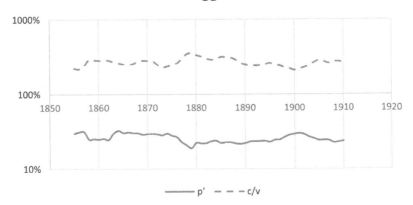

Fig. 3.   Actual Evolution of the Organic Composition and Rate of Profit in Victorian/Edwardian Britain. There Is a Negative Correlation of −61% Between Organic Composition and Rate of Profit. *Source:* Data Computed from the Bank of England (2017).

Fig. 4.   Left: The 150 hp Engine Designed for Tower Bridge by Armstrongs in 1886. Right: A 335 hp Turbine Made 1910 by Maschinenbau A.G., Prague. *Source:* Photos taken from "free to use and copy." Note how much more compact the more powerful later machine was.

(1) By how much did the average tonnage of a cargo ship rise?
(2) How much did the average crew size change?

For instance, the shift from sailing vessels to steam cargo ships would have reduced the crew requirement per ton displacement. This would correspond to a rise in the technical composition of capital.

(3) Most importantly, by how much did the price per ton of displacement change for new ships, whether measured in £s or in labor days?

Could a ship owner have bought a vessel like the Cheviot (Fig. 5) in 1870, used her for 30 years, and then with the depreciation money set aside have bought a larger vessel like the Ernst Woermann in 1900?

If productivity in the combined steel and shipbuilding industries had grown by 4% a year, he could have done. In fact growth in productivity was somewhat less:

> Between the late 1860s and the early 1890s the price of British iron ships declined about 40%. The fall in iron prices and the improvements in building technology were of approximately equal importance in explaining the price decline, while rising wages offset about half of their combined effect.[8]

This amounts to fall in the cost of constant capital for the shipping industry of about 1.7% a year. Between 1865 and 1895 British organic composition of capital fell at an average rate of 1.4% a year. If the general rise in productivity in what Marx called Department I of the economy, that producing means of production, was the same as in shipbuilding, then it was more than sufficient to account for the decline in organic composition of capital. The actual value of the capital stock per employee could have declined while its physical mass continued to grow at a modest rate.

This possibility was allowed for by Marx:

> Everything said in Part I of this book about factors which raise the rate of profit while the rate of surplus-value remains the same, or regardless of the rate of surplus-value, belongs here. Hence also, with respect to the total capital, that the value of the constant capital does not increase in the same proportion as its material volume. For instance, the quantity of cotton worked up by a single European spinner in a modern factory has grown, tremendously compared to the quantity formerly worked up by a European spinner with a spinning-wheel. Yet the value of the worked-up cotton has not grown in the same proportion as its mass. The same applies to machinery and other fixed capital. In short, the same development which increases the mass of the constant capital in relation to the variable reduces the value of its elements as a result of the increased productivity of labour, and therefore prevents the value of

Fig. 5. Size and Power of Typical Cargo Ships Increased During Late Nineteenth Century. Left: The Cheviot Built on the Tyne in 1870, 1226 grt, 120 nhp. Right: Ernst Woermann Built on the Clyde 1900, 4065 grt, 257 nhp. *Source:* Photos taken from "free to use and copy."

constant capital, although it continually increases, from increasing at the same rate as its material volume, i.e., the material volume of the means of production set in motion by the same amount of labour-power. *In isolated cases the mass of the elements of constant capital may even increase, while its value remains the same, or falls.*[9]

Taking into account the proviso shown in italics, the overall account given in Chapters 13 and 14 turn out to be consistent with what was actually happening to the British economy in the latter part of Marx's life.

- He gets right the inverse relation between organic composition and profitability.
- He gives an account of how the organic composition of capital can fall and the technical composition rise when, as was the case in the late Nineteenth Century, there is a steady rise in labor productivity in Department I.

One is left however with the feeling that this is not quite what he expected to happen. He seems to have regarded the cheapening of the elements of constant capital as the exception rather than the rule.

ACCUMULATION RATE

Although the organic composition of capital actually stayed relatively unchanged after 1855, this does not mean that no capital accumulated. Table 1 shows that the nominal value of constant capital stocks rose for 20 years, then stagnated from 1875 to 1885 before growth resumed.

Capital accumulation can be combined with a falling organic composition, and thus a rising profit rate, if the workforce is increasing. Marx indeed listed relative over-population[10] as one of the offsetting factors acting against a fall in the rate of profit in Chapter 14.

If we compare the growth of capital stock to the growth of the workforce in £s in Fig. 6, you can see that capital stock was rising faster than the employed workforce. Capital employed per worker was £65 in 1855 and had risen to £155 in 1910. Why then did the organic composition not rise sharply?

It is because Marx posed his argument in terms of real values (labor time), not nominal values in £s. His argument was that given a stable rate of exploitation, then dividing money capital stock through by wages amounts (subject to a constant of scale) to dividing the labor content of the capital stock by the living labor currently activating the stock. The relative constancy of c/v in the face of a rising nominal capital to labor ratio was possible because labor productivity rose.

This affected both wages and capital:

- In 1855, average daily wages were 39 (old) pence. In 1910 they had risen to around 81 pence. An index of real, inflation adjusted, earnings per day (taking 1900 as 100) rose from 55 in 1855 to 146 in 1910. The rate of surplus value was 67% in 1855 and 64% in 1910. Thus real wages had risen, even though the share of value added going to labor remained almost unchanged.

Table 1. The Growth of British Productive Capital Stock 1855 to 1910. Excludes Dwellings.

Year	Capital Stock	Average Growth Rate For Period	Employment	Average Growth Rate For Period
1855	994	0.2%	11,252,000	1.0%
1860	1,006	4.1%	11,818,000	0.8%
1865	1,213	2.1%	12,262,900	0.5%
1870	1,338	6.5%	12,584,300	0.8%
1875	1,772	−0.3%	13,090,500	0.2%
1880	1,749	−0.1%	13,236,600	0.7%
1885	1,743	2.0%	13,694,700	1.8%
1890	1,913	0.0%	14,935,500	0.4%
1895	1,909	7.2%	15,220,300	1.9%
1900	2,601	1.3%	16,690,300	0.3%
1905	2,765	1.8%	16,982,000	1.0%
1910	3,011	6.3%	17,867,000	1.9%

Source: Data computed from the Bank of England (2017).

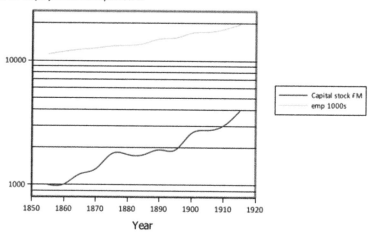

Growth of Uk employment and capital stock

Fig. 6. Growth of Capital Stock was Faster Than Growth of the Workforce. *Source:* Data computed from the Bank of England (2017).

- I have not been able to obtain time series for capital goods prices over the period so I will use the CPI shown in Fig. 7. Scaling to 1900 prices, this shows that the capital stock per worker in 1855 would have been £75 and in 1910 it would have risen to £159. So in real terms, in terms of productive equipment, it had risen. But what about in terms of labor values?

Consumer price index 1900=100

Fig. 7. Consumer Price Index for Late Nineteenth Century. Prices Were Generally Falling Until the Mild Inflation Caused by Rising South African Gold Production in the Early Twentieth Century. *Source:* Data computed from the Bank of England (2017).

- Consider Table 2. This computes the Monetary Equivalent of Labor Time (MELT) for the start and end years of our period. It can be seen that the value created by a year's work rose from £61 to £170 over the 55 years. If we use the MELT to convert the constant capital employed per worker given earlier into the number of years of labor needed to reproduce that constant capital, we see that the net capital stock per worker had risen slightly.

If we plot over time the relationship between the organic composition of capital c/v and the ratio of dead to living labor in worker years in Fig. 8, we see that they match very well.

It is notable that the broad trend of both is stable. There are short term fluctuations but no long term rising trend. We have accounted for this in terms of a cheapening of constant capital goods. But this is only a partial answer. At a deeper level the cause was the fact that the capitalist class, contrary to Marx's aphorism about accumulation being "their Moses and their prophets," actually spent only a minority of their income on accumulation.

Table 2. Estimating Capital Stock per Worker in Labor Time for the Start and End of the Period.

Year	Gross Domestic Product (£M)	Capital Consumption (£M)	Net Domestic Product (£M)	MELT (£ per Worker Year)	Capital Stock per Worker (in Labor Years)
1855	715	29	686	61	1.1
1910	22,122	108	2014	170	1.4

Source: Data computed from the Bank of England (2017).
Note: The MELT is obtained by dividing the Net Domestic Product by the number of worker years that were required to produce it. Similar methods were used to derive Fig. 9.

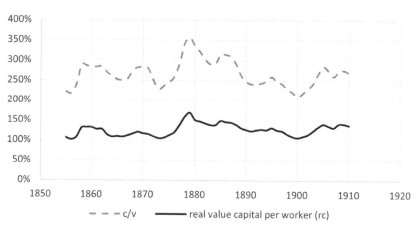

Fig. 8. Marx's Index of Dead to Living Labor *c/v* Correlates Well (Coefficient 86%) With the Value in Person Years of the Fixed Capital Operated by Each Worker. *Source:* Data computed from the Bank of England (2017).

A MODEL

If you look at Fig. 9, it is evident that the upper classes generally consumed more than 80% of surplus value, with accumulation rarely rising above 20%. Comparing the rate of accumulation out of surplus value with the movement of capital stock per worker measured in person years, it is clear that the former tended to drive the latter. We can systematise this with a little calculus.

Clearly if the rate of growth of capital stock dC/dt is higher than the rate of growth of the workforce $d\lambda/dt$, then c/v will rise, and c/v will fall if the workforce grows faster.

If the workforce and capital stock grow at the same rate then the organic composition and profit rate will stabilise. Let us ignore interest and rent, and

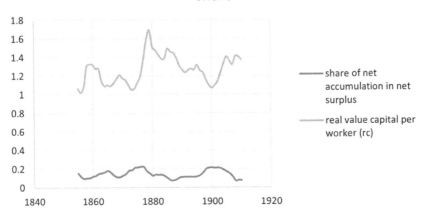

Fig. 9. Long Term Trends in Fixed Capital per Worker, Measured in Person Years, Are Driven by the Share of Surplus Being Accumulated. *Source:* Data computed from the Bank of England (2017).

assume all surplus value takes the form of profit. We will also initially abstract from depreciation and technical change.

Let $G = d\lambda/dt$ be the rate of growth per year of the workforce.

Let α be the share of net surplus value being accumulated.

Assume the rate of profit has stabilised, and denote this stable rate by p^*.

Clearly we must have relationship:

$$p^* = \frac{G}{\alpha} \qquad (1)$$

for profit to be stable.

Why?

Consider that the rate of profit is s/C, so $\alpha p^* = \alpha s/C$ is the rate of growth per year of the capital stock.

$$\alpha p^* = \frac{\alpha s}{C} = \frac{dC}{dt}$$

But we defined p^* to be the profit rate where $G = dC/dt$, so:

$$\alpha p^* = \frac{\alpha s}{C} = \frac{dC}{dt} = G$$

so $p^* = G/\alpha$, Q.E.D.

From Net to Gross Surplus

Now relax the assumption of no depreciation and not technical change. National income figures give us gross trading surplus and gross capital accumulation along with a separate figure for depreciation or capital consumption.

Let us use S for gross trading surplus, d for the annual depreciation rate as a share of capital, and $P = S/C$, be the gross rate of profit and A denote the share of gross surplus that goes to fund gross accumulation.

We can now modify eq. (1) to obtain a formula for the stable gross profit rate:

$$P^* = \frac{G+d}{A} \qquad (2)$$

Technical Change

If labor productivity grows at 5% a year, then clearly the labor value of capital stock at replacement cost also falls by 5% a year. Technical change thus acts on capital stock in the same way as depreciation – Marxist economists call this "moral depreciation."

Let the rate of growth of labor productivity be denoted by t for technical change.

A rapid rate of technical change tends to raise the stable rate of profit since it acts to slow down the accumulation process measured in real value terms: that is to say in terms of the worker years represented by the capital stock.

So our final equation is:

$$P^* = \frac{G+d+t}{A} \qquad (3)$$

One can consider P^* as the dynamic attractor of the profit rate. If the variables A, G, d, t remain unchanged then the real gross profit rate P' should asymptotically approach P^*.

This basic equation has been derived elsewhere (Cockshott, Michaelson, Cottrell, Wright, & Yakovenko, 2009; Cottrell & Cockshott, 2006; Zachariah, 2009) and tested against modern time series. In Fig. 10, we show how it can be applied to late Victorian British capitalism.

CONCLUSION

We have shown using old and recent UK data that key elements of Marx's theory of profit rates are valid.

(1) In both diachronic and synchronic cases the inverse relationship between organic composition and profit rate predicted by the labor theory of value is observed.

Profit rate against dynamic attractor

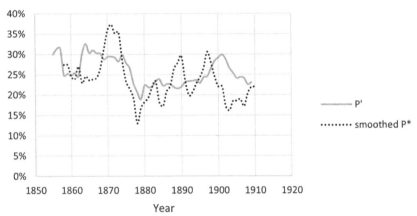

Fig. 10.   Profit Rate Against Dynamic Attractor. *Source:* All data calculated from the Bank of England (2017). *Note:* P' is the gross rate of profit and smoothed $P^{*'}$ is the 4 year average of the dynamic profit rate attractor.

(2) As Marx hypothesised c/v in money terms acts as a good proxy for the ratio of dead to living labor.
(3) One can, using the assumptions of his theory, derive a dynamic model of the rate of profit with non-negligible predictive power.

Fig. 10 shows how the dynamic attractor of the profit rate, whilst subject to high frequency noise from the business cycle, in absolute scale brackets and in its changes correlates (coefficient 42%) to the observed gross profit rate. It shows a tendency to lead the actual profit rate. This is quite striking given that the variables entering into it are all time derivatives – none of the original Marxian variables remains. The actual derivation of the calculus (eqs. 1–3) remains predicated on the assumptions of the labor theory of value. So although the new equation looks unfamiliar, it is axiomatically derived from that given in *Capital*.

NOTES

1. Since annual profit rate is an exponential of weekly profit rate so $1{,}310{,}363\% = (1.2^{52} - 1) \times 100$.
2. See for example: Cockshott and Cottrell (1998, 2003), Zachariah (2006).
3. See for example: Fröhlich (2013), Ochoa (1989), Petrovic (1987), in addition to those cited on the dispersion of profit rates.
4. For example the process described in Sraffa (1960).
5. Correlations are used here rather than a cosine metric since correlation is also numeraire independent and is also more widely used in the sciences. The correlation coefficient is in fact a cosine metric adjusted for shifts of origin.
6. Marx (1971), Chapter 13.

7. Computed from a wage share of 0.61 in Table A56 of the *Millenium of Economic Data*.
8. Harley, 1970.
9. Marx (1971), Chapter 14. My emphasis.
10. "Relative over-population becomes so much more apparent in a country, the more the capitalist mode of production is developed in it. This, again, is the reason why, on the one hand, the more or less imperfect subordination of labor to capital continues in many branches of production, and continues longer than seems at first glance compatible with the general stage of development. This is due to the cheapness and abundance of disposable or unemployed wage-labourers, and to the greater resistance, which some branches of production, by their very nature, render to the transformation of manual work into machine production. On the other hand, new lines of production are opened up, especially for the production of luxuries, and it is these that take as their basis this relative over-population, often set free in other lines of production through the increase of their constant capital. These new lines start out predominantly with living labor, and by degrees pass through the same evolution as the other lines of production. In either case the variable capital makes up a considerable portion of the total capital and wages are below the average, so that both the rate and mass of surplus-value in these lines of production are unusually high." (Marx (1971), Chapter 14, 4).

REFERENCES

Bank of England. (2017). Bank of England database *A Millennium of Economic Data. "A millennium of macroeconomic data for the UK,"* Version 3.1, London.

Cheng, H., & Li, M. (2020). Do labor values explain Chinese prices? Evidence from China's input-output tables, 1990–2012. *Review of Radical Political Economics, 52*(1), 115–136.

Cockshott, W. P., & Cottrell, A. (1998). Does Marx need to transform? In Bellofiore, R. (Ed.), *Marxian economics: A reappraisal* (pp. 70–85). Berlin: Springer.

Cockshott, W. P., & Cottrell, A. (2003). A note on the organic composition of capital and profit rates. *Cambridge Journal of Economics, 27*(5), 749–754.

Cockshott, W. P., Michaelson, G., Cottrell, A., Wright, I., & Yakovenko, V. (2009). *Classical econophysics.* London: Routledge.

Cottrell, A., & Cockshott, P. (2006). Demography and the falling rate of profit. *Indian Development Review, 4*(1), 39–59.

Fröhlich, N. (2013). Labour values, prices of production and the missing equalisation tendency of profit rates: Evidence from the German economy. *Cambridge Journal of Economics, 37*(5), 107–126.

Harley, C. K. (1970). British shipbuilding and merchant shipping: 1850–1890. *The Journal of Economic History, 30*(1), 262–266.

Marx, K. (1971). *Capital* (Vol. 3). Moscow: Progress Publishers.

Ochoa, E. M. (1989). Values, prices, and wage-profit curves in the U.S. economy. *Cambridge Journal of Economics, 13*, 413–429.

Petrovic, P. (1987). The deviation of production prices from labour values: Some methodolog and empirical evidence. *Cambridge Journal of Economics, 11*, 197–210.

Sraffa, P. (1960). *Production of commodities by means of commodities.* Cambridge: Cambridge University Press.

Zachariah, D. (2006). Labour value and equalisation of profit rates: A multi-country study. *Indian Development Review, 4*(1), 1–21.

Zachariah, D. (2009). Determinants of the average profit rate and the trajectory of capitalist economies. *Bulletin of Political Economy, 3*(1), 1–13.

APPENDICES

A. METHOD OF CALCULATION

The UK Office of National Statistics (ONS) publish capital stock data annually that give net capital stocks for distinct combinations of 12 asset types and some 90 sectors. Some sectors are given in both aggregate and disaggregated form so the total number of independently specified sectors is slightly less. Whilst the sector names are not identical to those used in the IO table, industrial sector codes are provided so it is relatively easy to translate to the IO table sectors. The data for 2015 was used as this corresponds to the most recent year that a British input output table has been published.

The capital data from ONS are in relational rather than matrix form so an expanded stock matrix was created such that for each column in the original stock matrix for which several sub industries exist in the io table the capital values in the original are spread among the new multiple columns in proportion to their share in the final output of this group of industries. The final output matrix has column names in the same order as the input output table. The resulting intermediate stock matrix has rows with the asset types:

- Dwellings;
- Other buildings and structures;
- Transport equipment;
- Computer hardware;
- Telecommunications equipment;
- ICT equipment;
- Cultivated biological resources;
- Research & development;
- Computer software and databases;
- Intellectual property products;
- Machinery, equipment and weapons systems;
- Other machinery, equipment and weapons systems.

It is again relatively easy to identify the input output table industries producing these categories of goods. The ones that were used in this study are documented in Table A1. Using this and the intermediate capital stock matrix produced by the previous step, software was used to produce an expanded stock matrix with the same layout as the iotable such that:

- For each row in the intermediate stock matrix for which several source industries exist in the source index file these are mapped to IO table rows using Table A1.
- Capital values in the original matrix are spread among the new multiple rows in proportion to the flows shown in the corresponding columns in the iotable.
- The underlying assumption for this approach is that the flows shown in the io table are replacement for depreciation and will be proportional to the corresponding capital stocks.

Table A1. Mapping From Capital Stock Types to Industrial Sector in the IO Table That Produces Them.

Dwellings	Construction			
Other buildings and structures	Construction			
Transport equipment	Manufacture of motor vehicles, trailers and semi-trailers	Building of ships and boats	Manufacture of air and spacecraft and related machinery	Manufacture of other transport equipment – 30.2/4/9
Computer hardware	Manufacture of computer, electronic and optical products			
Telecommunications equipment	Manufacture of computer, electronic and optical products	Manufacture of electrical equipment		
ICT equipment	Manufacture of computer, electronic and optical products			
Cultivated biological resources	Crop and animal production, hunting and related service activities	forestry and logging	Fishing and aquaculture	
Research & development	Scientific research and development	Other professional, scientific and technical activities	Scientific research and development NPISH	
Computer software and databases	Computer programming, consultancy and related activities			
Intellectual property products	Motion picture, video & tv program production, sound recording & music	Creative, arts and	Scientific research and development	Publishing activities	Advertising and market research	Motion picture, video & tv program production, sound recording & music	Creative, arts and entertainment

Table A1. (*Continued*)

Dwellings	Construction						
	publishing activities & programming and broadcasting activities non-market	entertainment activities				publishing activities & programming and broadcasting activities	activities NPISH
Machinery, equipment and weapons systems	Manufacture of fabricated metal products, excluding weapons & ammunition – 25.1-3/5-9	Manufacture of weapons and ammunition	Manufacture of computer, electronic and optical products	Manufacture of electrical equipment	Manufacture of machinery and equipment N.E.C.		
Other machinery, equipment and weapons systems	Manufacture of fabricated metal products, excluding weapons & ammunition – 25.1-3/5-9	Manufacture of weapons and ammunition	Manufacture of computer, electronic and optical products	Manufacture of electrical equipment	Manufacture of machinery and equipment N.E.C.		

B. HANDLING OF TAX AND IMPORTS

The IO table contains rows for taxes on products and production and for the import content of each column listed. Since we are concerned to do an unbiased comparison between prices of production and since Marx's Volume I and Volume III price theories ignore the effect of taxes we do not include them in the calculation. It should however be born in mind that in this and other studies of correspondence between labor values and market prices, the differential impact of taxes of industries will constitute a source of unaccounted for noise in the market prices.

Imports are dealt with by computing the labor content of £1 of exports and imputing the same labor content to each £1 of imports used by an industry.

C. VALUES AND PRICES OF PRODUCTION

Labor values and prices of production were computed via a Jacobi iterative procedure with 12 iterations. Two temporary vectors v, p are used. The vector v holds the labor content of each £1 of output of the corresponding industry, p holds the production price per £1 of output. Both vectors are initialised to zero.

On each iteration for each industry i the total labor content L_i is computed by adding the direct labor λ_i to $U_i^T \cdot v$, that is to the total obtained by converting the £costs in the ith column of the use matrix U into labor using v. Then v is updated by setting $v_i = L_i/F_i$ where F is the final output vector in £.

An analogous procedure is used to update p.

In this case the total production cost P_i for each industry is computed as:

$$P_i = \lambda_i + U_i^T \cdot p + r\left(K_i^T \cdot p\right)$$

where K is the capital stock matrix with the same shape as U and r the rate of profit for the whole economy obtained by dividing the Gross Operating Surplus of the economy as a whole by the total capital stock of the economy.

At the end of each iteration P, L are renormalised to ensure that their totals are equal to the total in £ of final output F.

ELEMENTS FOR A STUDY OF THE PROFIT RATE: FRANCE, 1896–2019

Weinan Ding, Zhiming Long and Rémy Herrera

ABSTRACT

Considering that the rate of profit constitutes a key indicator for the analysis of the evolution of capitalist economies, this chapter proposes to study the case of France from 1896 to 2019, that is, over 124 years in total. From a series of stock of productive capital reconstructed for the occasion, a rate of profit is calculated at the macroeconomic level within a conceptual framework faithful to Marx. Over this period of more than a century, three successive long waves are identified, as parts of a secular trend toward the fall in the French rate of profit. The latter, however, recovered several times during these three sub-periods, but finally reoriented downwards, with fluctuations of an amplitude tending to decrease more and more and a deployment in a decreasing spiral of French capitalism. This long-term downward trend is mainly due to the rise in the organic composition of capital.

Keywords: Rate of profit; long waves; productive capital; organic composition of capital; decomposition of the profit rate; France

INTRODUCTION

The idea of a downward trend in the rate of profit constitutes one of the central propositions of the Marxist theory of capitalist accumulation and crises. The accompanying debates have been and remain some of the most intensely polemical, when it is a question of knowing whether or not this "law" is justified in the element of theory or of showing empirically whether or not such a trend is observed. The literature devoted to the main capitalist economies reveals strong disparities in the estimation of profit rates, due in particular to the methodology for calculating this rate, different accounting perimeters relating to the variables

Value, Money, Profit, and Capital Today
Research in Political Economy, Volume 39, 189–195
Copyright © 2024 Weinan Ding, Zhiming Long and Rémy Herrera
Published under exclusive licence by Emerald Publishing Limited
ISSN: 0161-7230/doi:10.1108/S0161-723020230000039011

used (including that of capital) or even the problem of the transformation of values.

There are sufficiently abundant and quality statistical databases on France to try to shed light on this question in the case of this country. Trying to be as faithful to Marx as possible, we first present the methods mobilized to construct the stock of productive capital and to calculate the rate of profit, then our results, as well as a breakdown of the historical period studied into three successive long waves, and finally a brief analysis of the reasons for the evolution of the French rate of profit as we calculate it. It should be noted that this reflection is only a draft intended to identify some preliminary elements for a more in-depth research of this subject. Nevertheless, our provisional results are already sufficiently consistent and interesting to be presented to the readers.

METHODS OF CONSTRUCTING THE PRODUCTIVE CAPITAL STOCK AND CALCULATING THE RATE OF PROFIT

For our empirical study of the French economy, we use the World Inequality Database (various years),[1] which spans from 1896 to 2019 for the variables we need. The definition of "capital" used by this statistical database includes not only (net) foreign assets, but also domestic assets, which include, among others, agricultural land and other natural resources, as well as residential assets, taken as the sum of the values of the dwellings and those of their underlying land.

According to Marx, capital is fundamentally a relation of production. Things are only supports of it. Asking the question of whether or not an object constitutes capital therefore amounts to questioning the nature of this thing and the role it plays in the relation of production. Failing to distinguish between essence and phenomenon, mainstream (neoclassical) writers are mistaken in considering capital as a "factor" of a "production function" – alongside labor. For in order for money to be transformed into capital, it must first buy labor power, as well as materials and tools – the latter being themselves products of past labor.

The interpretation of capital retained by the database used here, which is that of the current Western national accounting system and which can be compared to the notion of "wealth,"[2] remains prisoner of this vision which we consider erroneous. This is the case when, for example, housing is included in the perimeter of the capital. However, contrary to this representation, the concept of capital in Marx has as its key the relation of production. For our part, we believe that these different connotations constitute a serious problem which requires reconstructing a series of stock of productive capital, as close as possible to Marx's original intention[3] – even if the available data do not allow us to separate unproductive labor from productive labor. We must therefore grasp the concept of capital from the productive sector alone.

Under these conditions, in the present empirical study, to get closer to the capital understood by Marx, we must proceed to two types of corrections: we decide, on the one hand, to deduce from the series of productive non-financial assets of the aggregated files the national accounts certain components, in this case, inventories, housing and armament systems; and, on the other hand, to retain the component of cultivated agricultural land drawn from the series of non-productive non-financial assets. It should also be noted that the capital defined here corresponds to private properties – the French State having net assets of zero, or even negative in certain years.

By retaining a hypothesis of homogeneity of the production and circulation processes, we can calculate a rate of profit, in the manner of Long and Herrera (2018) or Herrera and Long (2021), as follows:

$$r = \frac{\Pi}{K} = \frac{Y - (Z + T)}{K} \tag{1}$$

where Π is the profit, K the total capital advanced and r the ratio of these two variables, that is, the rate of profit. Profit Π is written as the difference between gross domestic product (GDP), denoted Y, and the sum of the remuneration of all workers, Z, and taxes T (import taxes included). The total advanced capital K is itself the sum of the fixed capital K_P, corresponding to the stock of productive capital, and the circulating capital, i.e., $Z + V$, with V representing the inventories. The data used to calculate the rate of profit is all expressed in current prices, with market prices as estimated in this database, World Inequality Database.

EVOLUTION OF THE PROFIT RATE OF THE FRENCH ECONOMY OVER 124 YEARS (1896–2019)

As can be seen in Fig. 1, the general profile of the evolution of the rate of profit of the French economy from 1896 to 2019 reveals a downward trend in the long

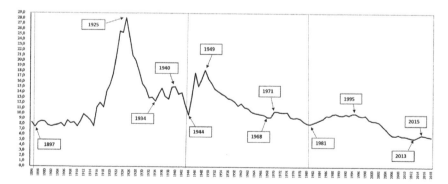

Fig. 1. Evolution of the Profit Rate of the French Economy From 1896 to 2019 *(percentage). Note:* Profit rate calculated by the authors from the *World Inequality Database* (various years).

term. But we also notice that this rate of profit fluctuates cyclically. Fig. 1 indeed exhibits three distinct long waves, quite complete, *à la* Kondratieff (1935). These successive waves, each of which lasts nearly four decades (respectively 47, 37, and 39 years, in chronological order) all have in common to contain two peaks and two troughs, alternating them according to a sequence that can be described as follows: from an initial low point identified at the very beginning of the subperiod, the rate of profit first begins by rising more or less quickly toward a peak, which corresponds to the maximum level of the wave, before to move clearly downwards toward a second low point, then to go up in the direction of a second high point, located however at a lower level than the previous one, and finally to go down again to reach a second trough (most often below the first).

The first long wave opens with the last year of the serious economic crisis that marked France at the end of the Nineteenth Century (i.e., 1897) and closes with the inflection point of the Second World War (that is, 1943). This period is characterized by the expansion of colonization and the completion of the transition of French capitalism from the free competition of markets to the oligopolistic concentration of capital. Over this subperiod, the rate of profit starts from its minimum level of 7.5% in 1897 (with the crisis ending the nineteenth century) to reach its maximum of 28.2% in 1925; then it fell to 12.4% in 1934 (real beginning of the Great Depression in France) and rose to 15.2% in 1940 (before the devastating effects of the defeat against Nazi Germany were felt). The second wave runs from 1944 – the year in which, during the Second World War, the rate of profit hit a low point of 9.8% – until 1980 – at the dawn of the neoliberal era in France. These limits correspond approximately to those of the *Trente Glorieuses* (the Glorious Thirty Years), the main feature of which was the strong intervention of the public authorities (including through planning) in order to accelerate the GDP growth rate and to set up the institutions of Social Protection. Over this subperiod, the maximum level was reached in 1949 at 18.3%, at the time of the post-war rebound, and the minimum level in 1968 at 9.4% ("May events"), just before the secondary peak of 1971 at 10.5%. The third wave of the French capital profit rate begins with the low point of 8.1% in 1981 and extends until the end of the sample. This is the period of neoliberal capitalism, which was not yet over in 2018. The peak of this wave is found in 1995 at 10.2% and its lowest trough in 2013 at 5.5%, located barely below the second peak of 2015 at 6.1% (Table 1).

The downward trend in the rate of profit of the French economy between 1896 and 2019 is reflected in the decrease in its averages by subperiod: 13.0% from 1896 to 1943, 11.9% from 1944 to 1980, 8.0% from 1981 to 2019. The amplitude of profit rate fluctuations is reduced over time: the strongest variations are observed in the first subperiod, with historical events of the magnitude of the two world wars and of the great crisis, then in the second subperiod, with the episode of May 1968 and the two oil shocks of the 1970s, and finally in the third subperiod (disturbances experienced by Europe; financial crisis of 2008).

Table 1. Long Waves of the profit Rate of the French Economy: Periods, Extrema, Averages.

Successive Long Waves	Periods	Profit Rate Extrema
First long wave	1897–1943 *(47 years)*	First trough in 1897: 7.5% *(minimum of the wave)* First peak in 1925: 28.2% *(maximum of the wave)* Second trough in 1934: 12.4% Second peak in 1940: 15.2% *Average of the subperiod 1897–1943:* 13.1%
Second long wave	1944–1980 *(37 years)*	First trough in 1944: 9.8% First peak in 1949: 18.3% *(maximum of the wave)* Second trough in 1968: 9.4% *(minimum of the wave)* Second peak in 1971: 10.5% *Average of the subperiod 1944–1980:* 11.9%
Third long wave	1981–2019 *(39 years)*	First trough in 1981: 8.1% First peak in 1995: 10.2% *(maximum of the wave)* Second trough in 2013: 5.5% *(minimum of the wave)* Second peak in 2015: 6.1% *Average of the subperiod 1981–2019:* 8.0%

Source: Our calculations on World Inequality Database.

DECOMPOSITION OF THE RATE OF PROFIT AND EXPLANATION OF ITS SECULAR EVOLUTION

To outline an explanation of the causes of these long-term variations in the profit rate, we use a method of decomposition of this rate of profit, inspired by the analysis proposed by Weisskopf (1979), but by calculating the organic composition of capital as the relationship between the stock of capital and remuneration, as close as possible to the vision given by Marx:

$$r = \frac{\frac{\Pi}{Z}}{\frac{K}{Z} + 1} \qquad (2)$$

where Π/Z represents the rate of surplus value and K/Z the organic composition of capital.

It can be observed that the organic composition of capital thus calculated for the French economy rose between 1896 and 1913, but that, at the same time, the rate of surplus value also increased rapidly, in fact at a much higher rate, which logically led to a rise in the profit rate. During the years following 1913, the rate of surplus value first decreased, then increased sharply until the peak of 1926, while the organic composition of capital decreased markedly, the two effects combined leading to the soaring of the profit rate to the maximum of the first long wave – and peak of the 124 years studied.

At the end of the Second World War, which marked the beginning of the second long wave, the French economy recovered fairly quickly and, with the rise in the GDP, the organic composition of capital and the rate of surplus value also increased, but from the year 1950, the rate of surplus value was oriented downwards, while the organic composition of capital continued to increase, at a good pace, and this until 1968, so that the combination of these two phenomena resulted by a very significant drop in the rate of profit.

At the beginning of the 1980s and the third long wave, that of the neoliberal era, the French profit rate recovered. As a matter of fact, during this same decade, from 1981 to 1989, the organic composition of capital increased, but the even faster increase in the rate of surplus value led to a rise in the rate of profit, which reached a peak in 1989 – a peak almost as high as that of this third wave, observed for the year 1995. But thereafter, the rate of surplus value having fluctuated only slightly, it is mainly the organic composition of capital which, by increasing, explains the most recent decrease in the rate of profit of the French economy.

In total, we observe, over the very long period, a downward trend in the rate of profit in France, but also several interludes of rebound or temporary stabilization, so that we are rather dealing with a downward spiral deployment of French capitalism. Consequently, we understand that the organic composition of capital, just like the rate of surplus value, fundamentally reflect the contradictions between the productive forces – therefore also productivity – and the relations of production of the economy. The successive attempts to resolve these contradictions inherent in the capitalist system, through the action in the short or medium term of counter-tendencies to the secular fall in the rate of profit in the long term, thus trigger the appearance of long waves giving to the accumulation of capital a tortuous trajectory.

CONCLUSION

In total, we observe, over the very long period, a downward trend in the rate of profit in France, but also several interludes of rebound or temporary stabilization, so that we are rather dealing with a downward spiral deployment of French capitalism. Consequently, we understand that the organic composition of capital, just like the rate of surplus value, fundamentally reflect the contradictions between the productive forces – therefore also productivity – and the relations of production of the economy. The successive attempts to resolve these contradictions inherent in the capitalist system, through the action in the short or medium term of counter-tendencies to the secular fall in the rate of profit in the long term, thus trigger the appearance of long waves giving to the accumulation of capital a tortuous trajectory.

NOTES

1. Alongside other specialists, Thomas Piketty was one of the designers of this database, on which his famous book, published in English in 2014, *Capital in the Twenty-First Century*, is based to a large extent. For a critique of the theses developed by Piketty in this book, read: Andréani and Herrera (2015) and Long and Herrera (2017, 2018).

2. See here: Herrera and Long (2021).

3. Marx (1987).

REFERENCES

Andréani, T., & Herrera, R. (2015). Thomas Piketty: "Réguler" le capitalisme. *La Pensée, 381*, 105–117.

Herrera, R., & Long, Z. (2021). *Dynamique de l'économie chinoise: Croissance, cycles et crises de 1949 à nos jours*. Paris: Éditions Critiques.

Kondratieff, N. D. (1935). The Long waves in economic life. *The Review of Economics and Statistics, 17*(6), 105–115.

Long, Z., & Herrera, R. (2017). Capital accumulation, profit rates and cycles in China from 1952 to 2014. *Journal of Innovation Economics & Management, 23*(2), 59–82.

Long, Z., & Herrera, R. (2018). The Laws of Capital in the twenty-first century in China. Piketty in Beijing. *China Economic Review, 50*(3), 153–174.

Marx, K. (1987). *Capital* (Vol. I). Moscow: Progress Publishers.

Piketty, T. (2014). *Capital in the twenty-first century*. Cambridge, MA: Harvard University Press.

Weisskopf, T. (1979). Marxian crisis theory and the rate of profit in the postwar US economy. *Cambridge Journal of Economics, 3*(4), 341–378.

World Inequality Database. (various years). Retrieved from https://wid.world/data/

PART IV

CAPITAL TODAY

FICTITIOUS CAPITAL, FICTITIOUS PROFITS, AND THEIR EXTREME FETISHISM

Mauricio de Souza Sabadini
and Gustavo Moura de Cavalcanti Mello

ABSTRACT

The purpose of this chapter is to characterize fictitious capital and fictitious profits as extreme expressions of the fetishism of capital. Considering the incessant search for valorization and allowing for fictitious forms of capital, the subject of this study is at the center of the dynamics of recent capitalist accumulation, especially when we take into account the capitalist crises over the last four or five decades. Its mechanism of fictitious valorization (M – M'), a decisive dimension of contemporary capitalism, is contradictory, based on the growing obstacles to the extraction of surplus value on an expanded scale, and therefore the real valorization of capital. At the same time, we support the idea that this mass of overaccumulated capital produces profits unrelated to surplus value, that is fictitious profits, further intensifying the fetishistic and contradictory nature of capitalism.

Keywords: Fictitious capital; fictitious profits; fetishism; capitalism; capitalist crisis; capital

INTRODUCTION

The debate surrounding fictitious capital has grown, mainly due to the recurring capitalist crises of the last decades of the twentieth century and the beginning of the twenty-first century. There were many in the 1990s, especially in underdeveloped countries, occurring again in 2008–2009 on a larger scale, this time reaching the core of the central capitalist economies. In this process, the flexibilization of financial rules, stemming from the spread of neoliberal policies, as

Value, Money, Profit, and Capital Today
Research in Political Economy, Volume 39, 199–214
ISSN: 0161-7230/doi:10.1108/S0161-723020230000039012

well as the development of the "microelectronic revolution," potentiated fictional valuation and changes in the pattern of accumulation, strongly led by speculative movements of capital.

It was in this context, in which fictitious capital assumed a determinative place, directly interfering with capitalist production and reproduction, either through the intensification of the extraction of surplus value in productive capital, or through the appropriation of wealth via the transfer of profits and interests as sources of income, that we suggest the existence of a type of profit, fictitious profit, as a remuneration derived from fictitious forms of capital.

As fictitious capital separates itself from the creation of value and surplus value, in a constant and contradictory search for total autonomy, the autonomisation of the functional forms of capital, which is at the origin of interest-bearing capital and fictitious capital, potentiates the fetish of capital, even if such an association has found little space in debates on the "financialization" of the economy.

"Financialization" attracts attention both in Marxist literature and in other currents of economic thinking, such as in post-Keynesian currents. Roberts (2018) correctly warns that this theme often appears disconnected from the study of forms of capital as a value that appreciates. Naturally, as will become clear through the text, our concept of fictitious profits means that we do not identify with those who deny or despise the Marxian theory of value. We maintain that the dynamics of the expanded reproduction of capital is based on the production of value and surplus value. We also suggest the existence of profits disconnected from the production of surplus value in the process of the expansion and growth of fictitious capital within the global cycle of capital, and that this corresponds to the extreme fetish of its fictitious forms.

These fictitious profits, which have been investigated in some of our recent works on the place of fictitious capital within the current dynamics of capital accumulation (Carcanholo, 2014; Carcanholo & Sabadini, 2014; Gomes, 2015; Mello & Braga, 2022; Mello & Nakatani, 2021; Mello & Sabadini, 2019; Sabadini, 2019, 2021), will be addressed in part two of this chapter. The following part briefly presents the links between the fetishism of the commodities, money, and capital, demonstrating that the exposition of fetishism accompanies each step of the exposition of the concept of capital at its core.[1] From this interpretative key, the fourth part will be dedicated exclusively to the presentation of the fetishism of interest-bearing capital and fictitious capital, followed by some brief final remarks.

It is worth emphasizing in advance that if the aforementioned fictitious profits do not express themselves as a transfigured form of surplus value, as in the profits related to the production and trade of goods, this does not mean ignoring the fetish of productive and/or commercial profits, which cloud the exploitation of labor and which points to the fact that the process of production-transfer-appropriation of wealth within the scope of competition between capitals were, and naturally continues to be, fundamental. At the same time, however, we recognize a reconfiguration of the dynamics of accumulation, in which the fictitious forms of capital and the mechanisms of income extraction acquire primacy.

We stated earlier that we agree with Roberts (2018), but, at the same time, we suggest an interpretation that seeks to advance the exposition of certain capitalist phenomena, without denying that the extraction of labor-value is its main support.

Our starting point, therefore, is that if the critique of labor-value lies at the center of the analysis and understanding of the capitalist mode of production, the theme of fetishism of the commodities, money and capital accompanies the process of the formation and empowerment of the functional forms of capital. In contemporary capitalism, these characteristics have been exacerbated by the growing economic weight of fictitious wealth, by the sophistication of financial operations, by technological investments, by the interconnection of markets, by new and complex financial products, representing commodity-capital, and by the shortening of space-time resulting from these phenomena.

So, fetishism is symbiotically linked to the development of value forms and accompanies their movement. Thus, the autonomisation and subjectivation of capital correspond to a process of the mystification of its own essence. Unlike interpretations of the "vulgar economy," so called by Marx, they are not disturbances of capital. On the contrary, they are part of the mystifying and contradictory nature of capitalist accumulation, and fictitious capital and fictitious profits are evident manifestations of this process. This is what we will try to expound in this text.

FICTITIOUS CAPITAL AND FICTITIOUS PROFITS

In this section, we will briefly expand on some of the central points we have discussed over the last two decades on the topic of fictitious capital and fictitious profits.[2] Fictitious capital is born from the process of the autonomisation of interest-bearing capital, in the development of the credit system, all wrapped in a kind of social illusion – well founded in the dynamics of capitalist reproduction – as it has no real substance. This implies that fictitious capital does not generate value and surplus value, but requires remuneration in the form of interests and, for us, also fictitious profits. Its logic is associated with the appropriation of a part of the surplus value produced which, apparently, develops independently of production, further disguising the connections with the real process of valorization, being, therefore, more complex, and more de-substantialized (Carcanholo & Nakatani, 2019; Carcanholo & Sabadini, 2014; Gomes, 2015).

Such characteristics further mystify the connections with the process of valorization, and it should be noted that the cycle of interest-bearing capital ($M – M – C – M' – M'$) gives the autonomisation of fictitious capital, in $M – M'$, as stated in Mello and Sabadini (2019):

> Unlike interest-bearing capital, which arises when a mass of capital is not directly invested by its owner but borrowed in exchange for its repayment plus interest, fictitious capital does not and never has possessed any value, it is a legal title which assumes an expectation of future

income streams and variations in the prices of financial assets themselves, based on the conditions of competition in the markets in which they circulate.[3]

As a result of the capitalization of future income, it should then be noted that even though it does not produce value and surplus value, it directly interferes with real accumulation, enhancing the mobility and centralization of capital, and pressing for the transfer of value from production to remunerate owners of property titles, such as shares. Such interactions between the productive and financial dynamics appear directly in the demand for greater labor productivity, in a constant relationship with so-called management and corporate governance policies, both in the macro and microeconomic spheres.[4]

Carson (2017) highlights the intensification of forms of capitalist domination in the face of the prominence assumed by fictitious capital, such as the central and classic subjection of the value-form, on the one hand, and subjection to future valuation, on the other. In addition, the author states that, "what is most striking about this analysis of 'fictitious capital', as a form facilitating the renewed emergence of directly personal power within the process of capital valorization, is the strong contradiction this implies" (p. 583). For him, personal power relationships hatch from fictitious capital, as they are launched by fetishism.

If the contradictory shortening of the cycle M – M′, as well as its incessant denial and inversion of the dynamics of real accumulation (Sabadini, 2019), apparently causes a detachment of the production of wealth in its entirety, intensifying its de-substantiated nature (Carcanholo, 2019; Carcanholo & Nakatani, 2019), then it should be noted that such a process does not deprive labor-value of its central position in the production of wealth in the capitalist mode of production, in what is clearly an illusory valuing of itself independent of labor. Therein lies its extreme mystification and, above all, the dialectical richness of this category which exudes the exponent contradiction of capitalism.

If, on the one hand, it seeks appreciation independent of labor, then, on the other hand, and from which we reaffirm the mainstay of the theory of labor-value, "this survival would not have been possible if, at the same time, an enormous rise in the exploitation of wage-earning workers had not taken place in both core and peripheral countries, in addition to a rise in the exploitation of non-salaried workers, especially in the poorest regions of the world" (Carcanholo & Sabadini, 2014, p. 146). As such, the theory of labor-value is radicalized through intensified exploitation of the workforce, concurrent with an attempt at the total autonomy of capital from labor.

Where does the notion of fictitious profits come from? Theorizing around fictitious profits emerged not only from the observation of the growth of fictitious capital, but mainly from the nature of the inversion and autonomisation of categories in the process of the logical-historical constitution of capitalism, associated with the consequent development of the mystification of wealth seen in the current dynamics. Despite signals in earlier texts, the concept truly emerges, in an embryonic form, in the early 2000s (Carcanholo, 2003), through the analysis of the process of the dissimulation of surplus value, in a clear allusion, even if not directly discussed in the work, to the fetishistic process of profits and, therefore, of the mystification of exploitation.

The main characteristics of fictitious profits are associated with fictitious capital, it is, after all, an income derived from it. Here we list some of these determinations. Fictitious profits are subject to this real/fictitious debate as they are real profits, from the individual point of view, and fictitious ones from the point of view of the totality. Therefore, they do not result from exploitation, are not associated with surplus value, and do not sustain the dynamics of expanded capital reproduction. If they do not resolve the current chronic over-accumulation of capital, since the accumulation of fictitious profits does not correspond to the increase in the production of value, then they postpone the explosion of the production-appropriation contradiction, at the same time that they potentiate it, since they widen the gap between the real and financial dimensions of accumulation. They appear, thus, as a new determinant of the dissimulation of surplus value, as another fetishistic element. They represent the negation of capitalist logic, expressed by the difference between the mass of value produced and the global profit, in a maximal antithesis with so-called "real/productive profits," which is an expression of a contradictory totality. So, fictitious profits appear as an "output" of speculation, disappearing with the reversal of the economic cycle and the outbreak of crises (see here Carcanholo & Sabadini, 2014; Gomes, 2015; Mello & Sabadini, 2019; Sabadini, 2019; Teixeira & Sabadini, 2022).

Despite all the contradictions present in this fictitious form of individual wealth, capital here does not fully realize its tendency to autonomise and deny living labor. It does not totally deny its source of wealth associated with labor, since the counter-tendencies of increasing exploitation of labor in various forms and the usual channels of production, appropriation, and transfer of value within the capital cycle continue to coexist alongside the creation of fictitious profits, which do not arise from this process.

We know that in conventional theory, the essence of economic and social phenomena is not fully understood and that the process of abstract wealth creation is ignored. And that, when we observe discussions involving the theme of "financialization," we find that even among those who use Marxist categories, there are analyses that point to the existence of profits arising from financial speculation, but without the required theoretical justification. Among the classic authors, Hilferding was one who suggested the existence of differential profits, profits that are disconnected from surplus value, but without any explanation for their contradictory existence (Sabadini, 2015). This led us to state that, as for Hilferding and several of his contemporaries, "in general, fictitious profits are under-theorised and disconnected from a more conceptual discussion about fictitious capital and its place in the concept of capital" (Mello & Sabadini, 2019, p. 155). Perhaps the fetish of fictitious profits had gone unnoticed until them.

THE FETISH OF COMMODITY, MONEY, AND CAPITAL

The term "fetish" has a multiplicity of meanings and determinants, including the meaning of "illusion" or "fiction" that is at the same time "real." The term was adopted by Marx to express, initially, the relationship of commodities, as the initial and apparent manifestation of wealth within the capitalist mode of production, with human beings.[5]

This expression indicates that fetishism crosses, or is transversally related to, the categories that Marx discovered and introduced in his *Critique of Political Economy*, as a commodity that contains use value, exchange value, and value, and its development with the forms of concrete and abstract labor that creates them. It is related to the exposition of the forms that value acquires through its mutations and inversions. It is expressed as money as a general equivalent, a special commodity, and the expression *par excellence* of value; and as capital, as a value that appreciates, "as a self-moving substance," *the substantivation of capital value* (Carcanholo & Sabadini, 2011), as the subject of the process, as we will see later.

The path does not stop there. The theme of fetishism, more specifically commodity fetishism, which was explicitly presented by Marx and which perhaps for this reason has received greater emphasis in literature, is, even so, relatively little debated (Netto, 2015; Prado, 2021). It has even been seen as "an objective and necessary phenomenon created by the very division of labor based on the commodity" (Antunes, 2018, p. 237), and is, therefore, of crucial importance. Furthermore, fetishism, albeit implicitly, accompanies the entire process of exposing the concept of capital, and can be understood as the very process of subjectivation and autonomisation of capital, of the constitution of capital as an "automatic subject" and as a complex and contradictory social totality. As such, the analysis of fetishism crosses all three books of *Capital*, enriching itself with certain determinations.

For the sake of delimiting the subject of study and accepting the risks that this demarcation imposes on us, since the fetish of money and the fetish of capital are present in the fetish of the commodity and are therefore part of a uniqueness, we will focus our attention on the autonomous and fetishized forms of interest-bearing capital, fictitious capital, and fictitious profits. By doing so, we believe that we will be able to point out some general aspects inherent to the fetish implicit in the "desire" of capital to free itself from labor, and in the magic of the multiplication of profits devoid of surplus value.

However, before that, it is important to set out, briefly, some determinations of the fetish of money and capital.

The Fetish of Money and Capital

If commodity, not coincidentally inserted by Marx at the opening of his work, makes possible the development of fetishism (indicating that the products of social labor are presented as acquiring a life of their own), the fetish of money, through the very development of the forms of value, appears as the development of capitalist relations from the general equivalent. Therefore, it is value taking on forms where the fetish of money manifests itself, because:

> What appears to happen is not that a particular commodity becomes money because all other commodities express their values in it, but, on the contrary, that all other commodities universally express their values in a particular commodity because it is money. The movement through which this process has been mediated vanishes in its own result, leaving no trace behind. Without any initiative on their part, the commodities find their own value-configuration ready to hand, in the form of a physical commodity existing outside but also alongside them (...). Hence the magic of money".[6]

In this sense, the fetish of money is not only expressed through the exchange of goods that represent social relations in and through money, but as power relations, which, in our view, are represented in economic, social, political forms of control over the work of other human beings, where labor-value occupies a central place. After all, according to a well-known passage from the *Grundrisse*, under the capitalist mode of production, "the individual carries his social power, as well as his bond with society, in his pocket" (Marx, 1993, p. 157). This becomes the totem, fictitious, and real at the same time, representative of this power.

With this, Marx manages to thoroughly understand, within the framework of the concept of capital, what he denounced in his first works, in the key to his critique of alienation; that under modern conditions, the individual "can be active practically, and produce objects in practice, only by placing his output, and his activity, under the domination of an alien being, and bestowing the significance of an alien entity – money – on them" (Marx, 1975, p. 174). So, we note the inseparability of fetishism and the theory of value, with money expressing its even more mystified source of value, thus "the riddle of the money fetish is therefore the riddle of the commodity fetish, now become visible and dazzling to our eyes" (Marx, 1982, p. 187).

When exiting simple circulation (see Section II of Book I of *Capital*), money as a form of capital is already clear, in the process of the valorization of value based on the extraction of surplus value. The fetishism of capital, according to Daremas (2018, p. 237), "is generated by the mode of inscription of the social process of 'appreciation' of the historically specific capital mode of production onto the social process of the production of use values through social labour."[7] Therefore, the dynamics of "things" expands to meet the incessant production of labor-value, mainly seeking to meet the needs of production and expanded reproduction of capital, which is already established on the solid foundations of capitalist production and circulation. In this context, therefore, the free purchase and sale of labor power between legally equal entities is already established, as well as "the labour-market in existence as a particular branch of the commodity-market" (Marx, 1982, p. 273).[8]

Still briefly, two fundamental tendencies of capital accumulation must be mentioned here: the increase in the organic composition of capital, and the formal and real subsumption of labor to capital. In its search for the extraction of relative surplus value, capital, especially, has the imperative of revolutionizing the means of production, which tends to be expressed in the relative and, in some circumstances, absolute increase of constant capital compared to variable capital. There is a tendency to replace workers with machines, a development of the negative relationship that lies at the heart of capital, which in the process of its valorization needs to simultaneously reduce living labor to the condition of variable capital and deny workers the full fruits of their labor (Grespan, 2012). This propensity, which leads to the tendency for the rate of profit to fall, within the scope of competition between capitals, already expresses the desire of capital to free itself, to become autonomous from its concrete contents and even its substance, completing the M – M′ cycle, without the mediations that are inherent to them.

Regarding the tendency to subsume labor to capital, suffice it to say that it corresponds to the historical process of the consolidation of a specifically capitalist mode of production. At first, capital finds an objective base in the past and, keeping the productive structures largely unchanged, formally submits workers to the condition of wage-earners, after dispossessing them of the means of production. In a second moment, manufacturing is consolidated, based on a rigorous technical and social division of labor, having the "total worker" composed of highly specialized "partial workers" as its material. All under a hierarchy and a despotic discipline dedicated to repetitive and demarked activities, as if they were automatons. Despite the startling increase of capital's control over labor under manufacturing conditions, it is with the introduction of machine tools and, above all, of automated systems of machines, that capital finds a truly adequate material base and really subsumes the workers, reducing them to appendages of the machine, and subject to the torture of labor devoid of content. It is under these conditions that "capital stands on its own feet," exercising totalitarian control over the production of goods, having already appropriated socially developed knowledge and productive capacities. These two tendencies reveal both the affirmation of capital as an "automatic subject," and its self-contradictory character: capital as "contradiction in motion" (Marx, 1993, p. 706).

It is because of this that we previously stated that the *substantivation of capital value*, in which a predicate becomes the subject of the process, expands, and goes beyond the notion of objectification to place the incessant quest to produce surplus value in its various forms at the center of the analysis, themes developed in later chapters of *Capital*. In this continuous process of the transformation of the productive forces of labor, which seeks to shorten required labor time and extend surplus labor time, the fetish involving the relationship between worker and capitalist is manifested in the appropriation of surplus labor in the form of surplus value, which, as Marx mainly develops in Book III, manifests itself in a disguised way in the form of profit and presents itself as the result of the work of the functioning capitalist.

If, in the fetish for money, the expression and representation of the domination and subordination of individuals are potentiated as it becomes the main objective of people's lives and expresses the economic, social, and political power of individuals, then we believe that its mystification gains new forms in the fetish for capital, that are even more potentiated, with new dimensions and concrete abstractions, with the autonomisation of its functional forms.

THE PAROXISM OF FETISHISM IN THE FICTITIOUS FORMS OF CAPITAL

From the forms of value in Book I, through the circulation of total social capital in Book II, to the autonomous functional forms of capital in Book III, the fetishization of the relationships of production acquires a specific character, specific forms, as capital becomes autonomous and increase the degree of fetishism. Each transfigured and autonomous form expresses the fetishistic character of the hidden relationships. This is why we have previously stated that the autonomisation of the functional forms of capital has an important place in understanding the dynamics of the fetish of the categories that Marx discovered and developed, based on the contradictory movement of capital, and that the fundamental trait of fetishism, according to Netto (2015, p. 74) is "the suppression of the social mediations that it operates, subsuming them in a substantive and autonomous conclusiveness" or, in the words of Marx (1971, p. 514), "the different relations and aspects not only become independent and assume a heterogeneous mode of existence, apparently independent of one another, but they seem to be the direct properties of things; they assume the material shape."

The fetishism of capital presents itself in the controlling of the individual's will, conscience, and their set of work capacities with the main purpose of the valorization of value, obeying the determinations of capital and "as conscious carriers of this movement," as Marx states, but it also acts on the development of science and production techniques, disguising the participation of workers in the productive process, where science and technique appear disconnected from social relations, breaking the dominance of the worker's knowledge of the production process (Moura, 2002). As we know, Marx also developed his investigative scope into the analysis of machinery and large-scale industry, where the dynamics of capitalist accumulation were consolidated into the formation of capitalism, especially in Western Europe, and by the expansion of the world market.

When moving forward, however, to consider the steps within the circulation of the global cycle of capital, represented initially by the functional forms of money capital and commodity capital, which then become autonomous as interest-bearing capital and fictitious capital, and commodity-trading capital and money-trading capital respectively, we find new determinations in the development of the fetish in each of these autonomous forms.[9] The theme of fetishism in Book III manifests itself in two decisive moments: firstly, when it deals with interest-bearing capital and, secondly, in the "Trinitarian formula." The following section addresses this theme.

Marx makes it clear, in several passages, that it is in interest-bearing capital that fetishism is to be found in its fullest form. We will not stop here to detail these passages, but a few, present in *Capital* and in the *Theories of Surplus Value*, are transcribed below for illustrative purposes. In the latter, especially in the annex entitled "Revenue and its sources. Vulgar political economy," we witness Marx's broader dissertation on the fetishism of capital, which supports the "Trinitarian formula" of Book III:

> In interest-bearing capital, the capital relationship reaches its most superficial and fetishised form.[10]

> The fetish character of capital and the representation of this capital fetish is now complete. In $M - M'$ we have the irrational form of capital, the misrepresentation and objectification of the relations of production, in its highest power: the interest-bearing form, the simple form of capital, in which it is taken as logically anterior to its own reproduction process; the ability of money or a commodity to valorise its own value independent of reproduction – the capital mystification in the most flagrant form.[11]

> On the other hand, *interest-bearing capital* is the perfect fetish. (…) In the form of interest-bearing capital only this function remains, without the mediation of either production process or circulation process.[12]

Interest-bearing capital is the consummate *automatic fetish*, the self-expanding value, the money-making money, and in this form, it no longer bears any trace of its origin. The social relation is consummated as a relation of things (money, commodities) to themselves.[13]

These statements would, themselves, be sufficient to justify that the fetish of capital attains its ultimate form in interest-bearing capital. We want to point to a different interpretation, that the fetish of capital presents itself most fully in fictitious capital, in actions, and not just in potential. To understand this, it is necessary to consider the global dimension of Marx's work, observing the constant developments and inversions of the categories which appear at the end of Book III, and which are frequently denied and reaffirmed, especially when it comes to the fetishism of capital and its autonomous forms.

That said, if the above quotes seem conclusive, we believe that there are some other elements that should be considered. The first is that, especially when Marx presents interest as a fraction of surplus value and the form of interest-bearing capital in direct relation to loan capital, based on the credit system, he methodologically deals with two moments that are simultaneously complementary and different. We refer to the functions of the money lender, the money capitalist, owner of money as latent capital, and of the borrower, the capitalist in function, who transforms money into capital in the production process, buying the means of production and the workforce.

If we look at lending in its totality, we have what Marx describes, in both the *1864–1865 Manuscripts* (Marx, 2016, p. 446), preparatory to Book III, and in *Capital* itself (Marx, 1991, p. 461), as the interest-bearing capital cycle, represented by the formula: $M - M - C - M' - M'$. If this is so, the fundamental assumption behind interest-bearing capital, exhaustively presented by Marx in numerous and even repetitive passages in his works, is that here money is placed as capital, and that the production of value and surplus value is a condition, a necessary presupposition of interest-bearing capital. This is understandable, since Marx, in addition to showing the antediluvian character of interest, shows that it is mystified in capitalism, in antithesis to labor, apparently originating from the property of money as capital, but which, in essence, is the result of the surplus value, a remuneration of the money lender arising from the exploitation of the workforce by the functioning capitalist.

So, what about the quotes from Marx above?

In our view, the answer to this question lies in the fact that many confuse the categories interest-bearing capital and fictitious capital, perhaps due to Marx's own explanation in his manuscripts, compiled by Engels and published in *Capital*, not understanding interest-bearing capital and fictitious capital and their necessary development in an in-depth way. To justify these hypotheses, we suggest that Marx's previous indications that the fetish of capital reaches its apex in the form of interest-bearing capital, are always associated with the shortening of the cycle, when money is valued by itself, that is, via M – M′. But, in this case, we believe that Marx is exposing the individual character of the loan made by the money capitalist, as the owner of money in its latent form, as an individual who sees his money being valued as a "pear tree that bears pears," a classic Marx statement (1991, p. 516), without going through the process of production because he has a property title: "Thus it becomes as completely the property of money to create value, to yield interest, as it is the property of a pear tree to bear pears. And it is as this interest-bearing thing that the money-lender sells his money."

It is also worth noting that it is common for Marx, especially in Book III of *Capital*, to present themes reporting this individual vision, the concrete forms of the movement of capital being observed in its appearance. This is not by chance, after all, the very objective of his book, presented at the beginning of Section I, reveals that "the configuration of capital, as developed in this volume, thus approach step by step the form in which they appear on the surface of society, in the action of different capitals on one another, i.e. in competition, and in the everyday consciousness of the agents of production themselves" (Marx, 1991, p. 117).

If not read carefully, the coming and going of forms and their contents can confuse readers and, moreover, it can seem that Marx is talking about the totality of the process, while, in fact, he is dealing with the way individuals view society, its appearance, which can lead to conclusions based only on the superficiality of the phenomena. The exposition of themes such as the dissimulation of surplus value in profit, or even the entrepreneur's concept of profit, for example, both in Book III, note that the capitalist

...[i]nevitably gets the idea into his head, therefore, that his profit of enterprise – very far from forming any antithesis with wage-labour and being only the unpaid labour of others – is rather itself a *wage*, 'wages of superintendence of labour,' a higher wage than that of the ordinary wage-labourer, *(1)* because it is complex labour, and *(2)* because he himself pays the wages.[14]

Marx shows this individual character in numerous passages. By doing so, he is signaling the fetish of capital in its various forms, such as interest-bearing capital and entrepreneur's profit. Without taking this into account, we would not arrive at interest-bearing capital, and to its general cycle (M – M – C – M' – M'); and this would make the necessary leap for the distinction and understanding of fictitious capital impossible.[15]

So, for us, it is in the form of fictitious capital that "the transubstantiation, the fetishism, is complete" (Marx, 1971, p. 494), since it represents the apotheosis of the autonomisation of capital in relation to its substance, abstract labor – "the pure form of capital expressed in the M – M' formula" (Marx, 1971, p. 494). Here the proposition of Marx seems to reach full validity, according to which

> ...[t]he pure form of capital expressed in the formula M – M'. The ossification of relations, their presentation as the relation of men to things having a definite social character is here likewise brought out in quite a different manner from that of the simple mystification of commodities and the more complicated mystification of money.[16]

It is also worth remembering that up to Chapter XXI of Book III, Marx was dealing with the emergence of interest and interest-bearing capital; fictitious capital appearing in Chapters XXIX and XXX. It is evident that interest-bearing capital was, until that moment, the most fetishized form of capital, not least because fictitious capital, as its autonomous form, only appears later. If we do not take these aspects into account, we are not only accepting Marx's quotes above without a systemic view of fetishism in the specific form of fictitious capital, but also confusing, or at least simplifying and restricting, the concept of fictitious capital. In our view, the fetishism of capital deepens with the appearance of fictitious capital, which forms the cycle M – M', the much-desired form of capital that valorizes itself, without mediation with labor, which we consider to be the extreme fetish.

Likewise, as remuneration arising from fictitious capital and resulting from the fetish of this autonomous form of capital, fictitious profits are nonsystemic profits; they do not arise from the dissimulation of surplus value in a competitive transfer process. Although illusory, they are real from the individual point of view, in the speculative movement of capital, but fictitious because they have no real substance. For this reason, they also appear as extremely fetishized, creating the illusion that they can definitively reverse the tendency for the rate of profit to fall, but they have in themselves the germ of crises, of capitalist crises that manifest themselves in the form of financial crises. They do not have the capacity, therefore, to sustain the dynamics of capitalist accumulation. They are also, therefore, from the point of view of remuneration, the purest manifestation of the contradiction, as the most concrete expression of fictitious capital in the circulation of markets and in speculative variations in the prices of financial assets.

In this way, the development of the understanding of the labor theory of value, the various forms that capital assumes, and the process of its autonomisation, to its most reified form of manifestation as fictitious capital, lead us to an analysis of fictitious profits that, in our view, serves as a basis for understanding some of the recent transformations of capitalism, with their particularities of both form and content.

CONCLUSION

If we accept the idea that the capitalist mode of production is in a historical moment where fictitious capital has decisively influenced the process of accumulation, then investigating the fetish of fictitious capital gives us the ability to see the contradictions and the crises posed by this simultaneously illusory and real form of capital. A form of capital that increasingly appropriates parts of the wealth created by the working class in the form of profits and interests. Thus, the transfer of substantive wealth, produced by labor, through the payment of interests and dividends, and the amortization of public debt, among others, shows the limits that the expansion of fictitious capital imposes on the global process of the valorization of value.

Its constant dynamic of the denial and inversion of the logic of accumulation, associated with the process of substantivation of value and autonomisation of functional forms, potentiates fetishism through fictitious capital, which is manifested in the contradiction of the existence of its form and its content. The phantasmagorical subject of the process of social reproduction becomes autonomous and assumes particularities, providing in its nature an extreme fetishized dimension, through the cycle $M - M'$, the apparent magic of money appreciating itself as money, without the necessary mediations with labor.

In the speculative dynamics of capital, where present and future are mixed in a homogeneous process, where commodity-capital in the form of financial assets is often bought and sold without effective production, but represented in the form of bonds and property rights that give the right to future income, two movements are generated, in our view, that are expressed through the appropriation of wealth created in production, as well as through interest payments, and through the production of fictitious profits unrelated to surplus value. If the dissimulation of surplus value appears in the form of productive and commercial profits, fictitious profits manifest themselves in even more fetishized movements, associated with the speculative movements of fictitious capital.

Recent financial crises, therefore, as expressions of a chronic over-accumulation of capital and characterized by intensified financial speculation, also acquire recurrent particularities in the global cycle of capital; specificities that must be properly analyzed, especially in relation to fetishism.

NOTES

1. Agreeing with Heinrich (2004, p. 185), "all members of bourgeois society are subordinate to the fetishism of social relations. This fetishism takes root as an 'objective form of thought' that structures the perception of all members of society. Neither capitalists nor workers have a privileged position that allows them to evade this fetishism." Nevertheless, it must be insisted in advance that fetishism has mental expressions but is based on a whole set of social practices involved in the valorization of value.

2. We refer here to a group of professors and researchers from the Department of Economics and the Post-graduate Programme in Social Policy at the Federal University of Espírito Santo (UFES). An article that summarizes in more detail the trajectory of our research can be found in Sabadini (2021).

3. Mello and Sabadini (2019), p. 153.

4. In an interesting article, Trenkle (2018) relates some changes in the world of work in what he calls the fictitious capital era. However, the author makes statements that are, in our view, at the very least problematic. Otherwise, see: "The production of value through the exploitation of labor has been replaced with the systematic anticipation of future value in the form of fictitious capital" (p. 101); or: "Capital also continues to be based on social mediation by labor because it has by no means abandoned the world of commodity production. However, to the extent that capital accumulates through anticipation of future value production (which is to say it uses the results of potential future work in advance), it frees itself from dependence on the exploitation of present-day labor and the sellers of labor power" (p. 109). It does not seem to us that there is strictly a "replacement of exploitation" by an "anticipation of future value," nor an emancipation of capital in relation to exploitation in the present. On the contrary, the centrality of fictitious capital, which has increased exponentially in recent decades, and which places obligations on the real dimension of capital accumulation, increases the excessive thirst for surplus value, being yet another stimulus to the precariousness of work, to increasing working hours and intensifying them, lowering the price of labor, destroying labor laws and social protection structures, and so on.

5. This phantasmagorical character of *commodity* and other social products of work are well discussed by Rubin (1982), for example when he argues that "a thing is an intermediary in social relations (. . .), the thing acquires specific social characteristics in a market economy" (for example, the properties of value, money, capital, and so on), due to which the thing not only hides the production relations among people, but it also organises them, serving as a connecting link between people" (p. 10).

6. Marx (1982), p. 187.

7. Grespan (2012, p. 109) reinforces that this fetishism of capital "consists not only of the illusion that capital is also an autonomous source of value production, but mainly in its effective power to subordinate work and the conditions of its self-valorization."

8. On the debate as to whether there is an antagonism between exploitation and fetishism or not, see Bonente and Corrêa (2021). For these authors, there is a false polarization between them, as "the categories *fetishism* and *exploitation* are linked and inseparable from the theory of value" (p. 134).

9. We have indicated in several of our works that the term *money trading capital*, in Chapter XIX of Book III of *Capital*, has been mistranslated as *finance capital* and that this concept does not exist in Marx. In addition to etymological issues, the term *finance capital* was, in fact, introduced and developed by Rudolf Hilferding in his work *Finance capital*, being most often used insufficiently to understand the current dynamics of contemporary capitalism.

10. Marx (1991), p. 515.

11. Marx (1991), p. 516.

12. Marx (1971), p. 454.

13. Marx (1971), p. 455.

14. Marx (1971), pp. 503–504.

15. Beyond the existence of several passages corroborating this interpretation throughout Section V of Book III of Capital, we should not forget the logic of Marx's dialectical exposition that demands an understanding of "the movement of capital as a whole," particularly the relation between essence and appearance, and between production and circulation, the subject of Book III.

16. Marx (1971), p. 494.

REFERENCES

Antunes, J. (2018). *Marx e o fetiche da mercadoria: Contribuição à crítica da metafísica*. Jundiaí (SP): Paco.

Bonente, B. I., & Corrêa, H. F. (2021). Entre o fetichismo e a exploração: Polêmicas sobre o Livro I de *O capital*. In J. L. Medeiros & E. S. Barreto (Eds.), *Para que leiam O Capital: Interpretações sobre o Livro I* (pp. 133–166). São Paulo: Usina Editorial.

Carcanholo, R. A. (2003). Sobre a ilusória origem da mais-valia. *Crítica Marxista, 16*, 76–95.
Carcanholo, R. A. (2014). The great depression of the twenty-first century and fictitious wealth: On the theoretical categories of fictitious capital and fictitious profit. In R. Herrera, W. Dierckxsens, & P. Nakatani (Eds.), *Beyond the systemic crisis and capital-led chaos: Theorical and applied studies* (pp. 153–175). Berlin: P.I.E. Peter Lang.
Carcanholo, R. A. (2019). Speculative capital and the dematerialization of money. In G. M. C. Mello & M. S. Sabadini (Eds.), *Financial speculation and fictitious profits: A Marxist analysis* (pp. 43–61). New York, NY: Palgrave Macmillan.
Carcanholo, R. A., & Nakatani, P. (2019). Parasitic speculative capital: A theoretical precision on financial capital, characteristic of globalization. In G. M. C. Mello & M. S. Sabadini (Eds.), *Financial speculation and fictitious profits: A Marxist analysis* (pp. 117–137). New York, NY: Palgrave Macmillan.
Carcanholo, R. A., & Sabadini, M. S. (2011). Sobre o capital e a mais-valia. In R. A. Carcanholo (Ed.), *Capital: Essência e aparência*. São Paulo: Expressão Popular.
Carcanholo, R. A., & Sabadini, M. S. (2014). Fictitious capital and fictitious profit. In R. Herrera, W. Dierckxsens, & P. Nakatani (Eds.), *Beyond the systemic crisis and capital-led chaos: Theorical and applied studies* (pp. 129–152). Berlin: P.I.E. Peter Lang.
Carson, R. (2017). Fictitious capital and the re-emergence of personal forms of domination. *Continental Thought and Theory, 1*(4), 566–586.
Daremas, G. (2018). The Social constitution of commodity fetishism, money fetishism and capital fetishism. Luxemburg International Studies in Political Economy. In J. Dellheim & F. O. Wolf (Eds.), *The unfinished system of Karl Marx: Critically reading capital as a challenge for our times* (pp. 219–249). New York, NY: Palgrave Macmillan.
Gomes, H. (Ed.). (2015). *Especulação e lucros fictícios: Formas parasitárias da acumulação contemporânea*. São Paulo: Outras Expressões.
Grespan, J. L. (2012). *O negativo do capital: O conceito de crise na crítica de Marx à economia política*. São Paulo: Expressão Popular.
Heinrich, M. (2004). *An Introduction to the three volumes of Karl Marx's Capital*. New York, NY: Monthly Review Press.
Marx, K. (1971). *Theories of Surplus-Value*. Moscow: Progress Publishers.
Marx, K. (1975). On the Jewish question. In K. Marx (Ed.), *Collected works* (Vol. III). London: Lawrence and Wishart.
Marx, K. (1982). *Capital: A Critique of Political Economy* (Vol. I). London: Penguin Books.
Marx, K. (1991). *Capital: A Critique of Political Economy* (Vol. III). London: Penguin Books.
Marx, K. (1993). *Grundrisse: Foundations of the Critique of Political Economy*. London: Penguin Books.
Marx, K. (2016). *Marx's Economic Manuscript of 1864–1865*. Historical Materialism Historical (Vol. 100). Leiden-Boston: Brill.
Mello, G. M. C., & Braga, H. P. (Eds.). (2022). *Wealth and Poverty in Contemporary Brazilian Capitalism*. London: Palgrave Macmillan.
Mello, G. M. C., & Nakatani, P. (Eds.). (2021). *Introdução à crítica da financeirização: Marx e o moderno sistema de crédito*. São Paulo: Expressão Popular.
Mello, G. M. C., & Sabadini, S. (Eds.). (2019). *Financial speculation and fictitious profits: A Marxist analysis*. London: Palgrave Macmillan.
Moura, M. C. B. (2002). Considerações acerca do fetichismo do capital. *Perspectiva Filosófica, IX*(17), 147–155.
Netto, J. P. (2015). *Capitalismo e reificação*. São Paulo: ICP.
Prado, E. F. S. (2021). Uma introdução à lógica da crítica da economia política. *Revista da Sociedade Brasileira de Economia Política, 59*, 217–238.
Roberts, M. (2018). Financialisation or profitability? *The Next Recession* [author's blog]. Retrieved from https://thenextrecession.wordpress.com/2018/11/27/financialisation-or-profitability/
Rubin, I. I. (1982). *Essays on Marx's Theory of Value*. Montreal/New York, NY: Black Rose Books.
Sabadini, M. S. (2015). O capital fictício e suas formas: Lucros de fundador, diferencial e fictício. In H. Gomes (Ed.), *Especulação e lucros fictícios: Formas parasitárias da acumulação contemporânea* (pp. 161–204). São Paulo: Outras Expressões.

Sabadini, M. S. (2019). A Teoria do valor-trabalho em Marx, os lucros fictícios e as crises capitalistas recentes. In J. Arancibia & A. López (Eds.), *Teoría del valor y crisis* (pp. 63–88). México: UNAM/UAZ.

Sabadini, M. S. (2021). A (crítica da) economia política, o capital fictício e os lucros fictícios. *Revista da Sociedade Brasileira de Economia Política*, 59, 175–202.

Teixeira, A. L. A., & Sabadini, M. S. (2022). Marx and the category of fictitious profits: Some notes on the Brazilian economy. In G. M. C. Mello & H. P. Braga (Eds.), *Wealth and Poverty in Contemporary Brazilian Capitalism* (pp. 105–142). London: Palgrave Macmillan.

Trenkle, N. (2018). Labour in the era of fictitious capital. *Contradictions – A Journal for Critical Thought*, 2(2), 101–113.

CRISIS AND FICTITIOUS CAPITAL

Rosa Maria Marques and Paulo Nakatani

ABSTRACT

This text analyzes the relationship between crises and the dominance of interest-bearing capital, with particular emphasis on fictitious capital, which forms a striking feature of contemporary capitalist economies. It discusses how capitalist crises are commonly viewed and how we should understand them, on several dimensions of reality, based on a comprehensive reading of Marx. We follow with a reflection on the nature and characteristics of interest-bearing capital and on fictitious capital and fictitious profit, given that the high activity of this last form of capital is a hallmark of current capitalism and is itself the maximum expression of the fetishism engendered by it. We conclude that what is understood as a crisis by people in general is, in fact, a source of enormous enrichment for the owners of fictitious capital.

Keywords: Capitalism; capitalist crisis; profit; interest-bearing capital; fictitious capital; fetishism

INTRODUCTION

One of the characteristics of contemporary world economies is the dominance of interest-bearing capital, especially in the form of fictitious capital. This dominance, as several authors have already analyzed (among which we highlight Duménil & Lévy, 2006; Husson, 2006), constrains the level of productive investment, promotes unemployment, and restricts the action of nation-states, among other negative impacts. According to Chesnais (2005), this capital is currently at the center of economic and social relations.

This is not the first time that interest-bearing capital has occupied this position. At the end of the nineteenth century and at the beginning of the twentieth century, when imperialism had been consolidated, it had equal importance. Such has been its expansion over recent decades, however, that the volume of resources involved and the value of fictitious capital in relation to current world gross

Value, Money, Profit, and Capital Today
Research in Political Economy, Volume 39, 215–229
Copyright © 2024 Rosa Maria Marques and Paulo Nakatani
Published under exclusive licence by Emerald Publishing Limited
ISSN: 0161-7230/doi:10.1108/S0161-723020230000039013

domestic product (GDP) cannot be compared to that of any previous period. The importance assumed by interest-bearing capital and its fantastic development were preceded by the loss of the conditions that had, for 30 years, allowed profits and real wages, among other indicators, to grow. When the loss of these conditions became evident, that is, when the rate of increase of profits began to decrease, investment retracted, and unemployment returned. In the mid-1970s, the United States and big European economies experienced a crisis. It was then that the Keynesian macroeconomic arrangements and policies in place at the time were questioned, and the foundations of neoliberalism were established, but not without first altering the conjunction of forces between the main social classes which imposed historic setbacks on US and British workers. It was with the active support of the United States of America and the United Kingdom that the practices and institutions created over the preceding decades fell away, giving rise to widespread deregulation, starting in the financial sphere. In place of the state, the new mantra claimed (and still claims) that the *market* was the locus for maximum efficiency to be achieved.

Since then, there have been several crises, the last one erupting in 2007–2008 (if we exclude the peak of the COVID-19 pandemic in 2020). Following these crises, countries considered to be more developed have never regained, in any sustained form, their previous performance levels, including regarding profit rates from productive activities.

This text discusses the relationship between crisis and the dominance of interest-bearing capital and, particularly, fictitious capital. The first part is dedicated to capitalist crises: how they are commonly perceived and how we should understand them from a comprehensive reading of Marx, that is, considering several dimensions of reality. The second part deals with fictitious capital and fictitious profit, since their high levels of activity are a hallmark of contemporary capitalism and because fictitious profit is the maximum expression of the fetish engendered by current capitalism. Finally, we end with a short concluding reflection.

CAPITALIST CRISIS

Argument around the nature of "capitalist crises" and their determinants has long motivated scholars in the field of political economy, especially those who have Marx as their inspiration for understanding them. Among many authors who place the principal cause as the development of unfavorable rates of profit, we highlight Husson (2014), Chesnais (2016), and Roberts (2022), all of them supported by the teachings of Marx, especially in some of his chapters of *Capital*.

In the political milieu, including among sectors of the so-called radical left and elsewhere throughout the world, i.e., those outside the social-democratic tradition, the crisis of capitalism is plainly evident, as high levels of unemployment and poverty persist and inequality has only increased globally in recent decades. This understanding of "crisis" is cemented by the fact that capitalism is responsible for extreme degradation of the natural environment, which places the reproduction of life on our planet at risk.

However, it is insufficient to focus on these aspects alone. Unemployment, poverty, and inequality have always been part of this mode of production, and we are far removed from a time when it clearly had progressive actions which benefitted the whole population in terms of advances in the organization and distribution of wealth compared with that seen previously. Clearly, it is important to denounce this tragedy, in which capitalism is built on the broad masses of workers who live by selling their labor force. It forms part of the struggle for the construction of a new world, in which the deconstruction of the rhetoric of the ruling classes is an essential element.

It so happens that these complaints often do not make it clear that there is no way to change this situation in a lasting way without overcoming capitalism. Proponents of capitalism understandably select as their reference points moments when political, economic, and geopolitical conditions permitted the reduction of unemployment to very low levels with significant reductions in both poverty and inequality, as was the case in the 30 years that followed the end of the Second World War (called the golden or glorious 30 years in the literature) or, in a much more limited and localized way, when more progressive governments took power in Latin American countries in the early 2000s.

The profit rate approach stems from the rationale by which capitalism exists to produce profits on invested capital in a continuous quest to expand the reproduction of capital. More than absolute profit, therefore, what matters is its rate (positive and increasing), without which capital cannot reproduce itself in an expanded form. When the rate of profit registers a fall, or worse, a tendency to fall, crises set in, because productive investment retracts, which generates unemployment and a reduction in income.

As Marx states in Chapter XV of Book III of *Capital*:

> A fall in the profit rate, and accelerated accumulation, are simply different expressions of the same process, in so far as both express the development of productivity. Accumulation in turn accelerates the fall in the profit rate, in so far as it involves the concentration of workers on a large scale and hence a higher composition of capital.[1]

> The periodical devaluation of the existing capital, which is a means, immanent to the capitalist mode of production, for delaying the fall in the profit rate and accelerating the accumulation of capital value by the formation of new capital, disturbs the given conditions in which the circulation and reproduction process of capital takes place, and is therefore accompanied by sudden stoppages and crises in the production process.[2]

A crisis is thus initiated, in which the difference between unpaid labor (surplus value, m) and invested capital (capital advanced, $C + V$), that is, $m/(C + V)$, ceases to be attractive to capital. It always results from overaccumulation, which is expressed in an increase in organic composition. The continuous rise in the organic composition of social capital throughout the history of capitalism is the result of the individual capitalists' quest to differentiate themselves from their competitors and thus guarantee extraordinary profits, beyond the average, reducing the cost of production through the incorporation of equipment and more up-to-date machines which, alongside human labor, increases productivity. This strategy is, however, adopted by all, so that, if there is no increase in the mass of surplus value to compensate for the change in organic composition and no reduction of the amount of work necessary to produce the constitutive elements of fixed capital and the value of force of work, the average rate of profit tends to fall, and a crisis is triggered.

Overcoming this requires recreating favorable conditions for a new cycle of capital expansion to occur, which must take place after the period of capital destruction that accompanies the crisis. The instruments for obtaining these conditions, as numerous as they have been in recent decades, are intended to provide an increase in surplus value and a reduction in the value of fixed capital and/or variable capital, to slow the fall in the rate of profit or even to reverse it.

In recent decades, especially since the 1990s, but starting in the previous decade in some countries, we have witnessed, alongside persistent unemployment, a reduction in the average real salary and a decrease in wages within the GDP of countries, reversing the trend observed in the golden 30 years. Shortly afterward, there was a large-scale relocation of companies from all over the world to countries where wages were significantly lower; a movement that benefited from the dissolution of the Union of Soviet Socialist Republics (USSR), the end of the Warsaw Pact, and the China's entry into the World Trade Organization in 2001. We are aware, of course, that the relocation of companies was driven by multiple factors and was not only to Eastern Europe and China,[3] but there is no doubt that the wage component was one of the most decisive in its early stages.

To gauge the importance of this factor, remember that, according to Cohen and Richard (2005, p. 211), the hourly cost of the workforce in French and German industries was, respectively, US$17, and US$24, while in that of Chinese it was only US$0.60. This, added to the strategy of importing raw materials and/ or commodities to reduce the costs of production, mentioned by Marx as one of the factors that acts against the tendency of the rate of profit to fall, led to the displacement of the whole or part of the production of countless companies to countries where conditions were more favorable for them. Furthermore, the process of capital globalization, which was being consolidated at the same time, facilitated the deepening of the functioning of a global network of oligopolized activities, which optimize the exploitation of the cheap labor located anywhere in the world.

In addition to a reduction in real wages and in the cost of the workforce achieved by shifting production to other countries or by adopting the network production strategy, other measures were taken which resulted in an increase in added value. These measures had the effect of increasing the effective weekly working hours of workers, despite advances in terms of statutory working hours that had been achieved by workers in some countries over recent decades. All this arises from the current conjunction of forces between workers and employers, resulting from low growth and high unemployment. In several countries the minimum age retirement was also raised, which increased *lifetime working hours*.

In the same period, new equipment and processes in microelectronics were introduced and expanded across many production processes to drive down labor costs, especially within those industries that had been reference points throughout the golden 30 years, such as the automobile industry, where the degree of organization of workers was stronger and, therefore, there was greater resistance to wage reduction and the worsening of general working conditions. The use of new technologies has not, however, been restricted to the automobile production or even to production as a whole: it has altered the set of economic activities, introduced new forms of communication, and even changed human subjectivity. In production and circulation, the result of this accelerated introduction of microelectronic equipment and processes significantly reduced the unit cost of goods and activities, but this was not reflected in an aggregate increase in productivity, as can be seen from Graph 1 presenting the evolution of productivity for some key countries (see Husson, 2014).

This apparent contradiction results from the fact that (1) companies, in replacing the workforce with machines, may have invested more than necessary, so that the maximum productivity potential would not be achieved. This explanation is corroborated by the fact that several sectors have been operating with a high rate of underutilization for a long period. Once again, the emblematic example is the automobile industry, but it is not restricted to it (Chesnais, 2013); (2) although there was destruction of the capital involved in the production and circulation of goods in the mid-1970s (when the crisis in the main world economies left no doubt that the expansion cycle of the golden years had ended), the destruction was very low compared to that of the 1930s and during the world wars. It is worth remembering that the USA, the epicenter of that crisis, only recovered from the Great Depression

Graph 1.   Profit and Productivity Rates. *Source:* Calculated from OECD database (available on: https://data.oecd.org/). *Note:* Weighted averages according to GDP for the USA, Japan, Germany, France, the UK, Italy.

during the Second World War, initially by producing weapons for France and the United Kingdom and, later, joining the conflict. The world economy only returned to the production levels of the late 1920s when the Second World War ended, and the process of rebuilding Europe began.

Instead of a massive destruction of capital, the value of which equates to that required to offset the crisis of the mid-1970s, capital was applied against workers (as evidenced by reduced wage levels, and increases in the exploitation of the workforce, poverty, and inequality over recent decades), and entered into a "regime" of low levels of investment and growth, but without negatively affecting profitability, which was increasingly obtained through the disproportionate expansion of fictitious capital. All this, within a framework of the proliferation of nuclear weapons and the imperative of not triggering a conflict on the scale of that experienced in the Second World War.

To facilitate this, it was necessary to attack the labor force globally, to dismantle the legal and economic apparatus that had been built through the Bretton Woods Agreement, and to promote the deregulation of markets, particularly the financial market. In fact, interest-bearing capital, which had previously been locked-in, and which had accumulated a significant volume, began, to take advantage of the opportunities presented by the crisis of the 1970s, to advocate the deregulation of all markets, that is, to be the "mouthpiece" for all types of capital, calling for the freedom for capital to "come and go," and for the State not to interfere in capital/labor relations or in social policies, or in other spheres of economic and societal activities.

Financial deregulation came first, with differing timeframes in different countries. A deregulation named the "3 Ds" by the specialized literature (Bourguinat, 1992), called for *Deregulation*, or monetary and financial liberalization, *Decompartmentalization* of national financial markets, and *Disintermediation*, that is, the opening of loan operations previously reserved for banks, to all types of institutional investor. As stated elsewhere, with the end of the fixed exchange rate regime, capital flows were deregulated until full liberalization by almost the entire world was achieved, forming integrated markets of currencies and capitals that, with the advance of computer networks, made it possible to conduct business between several countries in near real time. At the same time, capital transfers from one part of the world to another accelerated, with integrated financial markets operating 24 hours a day (Nakatani & Marques, 2020, p. 80). From then on, there was a surprising expansion of fictitious capital and the gains arising from its ownership.

Decades after the commencement of these capital actions and the change in the preferential "regime" of accumulation, the average rate of profit had not recovered to pre-1970s crisis levels and, more recently, it has been decreasing, as can be seen in Graph 2 (Roberts, 2022, p. 4). Despite this, the volume of profit not directly derived from activities involving the production and circulation of goods is overwhelming, and wealth is increasingly concentrated in the hands of a few.

Forbes magazine, following the evolution of the personal wealth of the world's richest individuals, estimated that in 2022 only 2,668 people, from a world population estimated at 8 billion, possessed fortunes of between 1 and 219 billion

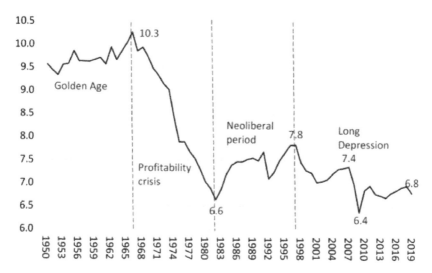

Graph 2. G20 Profit Rate. *Source:* Reproduced with the kind permission from the *Rebellion* website.

dollars, a total of 12.7 trillion (Forbes, 2022). According to the World Inequality Report, "the richest 10% of the global population currently takes 52% of global income, while the poorest half of the population earns 8.5% of it" (Chancel et al., 2022, p. 7). However, the concentration of wealth is much higher than that of income: "The poorest half of the global population barely owns any wealth at all, possessing just 2% of the total. In contrast, the richest 10% of the global population own 76% of all wealth." Forbes indicates that billionaires had suffered a loss of 400 billion dollars compared to 2021 and, nevertheless, became richer compared to the period before the COVID-19 pandemic. According to Oxfam's calculations, "an increase in real terms of US$ 3.78 trillion (42%) occurred during the COVID-19 pandemic. (. . .) The total wealth of billionaires is now equivalent to 13.9% of global Gross Domestic Product (GDP), up from 4.4% recorded in 2000" (Oxfam, 2022, p. 4).

However, recent decades have not been without crises. This attests to the fact that, although the latter first manifest themselves in the sphere of circulation, leading some to believe that to resolve matters it is enough to control the excesses of capital in the financial sphere, they, in fact, demonstrate that the contradictions that constrain capital have not been resolved and are even deepening.

It is true that during each crisis, capital is destroyed, but the framework in which capital acts allows fictitious capital to quickly reconstitute itself, and even create new modalities of this type of capital. All the while, the profits and fortunes of the holders of this capital grow, so that there is no crisis for them. Currently, when interest-bearing capital, especially in the form of fictitious capital, is dominant, crisis should not be confused with low economic performance, unemployment and all the ills associated with it.

The pertinent question is, who does the crisis benefit? Or, in other words, crisis for whom? Restricting our analysis to the behavior of the average rate of profit fails to consider that, with deregulation, capital has become totally intertwined, so that companies of all types produce goods, act as finance companies or banks, and may still be involved in commercial activities. Deregulation simply deepened a process already present in capitalist dynamics that, under the "new rules" of neoliberalism, gained strength, deepening both quantitatively and qualitatively.

But more important than that, is the understanding that capital is constantly changing forms and that there is no primacy of one form over another; continuous movement is a condition of its existence, that is, capital only exists if it is metamorphosing. In this sense, a crisis for capital is when this continuous process of change of form is interrupted. Analysis centered on the rate of profit prioritizes commodity-producing capital. It so happens that capital constitutes a unit in which money capital, productive capital, and commodity capital all act. This division is merely didactic, as capital is more than a social relationship and is constantly in process.

ACCUMULATION, CRISIS, AND FICTITIOUS CAPITAL

The continuous movement of capital is implicit to its existence, producing and realizing surplus value, while continuously accumulating a portion of this surplus. The movement of capital does not imply any temporal or geographical displacement, even though this also occurs, but is its changes of form or in its continuous process of metamorphoses. So, capital changes its form: from money form to commodity form, from commodity form to productive form, from productive form to the form of a new commodity and, finally, from commodity form to money form, in a continuous and incessant cycle.

Marx (1992) called these forms "autonomous" forms of industrial capital, considering them a more general form of capital with no reference to the manufacturing industry, but to all the forms of capital involved in the production of value and surplus value, whether in industry or services. Furthermore, we must pay attention to Marx's emphasis that there are productive activities that continue to exist in the sphere of circulation, such as those associated with the preservation of the use-value of goods and transport. We can consider industrial capital, therefore, as a form of expression of capital-in-general at a higher level of abstraction. The autonomous forms represent capital in different phases of its cycles, that exist concretely in the form of private capital or independent units of capital, in companies or in conglomerates, and in each unit we find the three forms coexisting simultaneously (Nakatani & Marques, 2020, pp. 11–28).

The inexorable tendency of capital, in its movement, is to accumulation. This occurs, as previously stated, in cycles of expansion and contraction with accompanying moments of acute crisis. Crisis is inherent to capital, from the metamorphosis of commodities to the most developed forms of capital. Crises constitute a moment in which capital disposes of its less productive elements to recover its rate of profit and resume accumulation. "The negative effects of this accumulation emerge when the forces that oppose the tendency to fall in the rate of profit are exhausted. (...) The function of the crisis is to allow capital to regenerate" (Salama & Mathias, 1983, p. 55).

Crises are also the moments when the centralization of capital accelerates, when smaller and less productive units are absorbed by more powerful capital in a process of mergers and acquisitions, where the State has historically intervened to save elements of the capital that are devaluing. As such, the weakest and least developed capital suffers from devaluation. Capitalists representing these devaluing units are impoverished at the expense of enriching other capitalists, while, simultaneously, the exploitation of labor and the impoverishment of all working classes increases.

Certain forms of capital, due to the particularities of their production, can interrupt the movement of capital as their production time is longer than their accumulation time. But, during its cycle, and for each unit of capital, there are other reasons why its movement might be interrupted. Portions of capital, in the form of merchandise, can be idle, either as stocks of raw materials or of unsold finished goods, as well as in the time taken to transport them; in its productive phase, production time paralyzes the movement of capital, which remains static, appreciating during this interruption; in the form of money, all idle or unapplied money capital ceases to appreciate. To counter these interruptions, developments in organization and methods of production always seeks to accelerate the movement in all forms of capital.

Moments of crisis are those in which, in addition to the inherent needs of the processes of appreciation, the movement of capital is interrupted. In these moments increasing portions of industrial capital cease to appreciate, and this is expressed through the behavior of profit rates. Capital finds itself in a position of overaccumulation in which it cannot find profitable investment options. In the first half of the Twentieth Century, the release for the overaccumulation of capital was the world wars and the great depression, when accumulated capital was physically destroyed. The second half on this same century saw the process of overaccumulation of the productive forms of capital being replaced by forms of interest-bearing money capital.

The name interest-bearing capital is extremely apt. To say that it bears interest means to say that it has been interest forever. This capital appears firstly in the form of money that has been accumulated as hoarded wealth, that is, not circulating. Furthermore, it does not matter how it was accumulated, whether it resulted from theft, extortion, or more noble activities. This money is potential capital because, although idle, it is seeking profitable opportunities and, when it identifies one, it launches into circulation. Assume that it "launches" itself in the form of a loan to an industrial entrepreneur who wants to expand his production, to buy new machines and to hire more workers. The moment this intention is carried out, there is no doubt that money has been transformed into capital and taken the form of machines, raw materials, installations and even the hiring of a workforce. The interesting thing is that, for the person lending the money, it was transformed into capital from the moment the loan contract was agreed, before the machines were purchased and the workers hired. This is because, regardless of the result of the use made of the money by the borrower, it must be repaid, within the stipulated time, plus interest, to the lender.

It should be noted that when the owner of money capital lends his or her capital to an industrial capitalist or a wholesaler, he or she is not carrying out any part of the cycle that capital passes through in capitalist production. When this happens, a metamorphosis is not taking place, such as when the commodity-producing capitalist hires wage labor and puts it to work in his or her company (production process); neither is the purchase or sale of commodities taking place (when the wholesaler buys the commodity from the commodity-producing capitalist). And the return of the borrowed money to its owner only completes the act performed by him or her, that is, the transfer of the money for a certain period.

Interest-bearing capital is rentier capital. Possession of money gives its owner the "right" to charge interest when allowing another to use it. In our example, buying machines. Just as landowners charge rent from those who use their property. With interest-bearing capital, money takes on a new function, to make a profit, money that generates money, without having to go through production. That is, to paraphrase Marx, it is just as a pear tree is expected to bear pears (Marx, 1981). Therefore, Marx calls this capital the most fetishized capital of all.

When we are referring to fetishism, we are saying that something is being attributed a quality that it does not possess. It is not the nature of money to generate money, just as it is not the nature of machines to generate new value. It is human labor that has the capacity to create value, which, in a capitalist society, takes the form of wage labor. If other forms of capital – involved in the production of goods and in their circulation – already show a high degree of fetishization, when one considers that their profit derives from their ability to organize and manage their business, then, with interest-bearing capital, this mystification reaches its zenith, as the presence of labor is no longer a requirement.

From the 1960s onward, the overaccumulation of capital in its money form was concentrated in international financial markets, especially those based in the City of London and in Wall Street in New York. This money capital, which expanded in the most familiar forms of eurodollars and petrodollars, was converted into a huge mass of public debts in developing and dependent countries. The crisis in the late 1970s, particularly in the United States, resulted in a change in monetary policy with a sharp rise in interest rates, the *prime rate*, and which also contaminated LIBOR in the City, London. The consequence was the long-term foreign debt crisis in developing and indebted countries, the effects of which lasted through the 1980s and 1990s. This was the period when neoliberal ideology and policies became dominant.

However, this overaccumulation did not only expand public debts, it also affected investment and pension funds that led to the enormous appreciation of shares on the stock exchanges and the expansion of public debts securitized by the renegotiations in which contractual debts were converted into bearer bonds tradable on stock exchanges. One of the key factors in this expansion was the change in criteria, or the valuation of companies, by share value. By this way, private units of capital, in the form of corporations, began to have their value measured through the prices of shares on the trading floors of the stock exchanges and the remuneration of executives was increased by *stock options*. These forms of capital, public debt, and equity, together with bank capital, constitute what Marx called fictitious forms of capital. The development and crisis of these forms, along with the development of new forms such as derivatives and the currency market, the *Foreign Exchange* (Forex), is detailed in Marques and Nakatani (2009) and in Nakatani and Marques (2020).

FICTITIOUS CAPITAL AND FICTITIOUS PROFITS

It is from the understanding of the nature of interest-bearing capital that one understands the existence and development of fictitious capital. In fact, the "origin" of everything can be found in the very emergence of money as a general equivalent, when, based on a historical process, a certain commodity is elected the equivalent of the world of commodities. It is at this moment that the general equivalent, instead of highlighting the value of the world of commodities, began to be seen as *The Value*, as if it alone encompassed value. In this way, money, already seen as a fetish, is now, as interest-bearing capital, capable of increasing its own value. The "right" to interest and its collection derives from the ownership of money. When employed by industrial or commercial capital, it constitutes a deduction from profit based on the new value created by the wage laborer, and which is appropriated by the person who hired him or her. In the case of fictitious capital, there is no direct relationship with the creation of new value; so it is fictitious, and the profitability associated with it constitutes "fictitious profit." When we speak of fictitious profit, we mean that it is not supported by or does not have any reference to new value created by the actions of the labor force used in the production of goods organized in a capitalist way. Despite this, it is real and concrete, filling the coffers of capitalists.

Interest-bearing capital has expanded enormously over the last 40 years and has imposed its logic and importance on both economic activities in general and on our subjectivity (Dardot & Laval, 2016). Although this process of accumulation and concentration began during the 30 years following the end of the Second World War, its return to the center of economic and social relations was only possible through deregulation in the global and national financial sphere (Chesnais, 2005). Some of the consequences of this imposition can be seen in Nakatani and Marques (2020), such as the persistence of low levels of investment in production, commercialization, and high unemployment, among others.

Although we have already looked at the forms taken by fictitious capital in the contemporary world in previous works, we will refer here to two of its modalities: public debt and cryptocurrencies, given their importance in countries such as Brazil and El Salvador.

Public debt is State debt, that is, regardless of its origin (whether it arises from the purchase of weapons, construction of infrastructure, maintenance of its current activities or the external indebtedness of companies that took on the debt). It becomes its responsibility to both administer and honor. The State borrows money and spends it, leaving only a debt bond representing something that no longer exists.

Public debt is inherent to the state, that is, indebtedness and the creation of national States are inseparable phenomena. The nature of the modern State is bourgeois and, therefore, it is, in essence, an instrument of the ruling classes. Nevertheless, activities that the State develops, and its employees, do not fall within the field of capitalist activity. Although they are useful and fundamental for the reproduction of capital, its "workers" do not produce surplus value. Because of this, by definition, public bonds are fictitious capital since the wealth they represent has been spent, consumed by the State.

However, its ownership gives its possessors power, especially today, when the dominant economic thinking, and its political manifestation, make debt a sword that hangs over society. A society where, on the one hand, they rhetorically advocate that public spending must be contained so that debt does not increase (thereby compromising social spending in general), while, on the other hand, they prioritize payment, especially interest, above the needs of the countries' working population. A part of this interest is commonly paid from new debt, thereby increasing fictitious capital through fictitious profits. In this way, the power of public debt creditors determines the State's fiscal policy, defining the level of public spending and its priorities, while, at the same time, these creditors pressure for a policy of upward interest rates, whereby they gain even more.

In contemporary capitalism, public debt, whether domestic or international, has thus become a strong instrument in subsuming workers to the interests of creditors. For example, in Brazil, subjection to debt creditors led, in December 2016, to a constitutional dictate that the central government budget should be frozen for 20 years, so that public accounts would generate, over time, an increased surplus which would guarantee the servicing of the public debt. It is important to clarify that this freeze applies to all forms of expenditure, including social spending, the only exception being debt payment, which unmistakably betrays the purpose of the freeze imposed in Brazil.

In the case of cryptocurrencies, the situation in El Salvador is emblematic. In September 2021, the government announced that it would adopt bitcoin as a new national currency and that it would exist alongside the US dollar. Twenty years earlier, El Salvador had renounced its monetary sovereignty and adopted the US dollar as its national currency. The first half of 2022 saw a severe devaluation of bitcoin (falling 54% by the end of June) and the profoundly shook this already fragile economy. In January 2021, bitcoin was quoted at US\$33,141; this increased to US\$58,796 in March (a growth of more than 77%), and fell to US\$34,655.10, then US\$37,305 in the months of May and June, respectively. This attests to the highly speculative component of the appreciation and devaluation of this cryptocurrency, as other ones.

This speculative component is also present in other forms of fictitious capital, such as on bond and stock markets, given that most of these transactions take place on the secondary market. In any case, upward or downward variations of the magnitude that have been observed in the value of cryptocurrencies on these markets would reveal a deep crisis, given how systemically these capitals are inserted.

In the case of cryptocurrencies, further to this speculative component, there are other elements that should be highlighted that make this mode of fictitious capital the fetish of all fetishes. What we mean by this is that, in cryptocurrencies, the level of fetish reaches its maximum, rivaling only the NFTs. But, unlike cryptocurrencies, these are not fungible (NFT meaning "non-fungible token").

Cryptocurrencies, unlike national and world currencies (among which the US dollar, which, although weakened, still constituted 59% of central bank reserves in 2021, and which remains the main currency for international transactions), are not guaranteed by any State. We can no longer view money as the only depository of value or even as a source of profit. It is that and more. Now, we can give it life, because of the individual will of a few. Although millions have flocked to cryptocurrencies, they are not the product of a historical process linked to the State decisions of sovereign nations. They are, rather, an expression of the place that money holds in contemporary capitalist society: of being the only depository of value, and that, therefore, their production can result from *will*, with no need for any reference to the existing relationships of production or the institutions created for maintaining these relationships. Those who bet on cryptocurrencies, as they exist today, forget that currency is power and that it is intrinsically linked to the State.

CONCLUSION

There is no doubt that capitalist economies are facing difficulties in maintaining previous levels of GDP performance, employment generation, and rates of profit derived from the production of goods. This perception is confirmed by weak growth in the world's principal economies, excluding China and India, and the most acute period of the COVID-19 pandemic; by the high and persistent levels of unemployment; and by continuing low and inadequate profit rates, to the point that Roberts (2022) qualified this period as the "long recession" (see Graph 2). Regarding this indicator, it is worth highlighting that, even in the period described by Roberts as the "neoliberal period" (actually, from the dawn of neoliberalism), profit rates were unable to attain the levels obtained during the golden 30 years.

However, as relevant as this approach to capitalist economies may be, it is partial and fails to consider the main component of contemporary reality: the dominance of interest-bearing capital, especially as fictitious capital, in defining economic and social relationships. This form of capital, whose freedom was restricted during the 30 years following WWII, but which became significantly concentrated and centralized, has, following the deregulation of the financial sphere, intertwined with other capitals and, in addition to expanding as never before, started to guarantee high profits not derived from the exploitation of the workforce.

So, in addition to asking "crisis for whom?", we ask "who benefits from the maintenance of this 'regime of accumulation' so strongly based on the development of fictitious capital?"

The beneficiaries are those who hold the various forms that fictitious capital takes in contemporary capitalism. They are nothing but rentiers. In a globalized world, with free mobility of capital both domestically and globally, their insatiable desire for "easy" and very short-term profits makes long-term government and company strategies for the production and commercialization of goods unfeasible. As for governments, their actions restrict the effectiveness of fiscal, monetary and exchange rate policies. On several occasions this has revealed that they are hostage to the interests of fictitious capital holders. We have highlighted the case of Brazil, where guaranteeing the servicing of the public debt has determined the federal government's budget.

As stated earlier, moments or periods of crisis are those in which, in addition to the needs inherent to the processes of appreciation, the movement of capital is interrupted. It is not the low growth of economies, the level of unemployment and the impoverishment of growing portions of the population that determine a crisis, from the point of view of capital. Nor is it caused by the increasing presence of fictitious capital. This set of indicators simply attests to the inability of capitalism to provide adequate living conditions for people, that is, it proves the historical need to overcome it and to build a different social arrangement which prioritizes the needs of the population and not the unbridled pursuit of profits.

NOTES

1. Marx (1990), p. 349.
2. Marx (1990), p. 358.
3. As recently as 2016, part of Renault's production was transferred to Morocco following resistance by French metal workers to the new working conditions proposed by the company.

REFERENCES

Bourguinat, H. (1992). *Finance internationale*. Paris: Presses universitaires de France.
Chancel, L., Piketty, T., Saez, E., & Zucman, G. (2022). World inequality report. Retrieved from https://wir2022.wid.world/
Chesnais, F. (2005). O capital portador de juros: Acumulação, internacionalização, efeitos econômicos e políticos. In F. Chesnais (Ed.), *A finança mundializada: Raízes sociais e políticas, configurações, consequências*. São Paulo: Boitempo.
Chesnais, F. (2013). As Raízes da crise econômica mundial. *Revista Em Pauta: Teoria social e realidade contemporânea*. Retrieved from https://www.e-publicacoes.uerj.br/index.php/revistaempauta/article/view/7556/5495
Chesnais, F. (2016). *Financial capital today*. Boston, MA: Brill.
Cohen, P., & Richard, L. (2005). *La Chine sera-t-elle notre cauchemar? Les Dégâts du libéral-communisme en Chine et dans le monde*. Paris: Mille et une nuits.
Dardot, P., & Laval, C. (2016). *A Nova razão do mundo: Ensaio sobre a sociedade neoliberal*. São Paulo: Boitempo.
Duménil, G., & Lévy, D. (2006). La finance capitaliste: Rapports de production et rapports de classe. In F. Chesnais (Ed.), *La finance capitaliste*. Paris: Presses universitaires de France.

Forbes. (2022). World's billionaires list. Retrieved from https://www.forbes.com/billionaires/

Husson, M. (2006). Finance, hiper-concurrence et reproduction du capital. In F. Chesnais (Ed.), *La finance capitaliste*. Paris: Presses universitaires de France.

Husson, M. (2014). *Apresentação de Michel Husson no Third Economics seminar of the IRRE*. Amsterdam. Retrieved from https://www.iire.org/node/640

Marques, R. M., & Nakatani, P. (2009). *O que é capital fictício e sua crise*. São Paulo: Brasiliense.

Marx, K. (1981). Capital. A critique of political economy. In *Book III: The process of capitalist production as a whole*. London: Penguin Classics.

Marx, K. (1990). Capital. A critique of political economy. In *Book I: The process of production of capital*. London: Penguin Classics.

Marx, K. (1992). Capital. A critique of political economy. In *Book II: The process of circulation of capital*. London: Penguin Classics.

Nakatani, P., & Marques, R. M. (2020). *O capitalismo em crise*. São Paulo: Expressão Popular.

Oxfam. (2022). *Lucrando com a dor: Relatório 2022*. Retrieved from https://www.oxfam.org.br/justica-social-e-economica/forum-economico-de-davos/lucrando-com-a-dor/#:~:text=A%20dor%20de%20muitos%20%C3%A9, conta%20de%20luz%2C%20um%20medicamento

Roberts, M. (2022). La Tasa de ganancia mundial: Nuevas evidencias importantes. *Rebelión*. Retrieved from https://rebelion.org/la-tasa-de-ganancia-mundial-nuevas-evidencias-importantes/

Salama, P., & Mathias, G. (1983). *O Estado Superdesenvolvido: Ensaios sobre a intervenção estatal e sobre as formas de dominação no capitalismo contemporâneo*. São Paulo: Brasiliense.

MONEY, FICTITIOUS CAPITAL, AND CRYPTOCURRENCIES: THEIR IMPACT ON THE WORLD ECONOMY

Ernesto Molina Molina

ABSTRACT

Without theoretically specifying the future of money as an equivalent commodity of other commodities, it is impossible to reveal the recent role of the emergence of cryptocurrencies, as a reflection of speculative competition increasingly sophisticated in its technological aspect and in response to the abusive use of the spurious competition of the big banks promoting the huge financial bubbles that have haunted the world economy, such as the one unleashed from Wall Street in 2008. The explosive growth of transactions in cryptocurrencies may mean, at some point, in the capitalist economic cycle, the possibility of a new financial bubble, as well as the emergence of new swindles to investors; but valid answers can also come from those actors who until now have had to endure the almost exclusive dominance of the international monetary system by the currency issued by the US government, the main exporter of inflation on a global scale.

Keywords: Fictitious capital; money; cryptocurrencies; financial bubbles; world economy; international monetary system

INTRODUCTION

Cryptocurrencies are global currencies, not always sensitive or amenable to the economies or politics of a specific country. They can be accessed by everyone and can be instantly transferred to anyone anywhere in the world. Cryptocurrencies are decentralized: there is as yet no official market, which means that they can be traded 24 hours a day, seven days a week.

Value, Money, Profit, and Capital Today
Research in Political Economy, Volume 39, 231–245
Copyright © 2024 Ernesto Molina Molina
Published under exclusive licence by Emerald Publishing Limited
ISSN: 0161-7230/doi:10.1108/S0161-723020230000039014

Cryptocurrencies often experience significant price movements suddenly. This makes them as speculative as securities, credit money, floating currency exchange rates, but at the same time, they constitute an alternative response to the almost exclusive domination over the international monetary system by the currency issued by the government of the United States, the main exporter of inflation on a global scale.

Without theoretically specifying the future of money as a commodity equivalent to other commodities, it is impossible to reveal the recent role of the emergence of cryptocurrencies in the world, as a reflection of the increasingly sophisticated speculative competition in its technological aspect and as a response to the abusive use of spurious competition by the big banks that promote the enormous financial bubbles that have plagued and harassed the world economy, such as the one unleashed from Wall Street in 2008.

THE MOVEMENT OF MONEY AND THE MOVEMENT OF FICTITIOUS CAPITAL

The most essential thing about money, as the general equivalent of other commodities, is explained by Marx (1973) through the simple form of value. But then he goes on to explain the historical passage from the simple form to the developed form of value.

Commodity A expresses its value in the use value of many other commodities (B, C, D, E, F...). For example:

$$A = 2B = 1/2\,C = 3D = 1/4\,E = 4F = \ldots = Y$$

When there was not yet an equivalent commodity of the other commodities, each producer considered the other commodities as special equivalents of his or her own, but since all commodity owners did the same, there was no commodity which was general equivalent, nor, thus, could commodities possess a relative general form of value that would equate them as values and allow them to be compared with each other as magnitudes of value. Marx expresses it this way:

> Every owner of commodities considers the commodities of others as special equivalents of his or her own, therefore seeing in this the equivalent of all the others. However, since all owners of commodities do the same, there is none that is general equivalent, nor can commodities, therefore, possess a relative general form of value that equates them as values and allows them to be compared among themselves as magnitudes of value. Consequently, commodities are not confronted, therefore, as such commodities, but simply as products or use values.[1]

At this stage of the development of the forms of value is what Marx calls: developed form of value.[2]

The state theory of money maintains that money is a product of state power and its basic function is that it serves as a means of payment – its other functions deriving from this basic one. For Marx, on the contrary, the basic function of money is to be a measure of value and all the other functions derive from it: means of circulation, means of hoarding, means of payment and world currency.

Capitalist society does not even know the mass of merchandizes to be sold or the sum of their prices, just as it cannot know the average speed of money turnover. Therefore, the law of the quantity of money necessary for circulation breaks through many fluctuations as an objective tendency. Something similar to what happens with the law of value.

If money only functions as a measure of value and a means of circulation, then this law is formulated by Marx as follows:

$$\text{Quantity of money} = \frac{\text{Sum of the prices of commodities}}{\text{Number of rotations of currencies of equal value}}$$

In Marx's time, in foreign trade, the weight of gold and silver, in bullion, had to be carefully checked. However, in internal trade, coins, even when they lost weight, were accepted, because in the commodity – money – commodity (C – M – C) cycle, the role of money is ephemeral. This made it possible to create the forced course of paper money.

Paper money does not represent all the gold which exists in the country, nor does it represent the gold found in banks. It represents only the amount of gold indispensable for circulation. Since paper money actually circulates instead of gold coins, it is subject to the laws of money circulation.

Only the proportion in which paper replaces gold can be the subject of a special law, which is: the issue of paper money is to be limited to the amount in which the gold represented by it would actually have to circulate.

If, for example, 5 million dollars are issued and circulation only needs 2 million, that mass of 5 million represents only 2 million. That is the reason why inflation is not possible with real money (gold or silver), it is only possible with signs of value.

Credit relations very often make money unnecessary, even as the final link.

One needs to know which commodities (C) are sold for money (M) and which on credit. And which of the latter are paid reciprocally or mutually and which balances must be paid in money.

If money not only functions as a means of circulation, but also as a means of payment, then this law is formulated by Marx as follows:

$$\text{Quantity of money} = \frac{\begin{array}{l}(\text{Sum of the prices of the commodities to be sold} \\ -\text{ Sum of the prices of the commodities sold on credit} \\ +\text{ Payments in bills of exchange} \\ -\text{ Debts that are compensated})\end{array}}{\text{Number of rotations of currencies of equal value}}$$

Credit money originates from the function of money as a means of payment, by the circulation of debt certificates in order to transfer these debts to others. Bills of exchange (B) function as credit money:

```
...C    CCCCC     C...
...M    BBBBBB... M  (circulation)
...C    CCCCC     C...
```

With the credit system, the function of money as a means of payment is also extended. In this capacity, money acquires its own forms of existence, in which it occupies the sphere of large-scale commercial transactions, while small change is mainly relegated to the sphere of retail trade.

In the world trade of the era of free competitive market capitalism, the local forms of money, fractional currency and paper money, were discarded, and only the form of money in ingots (gold [G]) was valid as world money.

```
...C        CCCCC        C...
...G        GGGGGG...    G    (circulation)
...C        CCCCC        C...
```

The gold that remains in circulation is hoarded. However, the signs of value cannot be hoarded because they have no intrinsic value.

The dollar has been and is still a strong currency because the US economy has a supply capacity that is very flexible to demand. The countries of the South have rigid production structures; therefore, their currencies are weak. In order to compete, they usually devalue their currency and raise the rate of inflation: this is spurious competition. The countries of the North can access technological change and strengthen their currency.

The law of the amount of money necessary for circulation that Marx discovered continues to apply in the stage of dominance of financial capital; but not all the money demanded by social capital responds to the needs of the circulation of real capital. The links between real capital and fictitious capital have become more complex and more decisive in the imperialist stage.

The interest rate and the movement of money, indeed, maintain a narrow relationship in this era, which is the result of the double link between real capital and fictitious capital:

• through stocks and bonds, among others; and
• through credit money, bank notes, and bills.

It is here that we are forced to use the contributions of John Maynard Keynes, in the way that Marx was able to recognize the contributions of bourgeois classical economists such as Adam Smith and David Ricardo.

According to Keynes (1968), the demand for liquid money, or cash, is governed by three different types of motives:

• transaction;
• precaution;
• speculation.

There is always a time interval between incomes and expenses. The greater this interval, more money should be saved to make these expenses. They can be consumption or business expenses. In either case, the transaction motive depends primarily on the amount of income and the normal length of the interval between incomes and expenses.

Since the level of income is an index of the level of transactions, the demand for money for the transaction motive is a function of income:

$$M_T = f(Y)$$

The precautionary motive is related to the impossibility of knowing with absolute certainty future incomes and expenses; there is always the probability that unexpected needs will arise, expenses will increase, incomes will be delayed, and uncertainties will arise in the face of future transactions, among others.

To a certain extent, the precautionary motive can be considered a variant of the transaction motive. In this sense, the precautionary motive is a function of income:

$$M_P = f(Y)$$

The speculative motive makes its influence felt on the demand for money, as changes occur in the prices of securities and debts of various maturities. In capitalist countries, the closest substitute to money is bonds – either one has money or one has bonds –; commercial bonds have fluctuating prices. If the interest rate decreases, the price of the bond increases, and vice versa. If the interest rate increases, the price of the bond decreases; thus, a capital gain or loss can be generated with the fluctuations of the prices of bonds.

This explains why increases in the demand for cash money are associated with decreases in the interest rate. That is, the money demand for the speculation motive is a function of the interest rate:

$$M_S = g(r)$$

As the money demand for the transaction and precaution motives is a function of income, while the money demand for the speculation motive is a function of the interest rate, Keynes simplifies the expression of these functions as follows. Let be the amount of cash held to satisfy the transaction and precautionary motives M_1, and the amount saved to satisfy the speculative motive M_2. Corresponding to these two cash money compartments, we have two liquidity functions L_1 and L_2. L_1 depends mainly on the level of incomes, while L_2 depends on the relationship between the current rate of interest and the state of forecasts. Thus:

$$M = M_1 + M_2 = L_1(Y) + L_2(r)$$

where L_1 is the liquidity function corresponding to an income Y (which determines M_1); and L_2 is the liquidity function of the interest rate r (which determines M_2).[3]

For example, let us suppose that a person has a given amount of wealth in excess of what he or she has set aside for M_1, which he or she wishes to hold in monetary assets (money in cash and bonds). Let us call this amount investment balance of this quantity. That person must decide whether to keep that investment balance in money or in bonds during the next period.

If he or she thinks that bond prices are going to rise and therefore the interest rate is going to fall, he or she is hopeful that the bonds will earn him or her interest plus a capital gain: he or she will prefer to hold bonds and the demand for money for the speculative motive will decrease. If he or she assumes that bond prices will fall and therefore that the interest rate will raise, his or her expectation will be to earn the interest minus a capital loss. If that net total is greater than zero, he or she will buy bonds; but if it is less than zero, he or she will retain his or her money in cash: the demand for money for the speculative motive will increase.

Fictitious capital is closely linked to joint-stock companies. It is a capital formed by public securities, which provides income to its holders and makes an independent movement in the public securities market, in which they are bought and sold.

Public securities do not in themselves create capital surplus value, but they give the right to obtain certain income in the form of interests or dividends. In the era of pre-monopoly capitalism, joint-stock companies and fictitious capital already arose, reaching their maximum development in the era of monopoly capitalism. The movement of finance capital comes to subordinate the movement of industrial capital, and even includes it:

$$\underset{\text{Industrial Capital}}{\underbrace{M-C\underset{R_M}{\overset{W_F}{\ldots}}P\ldots C'-M+d}} \quad \underset{\text{Fictitious Capital}}{\underbrace{\overset{G.e-G.e/i-S}{\underset{Rt-R/i}{}}}} \quad \underset{\text{Industrial Capital}}{\underbrace{-M-C\ldots P\ldots C'-M'}}$$

$$\underset{\text{Financial Capital}}{\underbrace{}}$$

In this scheme, where W_F represents the workforce and R_M raw materials, industrial capital is written in a synthetical form (as money capital) as follows:

$$M-C\ldots P\ldots \acute{C}-\acute{M}.$$

If it was expressed in developed form, that is:

$$M-C\ldots P\ldots \acute{C}-\acute{M}\ldots M-C\ldots P\ldots \acute{C}-\acute{M},$$

the scheme would have been too broad.

Fictitious capital is also presented in synthetical form, as the entrepreneur's capitalized profit (G.e/i) to access external capital in the form of fictitious shares and securities of all kinds as a source for real investment.

The fictitious capital can also be presented as the average capitalized profit (G.m/i), but we have to keep in mind that the average profit is broken down into the profit of the entrepreneur and loan interest, and the latter is destined to the sources of capital that come from credit, and not directly from the issue of shares (stocks).

We know that, expressed in synthetical form, the price of a standard share is equal to the capitalized dividend (D/i). The entrepreneur who decides to create a joint-stock company cannot issue any magnitude of shares that comes to mind.

In this scheme, it can be observed that the supply of capital for investment is enhanced thanks to the capital market. In turn, the division of the average profit into the entrepreneur's profit (G.e) and loan interest (i) serves as the basis for the creation of shares or securities (S) based on the capitalized expected dividends (D/i), very similar to the category of "land price," which, without being the result of social labor, when it is a commodity, assumes a capitalist price based on capitalized rent (R/i).

But how does the central bank manipulate the price of securities?

The price of a share is the capitalized dividend: $P_A = D/i \times 100$.

The central bank can lower or raise the interest rate, and in doing so, it modifies share prices and thus can create financial bubbles. The "bubble economy" refers to that excessive increase in asset prices, based on expectations of future price increases, not supported by economic fundamentals and, therefore, followed by a reversal of expectations and the collapse of prices.

Keynes (1968) perceived the dangers involved in the correlation between the movements of industrial capital and fictitious capital; at the same time, he recognized the need to mobilize that source of investment, without which the dynamics of capitalism are severely restricted. As a consequence, he did not renounce the manipulation by the state of the movement of fictitious capital.

Criticism of the Keynesian conception demands recognition of its practical importance in developing a certain model of capitalist accumulation in which the relations between the "real economy" and the "financial economy" are regulated. The existence in the United States, after the Great Depression and since 1934, of a regulatory body created for these purposes is not accidental: The Securities and Exchange Commission (SEC).

Simplifying the analysis that this regulatory institution can carry out, the businessman who aspires to create the joint-stock corporation assumes as a criterion the expected normal annual profit, otherwise he or she would not be able to fulfill the commitment to pay the dividends to the shareholders. Let us assume an industrial company with a capital of 1 million dollars and an average corporate profit of 15%. The sum of 150,000 dollars, capitalized as an annual rent at 5%, will be priced at 3 million dollars. A careful audit must really calibrate all the factors that determine the "fair value" of the possible shares to be issued.

When presenting the price of land as capitalized rent (R/i), real estate capital may be subject to the movement of a bubble economy.

DOLLARIZATION AND SPURIOUS COMPETITION IN THE UNITED STATES

Currencies are not money because the state mints them. And yet, after the Second World War, the US dollar ($) gained such preponderance over the international monetary system that since then, it has given the impression that the US state has the ability to mint money:

$$\ldots \quad \text{CCCCC} \quad \ldots$$
$$\ldots \quad \text{\$\$\$\$\$\$\$\$} \quad \ldots \text{(circulation)}$$
$$\ldots \quad \text{CCCCC} \quad \ldots$$

According to Milton Friedman (1993), the cause that triggers inflation is poor management or control of money by the state.[4] For him, not all public spending generates inflation. If public spending is financed by taxes or private money borrowed through loans, there is no inflation. Why? Because the state has more money and the citizen less, but it is the same amount of money. On this precise point, we could perhaps agree with this criterion of the 1976 Nobel laureate.

Nonetheless, if the state decides to finance public spending with inflation, what does it do?

The US administration orders the Treasury to sell bonds to the reserve system (central bank, or "Federal Reserve System"). The latter, in exchange for the bonds, delivers notes that it has just printed, or underwrites them into the accounts that the Treasury has in the Federal Reserve. The Treasury can now pay for public spending.

Obviously, Friedman declares innocent the monopolistic corporations and recognizes only one culprit: the discretionary state, which manipulates the signs of value and credit money to regulate the money supply. The capitalist system is also absolved and, very particularly, in its monopoly phase. M. Friedman, co-author of *A Monetary History of the United States* (1963),[5] does not take into account the following historical facts:

• With monopoly capitalism, the development of credit reached such a level that practically real money – i.e., gold – was replaced in circulation not only at the national level, but also internationally.
• Of the three monetary forms – metallic money, paper money and bank deposits–, the latter became predominant.
• As it is only possible from the representatives of money or signs of value, inflation becomes a chronic phenomenon with monopoly capitalism.
• State monopoly capitalism further aggravates this situation, since the system of state economic regulation affects, precisely, the monetary sphere through directed credit.
• The competitive speculation of private banks, of the monopolies, on the one hand, and, on the other one, the development of the public debt by the state, aggravates the inflationary mechanism.

Military spending is covered for with an inflated budget. The international financial system created after WWII, i.e., the Bretton Woods system, gave the possibility for each national state and especially the most developed states, to regulate their economic and industrial policies, since the international monetary system guaranteed stability and certain security in expectations. One was not in an unpredictable turbulent financial world.

The exchange rate came to play the role of a variable of state decision in competition on a worldwide scale. So, to take advantage of this regulating magnitude within global competition, the United States began by abandoning the Bretton Woods fixed exchange rate regime and introduced a generalized floating exchange rate regime, in which:

$$1 \text{ ounce of gold } = \text{US\$35} \ldots \rightarrow \ldots 1 \text{ ounce of gold } = ?$$

There was a strong economic rationale in this unilateral decision of 1973: the United States hoped to compensate for declining competitiveness and growing indebtedness by exporting macroeconomic imbalances. The floating exchange rate regime provided the US authorities with a light and effective monetary tool, allowing them to escape the adjustments that their new debtor status would have implied.

In a fixed exchange rate and gold-convertibility regime, the United States would have been forced, as currently happens to all Third World countries, to pay the price with a relative loss of sovereignty and very unpopular internal austerity measures.

The new regime has allowed the United States to take advantage of the world's savings reserves to maintain a high level of spending. Thanks to its political power and the dollar – the world's only reserve currency –, it has safeguarded full and complete sovereignty in the monetary field: its allies could not question its general policy without destabilizing the institutional framework and security structures of the Cold War, from which they obtained multiple benefits.

Since the money supply is regulated by the state and the exchange rate became floating, both the interest rate and the exchange rate, together with all forms of financial derivatives in the world capital market, are regulatory magnitudes at the service of the transnational corporations and the states of the North – but above all that of the United States (See: Lebowitz, 2005).

The unequal process of "dollarization" of the global economy plays an important role in the geographical "distribution" of the global crisis. An abstract possibility of getting out of the crisis lies in the growth of the internal market in China and in general in the internal market of all the large creditors of the United States. However, is the United States willing to pay off debts by exporting high technology to its creditors? Can the US government stop US corporations from exporting advanced technology to China, Russia, India and the rest of the world?

THE MOVEMENT OF CRYPTOCURRENCIES AGAINST DOLLARIZATION

Cryptocurrency is a digital means of exchange, which uses encryption techniques to regulate the generation of units and verify the transfer of funds. It operates independently of a central bank and is converted into "digital money" through various ways, with the so-called Exchange platforms being one of the options (See: Infante Ugarte, 2018).

The emergence of multiple digital currencies on a global scale as opposed to the US dollar constitutes a challenge, not yet strong enough against the international currency that has monopolized this function for decades.

In a certain way, cryptocurrencies come to play the role of "equivalents" of the other commodities, with the aggravating circumstance of being, for most of them, signs of value. And the fact that crypto-currencies experience significant price movements in a speculative manner introduces in the four markets (those of labor, commodities, capital, and technology) a price movement that is difficult to predict and control, which makes very vulnerable the accounting of inflation or deflation.

Consequently, cryptocurrencies turn out to be as speculative as securities, and constitute a sign of value as inflationary as credit money, especially since they are used as an alternative response to the almost exclusive domination over the international monetary system by the currency issued by the US government – i.e., the main exporter of inflation on a global scale. The inflation of the dollar is fought through the inflation or deflation of prices thanks to the use of cryptocurrencies.

The first cryptocurrency was bitcoin, created in 2009 – one year after the liquidity crisis that rocked the world economy. Bitcoin has had an accelerated increase that worries specialists, since they reason that its valorization could plummet with just one click, because it has no support, nor it is derived from other assets, and since that date many other cryptocurrencies of this type have appeared, with different characteristics. It is estimated that today, there are several thousand varieties.

Something very particular about cryptocurrencies is that they eliminate intermediaries (banks) by decentralizing all operations. Control of the process belongs to the users. Is it really so? Or are we in the presence of digital banks that each control the cryptocurrency they issue? Everything seems to indicate that we are dealing with very real banks (which have nothing imaginary) that benefit from the operations carried out by their clients.

Their growth has been such that entities (banks) such as Goldman Sachs and Black Rock already offer management services to hedging organizations that are investing aggressively in them and their value depends on the requests, taking as reference the most influential currencies. Some of the digital currencies are backed by specific commodities (oil, gold or diamonds); some others are not controlled by any state; others are controlled by states that are adversaries to the

US dollar, including the so-called "failed states," and, therefore, are seen as a danger by the "owner" of the dollarized system of the world economy.

Today more than 100 recognized cryptocurrencies are ranked by their market capitalization volume and valued by their demand and the number of coins issued or created. Many cryptocurrencies are limited edition, such as bitcoin, that is, the code with which they are "mined" is programmed to create a certain amount as a limit. This process is slow and increasingly complex as the code becomes more difficult to mine a coin to ensure its security and prevent fraud or duplication. Thus, it requires more hardware equipment (miners) who work longer to create them; although cryptocurrencies created by algorithms are already beginning to emerge.

We can present a few examples that just illustrate the recently started path of the emergence of these digital currencies, which, it seems, are going to flood the world monetary circulation.

- Bitcoin is the most widely used cryptocurrency in the world.
- Ether is a cryptocurrency that outperforms bitcoin, because it has no limit to create coins, while bitcoin has a limit of 21 million coins.
- Litecoin has a network to handle 84 million litecoins, that is, four times more than bitcoin. In addition, just like that of Etherum, the litecoin network is also faster. It only takes 2 minutes and 30 seconds to generate a transaction, when the bitcoin network requires 10 minutes.
- Ripple is a cryptocurrency that offers practically instantaneous and cheap money transfers, since it reduces the transaction time to a few seconds and the costs to a few hundredths of a dollar.
- Bitcoin Cash resulted from an evolution of bitcoin, which allowed the creation of a new digital currency with the possibility of being stored in a larger data network. It increases the capacity of 8 Mb every 10 minutes, while bitcoin has a limit of 1 Mb every 10 minutes.
- Cardano is a cryptocurrency that lacks miners, since it operates through a new algorithm called "Ouroboros." This protocol guarantees the maximum possible security on the platform. It also allows a new generation of smart contracts through a new language developed for the use of Cardano.
- On December 3, 2018, President Nicolás Maduro announced the creation of a cryptocurrency called Petro and backed by 5,342 million barrels from the Orinoco Oil Belt. This cryptocurrency is established with the power to carry out international procedures, overcoming the difficulties that the sanctions established by the US government have implied for Venezuela, and thus being able to finance its economic and social development through a fast, direct digital resource without intermediaries.

Today there are many types of digital currencies. We present below some of the most used, nationally and internationally:

Table 1. Most Used State Digital Currencies.

State Digital Currencies
Petro (Venezuela)
Turcoin (Turkey)
Cryptoruble (Russia)
Cut and Carat (Israel)
CriptoBRICS: In process

Table 2. Most Used Private Digital Currencies.

Private Digital Currencies
Bitcoin
Bitcoin Cash
Ether
Ripple
Cardano

There is something even newer in the field of speculation: cryptocurrencies function as fictitious capital and, consequently, attract external capital for investment: they are bought with normal currencies and bring benefits or capital gains like securities.

CRYPTOCURRENCIES AND INTEREST RATE

Whatever it is, the interest rate plays such an important role in the capitalization of cryptocurrencies in the stock market that it is necessary to know the changes that the movement of the interest rate has undergone.

In the time of Marx, the interest rate was not subject to state regulation, it was governed by the supply and demand for credit. In the time of imperialism, Keynesian monetary policies already promoted low and stable interest rates in order to regulate the speculative movement of securities. Later, neoliberal monetary policies decided to raise interest rates to attract foreign capital.

Currently, interest rates are governed by the supply and demand for credit on a global scale and, therefore, there is a struggle of forces between the monetary policies of the states and corporations fighting to access foreign capital. Each new cryptocurrency is an opportunity to access global foreign capital for the investment of one state or another or for the benefit of some corporation.

Of course, a financial bubble of cryptocurrencies can burst and a sudden financial crisis ensues, something that still seems early, given the phase of the capitalist economic cycle, which has not advanced sufficiently toward the boom phase, since it is known that the crisis occurs after the boom.

Another novelty of cryptocurrencies as fictitious capital is that, being global virtual money, they do not have a national central bank that can manipulate their prices through the movement of the interest rate. Consequently, as long as there is no global central bank, the interest rate will move spontaneously in the global capital market. The national companies that will preferentially attract foreign investment capital will be those that provide some very advanced technology on a global scale, as well as unique products and services.

It is necessary to distinguish the demand price of a cryptocurrency from its supply price. Once the cryptocurrency is created and supplied, there will be those who will be willing to obtain it for its demand price. Financial investment, according to Keynes, is closely related to the current demand price of a capital good (P_D):

$$P_D = \frac{Q_1}{1+i} + \frac{Q_2}{(1+i)^2} + \ldots + \frac{Q_n}{(1+i)^n}$$

where Q_n represent expected returns; and i the interest rate.

The movement of financial capital thus subordinates the movement of cryptocurrencies as fictitious capital, since there is now a new competitive way of accessing foreign capital for real investment:

$$M - C \begin{matrix} W_F \\ \ldots P \ldots \\ R_M \end{matrix} C' - M + d \quad Sv \text{ in cryptocurrency} / i \quad -M - C \ldots P \ldots C' - M'$$

Industrial Capital	Fictitious Capital	Industrial Capital

Financial Capital

with S_V in cryptocurrency/i = fictitious capital expressed in cryptocurrency securities of value relative to the interest rate.

The supply price of a cryptocurrency, therefore, corresponds to a financial investment, although such cryptocurrency is a technological mathematical result that facilitates its double function as a sign of value and speculative capital.

It is not easy to forecast in the short term if there will be a change in the universal financial power, but many analysts point out that the situation that has opened the existence of cryptocurrencies will provide an alternative market and offer greater opportunities. Reactions in Europe have been quick. The European Central Bank is already planning to use the yuan as a reserve. This is the backdrop in the great battle for the new division of the world: the loss of unipolar power is obvious and this process, without a doubt, can help to weaken the financial and monetary subordination of the states and peoples of the political global South to the Northern countries and their corporations.

CONCLUSION

Money became capital under certain historical conditions, hence the movement of money, although it is intertwined with the movement of capital, has its own internal logic. And yet, once the movement of capital is consolidated, it subordinates the movement of money to such an extent that it leads it to fulfill increasingly complex and risky speculative functions, leading to explosive financial bubbles.

The current rise of virtual currencies or cryptocurrencies has been possible thanks to modern computer and communication technologies that, together with the generalized application of robotics, artificial intelligence, telerobotics and telepresence, have allowed to modify the movement of money and capital, above all, in the speculative sphere.

However, the need for the emergence of cryptocurrencies is associated with the complex deployment of contradictions on a world scale between the gigantic global corporations, the capitalist states of the North and the South, and the struggle to dominate the four fundamental global markets: the commodity market, the capital market, the technology market and the labor market.

Using other means of payment is obviously a rejection of the control by the United States of the dollar as the world currency. Sanctions and boycotts have achieved nothing other than guiding and pushing toward the option of multipolarism. Countries like Russia, Iran, China and others follow a de-dollarization strategy to escape the dominance of the US dollar. The European Union itself follows this path with the euro. With the current global crisis, new-born alliances are being produced at great speed, with different levels of agreements, such as between Russia and China, on the one hand, or Brazil, Russia, India, China and South Africa (BRICS), on the other one, and, therefore, the United States is forced to counterattack.

Simón Bolívar and José Martí referred early on to the balance of the world as an option for the development and independence of the peoples of "Our America" (*Nuestra América*). However, the balance of the world is only possible if, in the great diversity of global interests, the forces in favor of peace prevail. One of the links of the historical events that can define this world situation can be related to the following question: Does the United States have the political capacity to prevent modern China from advancing with its peaceful Silk Road project toward the rest of the world? (See: Molina, 2007)

NOTES

1. Marx (1973), p. 53.
2. *Idem*, pp. 31–32.
3. Keynes (1968), p. 194.
4. Friedman (1993), pp. 105–131.
5. See: Friedman and Schwartz (1963). Also: Friedman and Friedman (1980).

REFERENCES

Friedman, M. (1993). *Why government is the problem*. Essays in Public Policy, 39. Stanford, CA: Hoover Institution Press.

Friedman, M. R., & Friedman, R. (1980). *Free to choose*. New York, NY: Harcourt.

Friedman, M., & Schwartz, A. J. (1963). *A monetary history of the United States: 1867–1960*. Princeton, NJ: Princeton University Press.

Infante Ugarte, J. (2018). Las monedas digitales o criptomonedas; actualidades y perspectivas. Paper presented at *the Third Congreso Internacional de Gestión Económica y Desarrollo*, Havana, May 29–June 1.

Keynes, J. M. (1968). *Teoría general de la ocupación, el interés y el dinero*. Instituto del Libro, Havana: Edición Revolucionaria.

Lebowitz, M. A. (2005). *Más allá de El Capital*. Madrid: Ediciones Akal.

Marx, K. (1973). *El Capital*. Book I. Havana: Editorial de Ciencias Sociales.

Molina, E. (2007). *En Busca de una teoría crítica para el desarrollo de América Latina*. Havana: Ruth Casa Editorial.

INDEX

of exploitation, 68, 172–173, 203,
    218, 220
inter-individual, 134, 157, 217–218
monetary, 40
social, 75, 208, 215, 225
technical, 13, 134, 174–175, 181,
    206
Relocation, 106, 218
Reproduction, 6–7, 10, 47, 75, 156,
    200, 205, 217
Resource mobilization, 132–135

Sovereignty, 62, 66, 69, 239
Speculation, 9, 11, 105, 203, 211, 235
State, 4, 6, 9, 11–12, 14, 19–20, 24–25,
    58, 69, 79, 130, 147,
    190–191, 202, 225–227,
    232, 238, 242
Substance, 23–24, 201, 205–206, 210
Supply, 6–7, 49, 60, 121, 129,
    134–135, 158, 234, 242–243
Surplus value, 11, 13, 19–20, 75,
    85–86, 124, 126, 146,
    150–151, 155–156, 173,
    176, 178, 193–194, 200,
    202, 208, 217–218, 236

Theory, 20, 26–27, 32–33, 39–40, 68,
    75, 131–132, 135–138, 160,
    167, 189–190, 200, 210, 232
Trade war, 31–33, 35, 42
Transformation, 62, 97, 133–134, 147,
    155, 169, 189–190, 210

surplus value, 146–147, 155–156
Transnational corporations. *See*
    Multinational firms
Trend, 44, 74, 79, 87–88, 108, 124,
    172–173, 176, 194, 218
Trust, 132–135
Turnover of capital, 153, 160

Unequal exchange, 33, 36, 38–39, 44,
    47
Unit of account, 111–113
Utility, 76, 151, 219–220

Valorization, 9, 22, 74, 79, 86, 100,
    104, 139, 153, 240
Value
    chains, 49, 122
    composition of capital, 49, 97,
        121–122, 129
    criticism, 19–20, 23, 25
    exchange, 39–44
    labor, 36–38
    use, 5, 118, 120–121, 123, 204, 222,
        232

Wage Earner, 110, 206
Wealth, 9, 11, 32–33, 39, 62, 118,
    123–124, 128, 131, 190,
    200–201, 203, 217, 235–236
World economy, 65, 74, 122, 219–220,
    240